Paul Cézanne

Masterpieces of Art

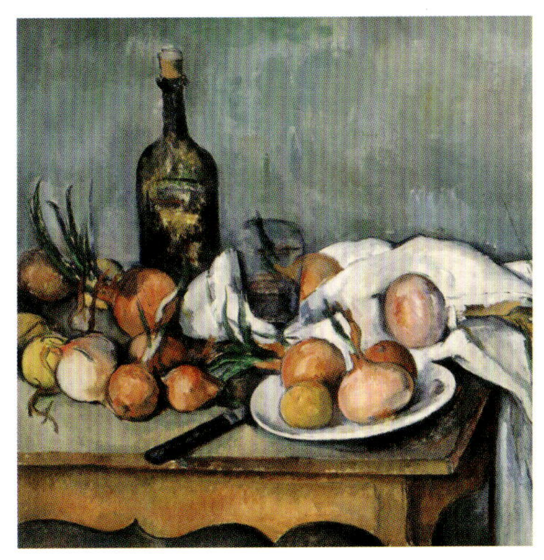

Publisher & Creative Director: Nick Wells
Senior Project Editor: Catherine Taylor
Copy Editor: Anna Groves
Art Director: Mike Spender
Layout Design: Jane Ashley
Digital Design & Production: Chris Herbert

Special thanks to Dawn Laker, Helen Snaith, Frances Bodiam.

FLAME TREE PUBLISHING
6 Melbray Mews
Fulham, London SW6 3NS
United Kingdom

www.flametreepublishing.com

First published 2020

20 22 24 23 21
1 3 5 7 9 10 8 6 4 2

Image credits: Courtesy of **National Gallery of Art, Washington:** Gift of the W. Averell Harriman Foundation in memory of Marie N. Harriman: 1, 43; Chester Dale Collection: 4; Gift of Eugene and Agnes E. Meyer: 47; Collection of Mr. and Mrs. Paul Mellon: 80, 91. Courtesy of **Metropolitan Museum of Art, New York:** The Walter H. and Leonore Annenberg Collection/Gift of Walter H. and Leonore Annenberg, 1993/Bequest of Walter H. Annenberg, 2002: 7 & 81, 67, 97; Bequest of Joan Whitney Payson, 1975: 24 & 108 & 113; H. O. Havemeyer Collection, Bequest of Mrs. H. O. Havemeyer, 1929: 55; Bequest of Stephen C. Clark, 1960: 78 & 95; The Mr. and Mrs. Henry Ittleson Jr. Purchase Fund, 1962: 90; Bequest of Stephen C. Clark, 1960: 92. Courtesy of **The J. Paul Getty Museum, Los Angeles**/Courtesy of the Getty's Open Content Program: 11, 100. Courtesy of **Bridgeman Images:** Private Collection: 13 & 65, 31, 32, 38, 74, 84, 101; Hamburger Kunsthalle, Hamburg, Germany: 20; © CSG CIC Glasgow Museums Collection/Burrell Collection, Glasgow, Scotland: 21 & 54; Samuel Courtauld Trust, The Courtauld Gallery, London, UK: 40, 56, 62, 69, 94, 96; Musee d'Orsay, Paris, France: 42, 51, 75, 98, 112, 120; Louvre, Paris, France: 44, 118; Grand Palais, Paris, France: 46; Museum Folkwang, Essen, Germany: 64, 68; State Hermitage Museum, St. Petersburg, Russia: 70, 105; Philadelphia Museum of Art, Pennsylvania, PA, USA: 73, 88, 125; Cincinnati Art Museum, Ohio, USA: 77; Museum of Fine Arts, Boston, Massachusetts, USA: 85, 102; Musee de l'Orangerie, Paris, France: 87; Pushkin Museum, Moscow, Russia: 89; Musee de la Ville de Paris, Musee du Petit-Palais, France: 104; Museum of Modern Art, New York, USA: 114. Courtesy of **The Art Institute of Chicago:** Mr. and Mrs. Martin A. Ryerson Collection: 14 & 48 & 60; Helen Birch Bartlett Memorial Collection: 36; Amy McCormick Memorial Collection: 121. Courtesy of **The Barnes Foundation**: 15 & 58, 21, 122; Courtesy of **National Gallery in Prague**/sbirky.ngprague.cz: 16. Courtesy of **akg-images:** 17, 26 & 116, 37 & front cover, 52, 93, 103, 106, 110; André Held: 6 & 83, 22, 23 & 76; Erich Lessing: 8, 71, 72, 117; © Sotheby's: 9; Laurent Lecat: 10 & 128, 18 & 35, 28 & 41, 30, 50, 53; Heritage Images/Fine Art Images: 25 t & 111; Album/Joseph Martin: 34; Mondadori Portfolio/Laurent Lecat: 82; The National Gallery, London: 86, 99, 124; De Agostini Picture Lib./M. Carrieri: 107. Courtesy of **Kunstmuseum Basel**/Sammlung Online: 19 & 63, 25b & 115, 27. Courtesy of **Dallas Museum of Art**: The Wendy and Emery Reves Collection: 45. Courtesy of **DIRECTMEDIA Publishing GmbH**/GNU Free Documentation License: 57. Courtesy of **Minneapolis Institute of Art (Mia):** The William Hood Dunwoody Fund: 61. Courtesy of **Museu de Arte de São Paulo (MASP):** Doação, João Chammas, Antonio Adib Chammas and Geremia Lunardelli, 1951/Photo: João Musa: 66.

ISBN: 978-1-83964-160-2

Printed in China I Created, Developed & Produced in the United Kingdom

Paul Cézanne
Masterpieces of Art

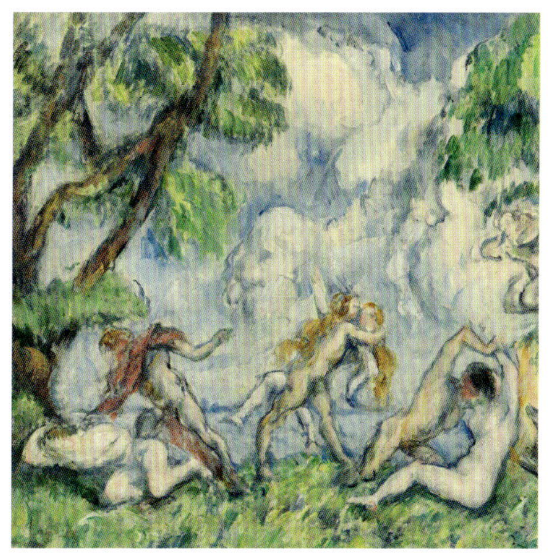

Julian Beecroft

FLAME TREE
PUBLISHING

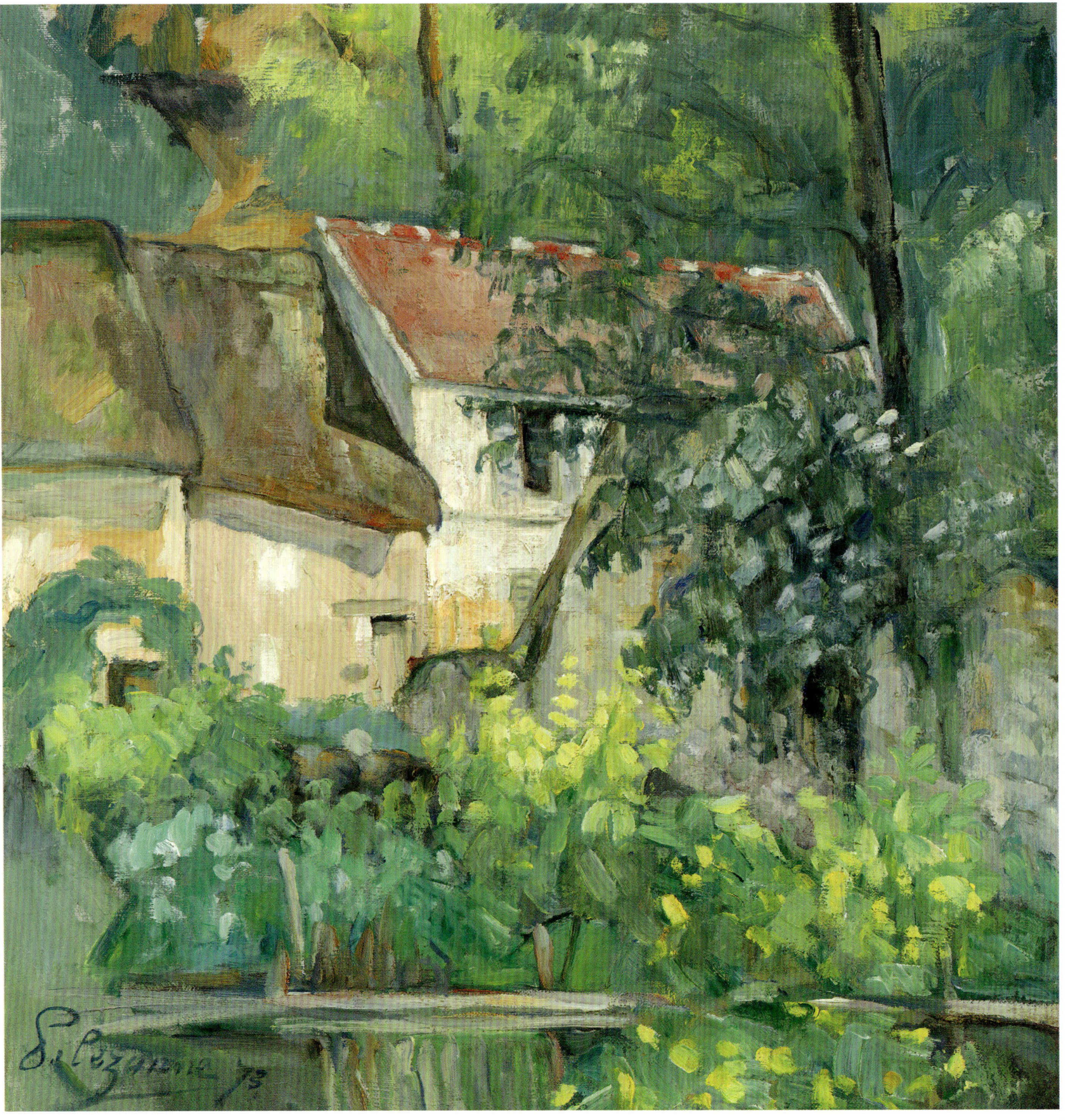

Contents

Paul Cézanne: The Moses of Modern Art

6

Still Life

28

Landscapes

48

Portraits

78

Nudes

108

Index of Works

126

General Index

127

Paul Cézanne: The Moses of Modern Art

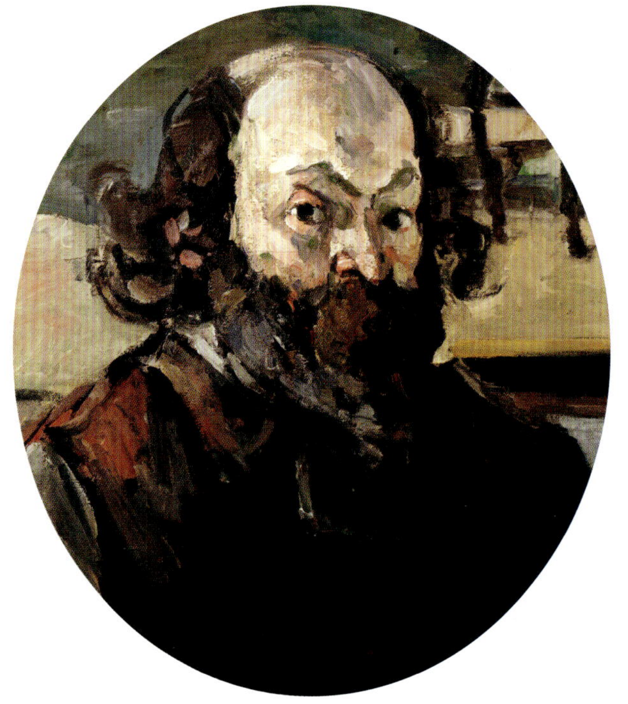

Paul Cézanne (1839–1906) was a difficult man who loved nothing better than to be left alone to paint. As he aged, he increasingly withdrew to the childhood haunts around his home city of Aix-en-Provence – in particular the great peak, Mont Sainte-Victoire, which dominates the region. Plagued by self-doubt, he was keenly aware of the distance between the lofty aesthetic goal he had set himself and his own ability to reach it. But the 'hermit of Aix', as he came to be known, could also sense his own worth as an artist and the place in history he would one day assume as the 'Father of Modern Art'. Indeed, in a letter to a friend written late in his life, he claimed that he could 'glimpse the Promised Land. Will I be like the great leader of the Hebrews,' he wrote, 'or will I be able to enter it?'

A Bourgeois Background

Cézanne was born on 19 January 1839, into a well-to-do family living in an affluent but conservative city which in pre-revolutionary times had been the capital of the region of Provence. His father, Louis-Auguste (1798–1886), began as a hat maker who, by 1838, when he met his much younger wife, Anne Elisabeth Honorine Aubert (1814–97), was running a prosperous business from premises on the main boulevard of Aix. Having a keen sense of any opportunity to advance himself, in 1848 he took advantage of an economic downturn, and the failure of a local bank, to begin loaning out money, with interest, to local businesses, and had soon established his own bank to fill the gap. Over the next three decades he made such a success of it that his son would never have to work for a living.

By 1859, Louis-Auguste was wealthy enough to be able to buy the Jas de Bouffan, a 45-acre estate a mile or so to the west of Aix, which he was already renting and where Cézanne had spent the latter years of his childhood. By this point, the young man had managed to scrape through his baccalauréat at the second time of asking and had enrolled in the law school of the University of Aix to study for the respectable career his father expected him to pursue. But for several years, young Cézanne had also attended drawing classes at the local art school and had executed a series of murals on the walls of the bastide (Provençal manor house) of the Jas de Bouffan, of whose garden and surrounding lands Cézanne would paint more than 50 oils and watercolours over the next 40 years. Then, in 1861, after a frustrating delay, his father consented to let him leave for Paris, the artistic centre of France, to try his luck in what was clearly his true creative passion.

Drawn to Paris

He would not be alone there, as his friend, the writer and future novelist Émile Zola (1840–1902), had already left Aix to follow his own calling in the great metropolis. The pair had been inseparable through their teenage years in Aix, roaming the countryside around the city. Zola was hugely ambitious and had moved to Paris as soon as he had finished school in 1858. From then on, the younger man would continue to outstrip his painter friend in worldly success and social ease, an imbalance that grew ever wider over the next quarter of a century, distilling in the writer a slow-growing pity for Cézanne.

The young painter's first stay in Paris would last only a few months before he abandoned his studies and sloped back to Aix in disappointment, setting a pattern of restless oscillation between the capital and the landscape of his childhood which would persist for some three decades. Returning home that first time, Cézanne accepted desultory employment in his father's bank while resuming drawing classes at the local art school in Aix. But it was clear to Louis-Auguste, as it was to his more sympathetic mother, whose temperament Cézanne shared, that he was not cut out for a life in business. So in November 1862, he set off again for Paris, this time with an allowance from his father sufficient to enable him to make a serious go of his chosen profession.

Friends and Influences

As in the previous year, he enrolled in classes at the Académie Suisse and met fellow painters such as Armand Guillaumin (1841–1927), Antoine Guillemet (1843–1918) and Camille Pissarro (1830–1903), who would become firm friends. He also sat, but failed, the entrance exam for the prestigious École des Beaux-Arts, while also establishing the lifelong habit of going to the Louvre every day whenever he was in Paris to copy from the Old Masters he most admired: the 'Venetians', by which he meant Titian (*c.* 1488/90–1576), Tintoretto (1518–94) and Paolo Veronese (1528–88), as well as the Spanish Baroque painters Francisco de Zurbarán (1598–1664) and Diego Velázquez (1599–1660).

In 1863, he attended the Salon des Refusés, the exhibition established by Emperor Napoleon III (1808–73) for just that year to show paintings by artists whose work had been rejected by the official Salon of the Académie des Beaux-Arts. Included in the selection was *Le déjeuner sur l'herbe* (1862–63) by Édouard Manet (1832–83), a *succès de scandale* whose audacity astounded the young Cézanne and persuaded Zola to use his own gift to champion the new art this shocking masterpiece seemed to announce. Manet caused even more of a shock two years later when his canvas *Olympia* (1865) was exhibited at the official Salon. By then the confident sensuality of the *enfant terrible* of French painting, but also the ripe Romanticism of Eugène Delacroix (1798–1863) and the brooding Realism of Gustave Courbet (1819–77), had firmly imprinted an influence on the painting style of the young Cézanne, which would inflect his work for the next several years.

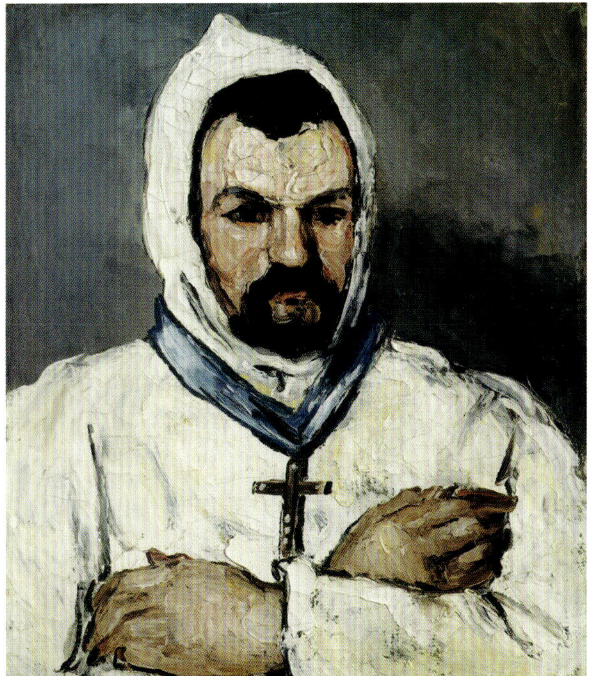

Romantic Visions

This period, known as Cézanne's *couillarde* or 'ballsy' period and sometimes as his dark period, is marked by a series of atmospheric portraits, including the picture of Louis-Auguste, *The Artist's Father, Reading L'Evénement* (1866, *see* page 80), or that of his mother's brother, *Uncle Dominique as a Monk* (1866, *see* left and page 81), both painted in thick impasto applied with a palette knife, after the manner of Courbet. From the same period, and showing the influence of the same artist, are still lifes like *The Black Marble Clock* (*c*. 1870). But there are also dramatic if rather crudely executed figure compositions clearly influenced by Delacroix, fantasies based on imagination rather than observation, often with sexual or violent content, as in *The Murder* (*c*. 1870) or *The Temptation of St Anthony* (*c*. 1870, *see* page 110). St Anthony's battles with the desires of the flesh is a theme Cézanne would return to some years later, but the more general theme of the female nude is one that would eventually provoke his most monumental works, in part because it was an area of personal experience with which he was never wholly comfortable.

Indeed, he sometimes found himself unable to draw from a live model, disturbed by their nakedness, which on occasion caused him to fly into a rage. He could be just as volatile in the company of his young painter friends, who met regularly at the Café Guerbois in the Batignolles district of north-west Paris. The Groupe des Batignolles, as they became known, which formed around the figurehead of

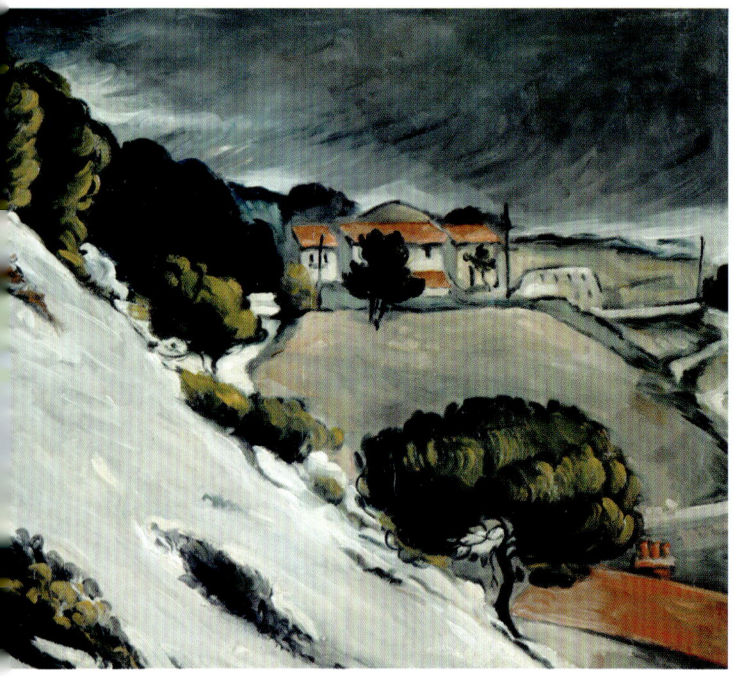

Manet, included all the young tyros who would later be associated with Impressionism – Pissarro, Claude Monet (1840–1926), Pierre-Auguste Renoir (1841–1919), Alfred Sisley (1839–99), Frédéric Bazille (1841–70) and Edgar Degas (1834–1917) – along with Zola and various others working in different creative fields. Often overcome with timidity in the company of his far more gregarious friends, Cézanne was prone to sudden outbursts – gratuitous expletives or even personal insults – in particular when reacting to heated arguments or disquisitions on art, which he feared would influence him against his will and deflect him from his true path.

Hortense

Throughout this period, the paintings Cézanne sent to the Salon were repeatedly rejected, even in 1868 when works by most of the other painters of the Batignolles group were officially accepted. Throughout the 1860s, he returned for a period every year to his home city, painting a number of notable portraits, including an especially wistful image (*c*. 1866–70) of his much older friend from the art school in Aix, the painter Achille Empéraire (1829–1898). This painting today is acknowledged among Cézanne's early masterpieces, though it too was rejected by the Salon in 1870. It was against such a background of discouragement that, the previous year, he had fallen into a relationship with the artist's model Marie-Hortense Fiquet (1850–1922). But his prospects were bleak: his work was still unrecognized, unsought-after and, most significantly, lacking that singular vision which, perhaps more than that of any artist of his generation, it would later go on to develop.

In July 1870, France went to war with Prussia and Cézanne fled with Hortense to L'Estaque, a village on the French Mediterranean coast close to Marseille, where he hid from the draft until the end of first the war and then the violence and disorder of the Paris Commune the following spring. It was in this southern seaside village that he painted his first significant landscapes, such as *Melting Snow at L'Estaque* (*c*. 1870, *see* left), a brooding snowscape executed with the same vigorous impasto brushwork as the other paintings of his *couillarde* period.

The Birth of a Son

This avoidance of military or political action was entirely characteristic
of Cézanne, who never once voted in an election, and in general was
extremely conservative in his social attitudes – another source of
frustration for Zola, an avowed and life-long socialist. Nonetheless,
once the fighting was over and peace had been restored, Cézanne
made his way back to Paris to live for a time with another childhood
friend from Aix, the sculptor Philippe Solari (1840–1906). Hortense
moved with him to the same address and on 4 January 1872 gave
birth to a son, also called Paul, whose fragile infanthood Cézanne
captured in a painting of mother and child, *Hortense Nursing Paul*
(1872, *see* right), which has the tenderness of a true nativity. For years
afterwards, as they moved from one address to another, the couple
remained unmarried and Cézanne kept both partner and child a secret
from his father, for fear of losing the allowance that was still the only
means he had of pursuing his vocation.

The first of these moves, in April 1872, was to the village of Pontoise,
some 20 miles north-west of Paris, where Pissarro was leading a
group of slightly younger landscape painters, all working *en plein air*
(outdoors) directly on to canvas, trying to master what would come to
be called Impressionism, a new way of depicting the world through the
effects of light, which was then emerging in the work of the leading
artists of the Batignolles group.

Impressionism

The kindly Pissarro soon became a father figure for Cézanne, who even
decades later still referred to himself as a 'pupil of Pissarro'. The older
man encouraged him to lighten his palette, to swap heavy, earthy tones
such as sienna and ochre for light grey, to paint winter scenes to oblige
him to make use of white, and above all to ditch the black bitumens he
had been accustomed to using. He also directed Cézanne to trade the
sweeping Romantic energy of his early brushwork for a more cautious
deployment of short, deliberate marks. The change of scenery, subject
matter, means and mode of depiction had a decisive effect on his art.
Now committed to painting the subject from direct observation – *sur*

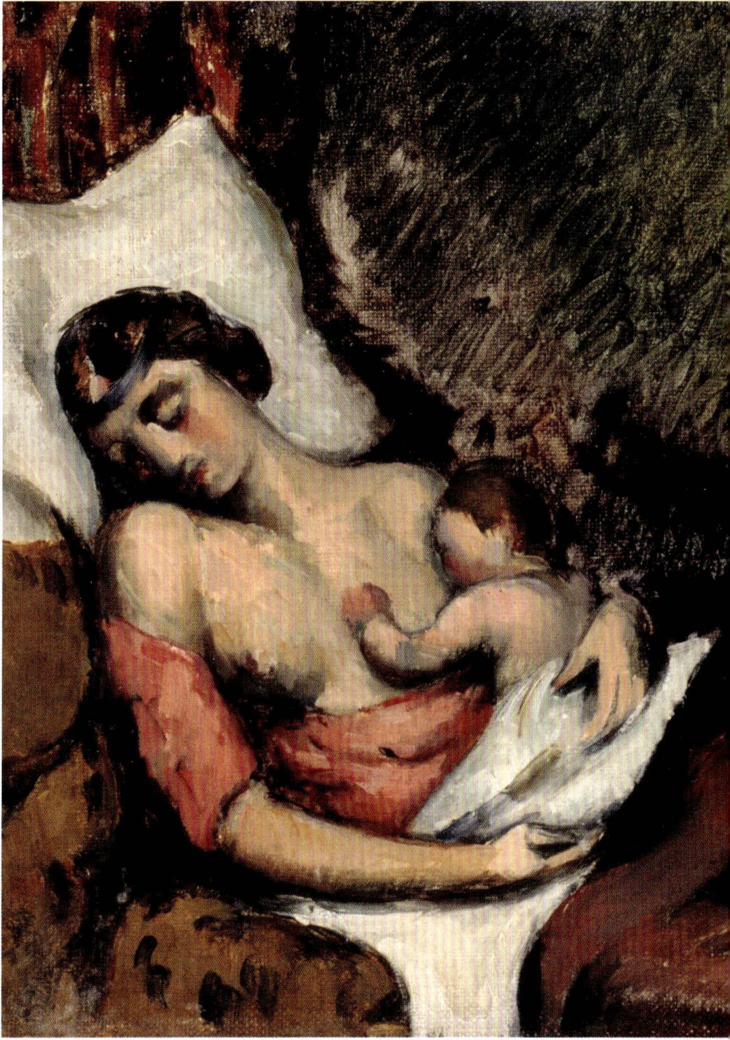

le motif – Cézanne's new works, such as *The Hanged Man's House*
(1873, *see* page 50) or *House of Père Lacroix* (1873), were sober
meditations on ordinary, everyday subjects in the manner of Pissarro
himself, executed with the high-keyed palette Pissarro recommended,
based on the three primary colours and their immediate derivatives,
which became indispensable to the Impressionists' stated aim of
capturing fleeting moments in time.

The following year, Cézanne moved to the nearby village of Auvers-
sur-Oise, to live with Dr Paul Gachet (1828–1909), already a keen

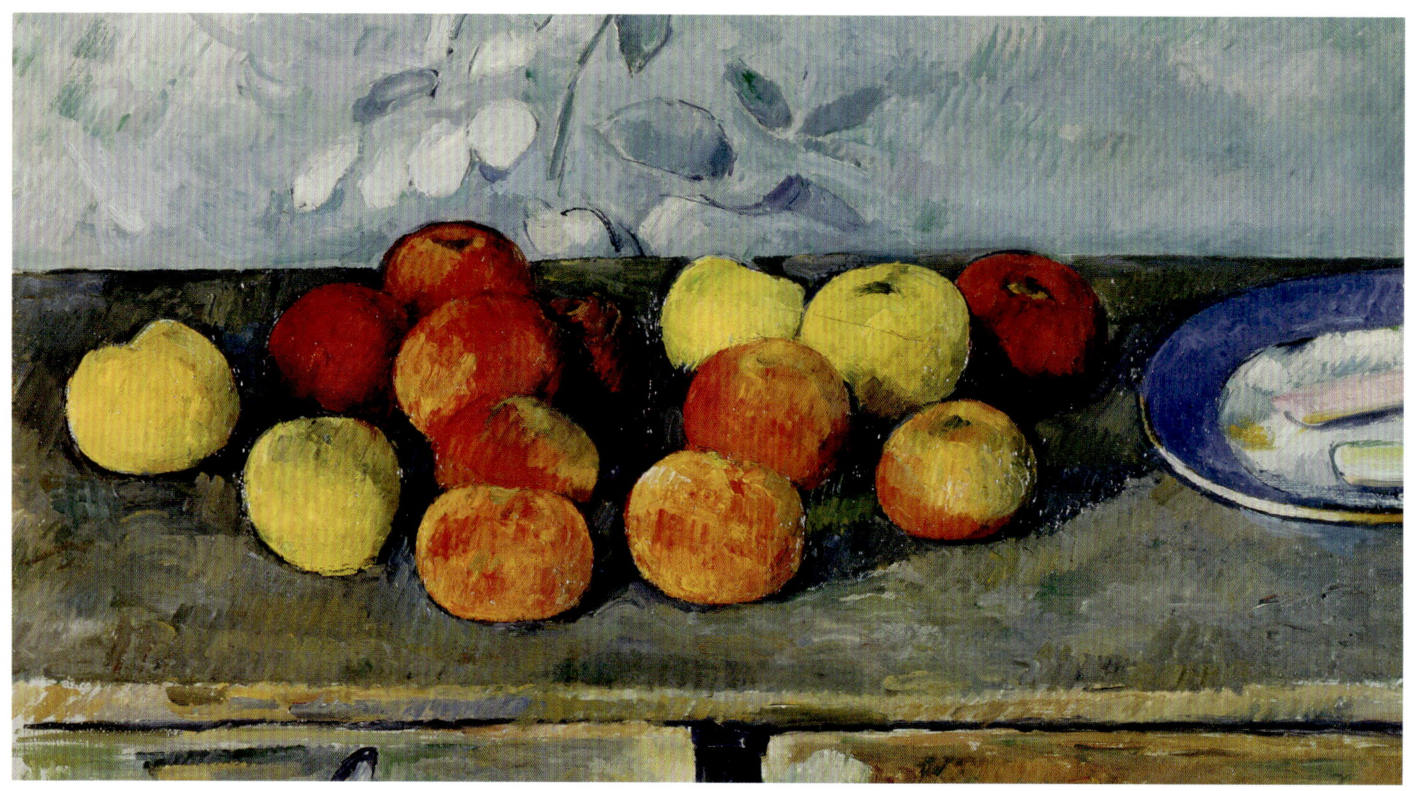

supporter of modern art, who would later be depicted in a famous
portrait by Vincent van Gogh (1853–90). It was here that the young
painter began to apply his bright, new, optimistic palette to still life,
a genre he had pursued more assiduously than anyone else in his
circle, in which the black shadows and impenetrable backgrounds of
the previous decade were replaced with coloured shadows and bright
subjects taken from the natural world, as in *Bouquet in a Small Delft
Vase* (1873, *see* page 30). The good doctor, seeing that Cézanne's
allowance was not enough to provide for his young family, helpfully
purchased a large number of these works from him.

The Male Gaze

As well as landscape and still life, Cézanne continued to be drawn
to the sensual visions of the previous decade, which in canvases
like *A Modern Olympia* (1873–74, *see* page 112), a clear homage to
Manet's painting, seem almost joyful under the influence of the new

Impressionist palette. A new version of *The Temptation of St Anthony*
(*c.* 1877, *see* pages 25 and 111) is a somewhat sunny encounter with
a sensuality which had previously been depicted in threatening terms.
While painting from life – *sur le motif* – became his guiding principle,
Cézanne continued to make sensual fantasy paintings throughout the
1870s and beyond, such as *The Eternal Feminine* (1877, *see* right) or
The Battle of Love (*c.* 1880, *see* page 3), as well as a growing series
depicting bathers (mostly female bathers), a paradisiacal theme that
would come to dominate his last decade. It seems that none of these
nudes were painted from life, but instead from copies of Old Masters
and photographs of nudes he managed to acquire.

His portraiture, both of himself and at this stage mainly Hortense, was
also transformed by the new bright palette. By the time he came to
paint *Madame Cézanne in a Red Armchair* (1877, *see* page 85), his
understanding of the coloured shadows he had learned to integrate
into landscapes and still lifes led him to distribute mottled patches of

green across the shaded areas of her face in a way that is reminiscent of the Fauvist portrait Henri Matisse (1869–1954) made of his own wife some three decades later. By the late 1870s, Cézanne was probing a new approach that broke away from the dappled light effects of Impressionism, a clear demonstration of his famous statement of intent from this period: that he wanted 'to make Impressionism something solid and lasting like the art of the museums'.

A Great Patron

By then he had shown work in both the first and third Impressionist exhibitions, in 1874 and 1877, and while on the first occasion he had not been alone in selling very little and being the target of ridicule from press reviewers, still he seemed to be singled out for particular scorn. One of those who defended Cézanne and the other exhibitors against these attacks was Victor Chocquet (1821–91), a civil servant who expended all his spare income on paintings by the Impressionists, and one of a handful of collectors, including writer and art critic Théodore Duret (1838–1927) and wealthy fellow Impressionist painter Gustave Caillebotte (1848–1894), who bought work from Cézanne during these

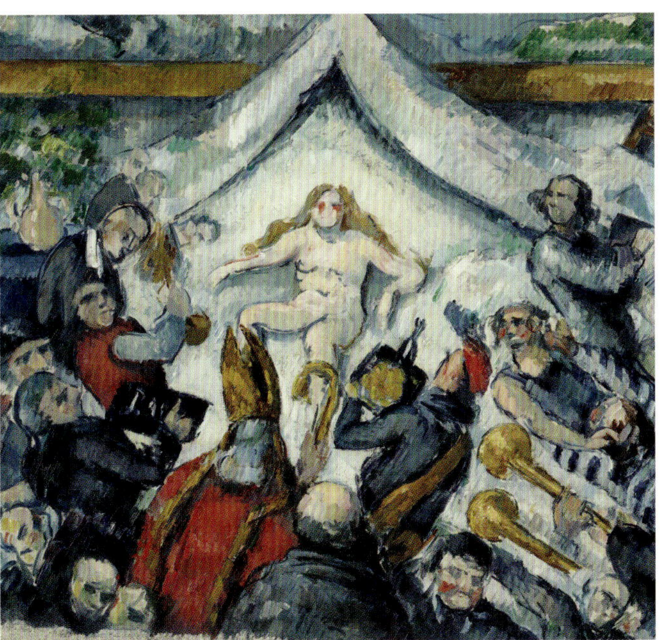

difficult early years. Cézanne had met Chocquet through Renoir, from whom Chocquet bought many works. But the government official soon recognized the aesthetic seriousness of Cézanne's intentions, and over the years bought more from him than from any other painter, some 35 works in all. Like Renoir, Cézanne also painted his patron on more than one occasion during this period (*see* page 84). These portraits convey a sense of the sitter's personality with more immediacy than perhaps any others he ever painted, a convention which in later portraits he more or less abandoned.

Above all, though, it is in the landscapes done throughout the 1870s that the slow development of Cézanne's method is most evident. Thus in *The Road at Pontoise* (1875–77, *see* page 52), instead of the variegated treatment of colour and atmosphere we would expect in an Impressionist work in order to suggest the fleeting effects of light, here the foliage of the trees and the green of the grass are dealt with summarily, almost as an idea or concept of grass or foliage. In doing so, Cézanne draws our eye towards the cluster of more carefully rendered monastery buildings to the left of the picture. It is clear that in his treatment of different parts of this image Cézanne is telling us something about how the eye, in fixing on a certain object as the focus of its gaze, apprehends the remainder in far less detail. The overall effect is neither conventionally representational nor Impressionist, but something else.

The Construction of Vision

In *The Bridge at Maincy near Melun* (1879, *see* page 53), an out-and-out masterpiece from the end of the decade, this summarizing tendency has been taken further towards the abstraction of vision that came to dominate Cézanne's thinking, particularly with regards to landscape. While the foliage has been painted with deliberate vagueness using the short, even strokes that became his most distinctive marks, the very definite intersecting lines of the bridge, the overhanging tree branches and the slim tree trunks – including the foreground saplings which in a break with conventional pictorial piety split the canvas and its ostensible subject, the bridge, boldly in two – emphasize the underlying structure of the picture as its most salient meaning.

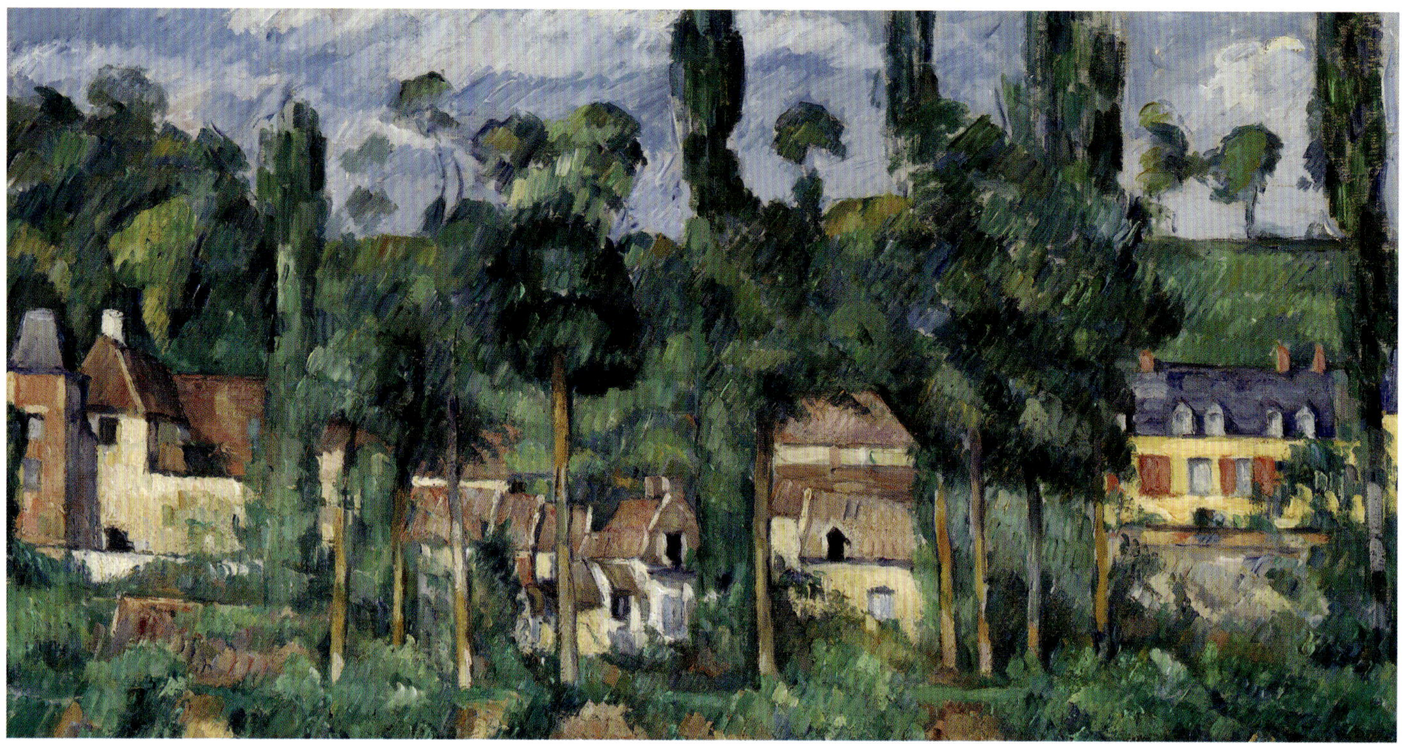

This canvas signals something new in Cézanne's perception at the beginning of what is usually known as his 'constructive' period. Melun near Fontainebleau, the favoured forest haunt of the Barbizon painters of the previous generation, was one of a number of sites around Paris where Cézanne spent time during the later 1870s and early 1880s. Others included Chantilly to the north and, on several occasions while staying at Zola's mansion (*see* above and page 54), Médan to the north-east on the banks of the River Seine. But Cézanne was also making regular visits back to Aix to see his family throughout this decade, to paint on the coast at L'Estaque and make surreptitious visits to Hortense and Paul, who from 1878 lived for some of the year at a house Cézanne had rented for them in Marseille, close to L'Estaque.

Found Out

By this point, the subterfuge by which he had been trying to keep his father from learning of the existence of his partner and son had begun to unravel. Still in total control of Cézanne's income, Louis-Auguste thought nothing of opening any correspondence addressed to him that arrived at the Jas de Bouffan, and in a letter from Chocquet that year Louis-Auguste discovered a clear reference to this secret family. He confronted his son, who denied their existence. As a result, either from social shame or because of such an obvious and disrespectful lie, his father summarily cut in half Cézanne's allowance, which by then had risen to 200 francs per month. For a time the painter was reduced to asking Zola for regular amounts to keep the family from destitution until, perhaps under pressure from his mother, his father reinstated the former sum. It would still be a further eight years before Cézanne saw fit to do as Marie (b. 1841), the older and more religious of his two sisters, kept urging and make Hortense his wife and young Paul, by then a teenage boy, his legitimate heir.

The Crisis of Impressionism

By the late 1870s, Impressionism was in crisis, with canvases hardly selling to an art-buying public not only still wary of the novelty of the style but suffering the effects of a global recession. In France this had begun with an economic crash in 1873 and a subsequent recession that continued, more or less unbroken, until the end of the following decade. But there was also a more specific, aesthetic crisis, keenly felt by all the artists associated with the style, which they responded to in different ways; a crisis which Zola, previously so supportive of the group, described in a withering critique published in the newspaper *Le Voltaire* in 1880. Concluding that all of them were 'forerunners' – that 'Their artist of genius has not yet been born' – Zola was in fact echoing their own collective doubts about the incidental nature of the style: that the spontaneity and immediacy that made Impressionism so fresh would ultimately render it disposable. Cézanne had always harboured these same reservations, with his adoption of an Impressionist palette and methods under the tutelage of Pissarro more a way of escaping the morbid Romanticism of his early period. Impressionism was merely the means by which he would learn to truly look at a motif and bind himself to the world beyond his own imagination.

Cézanne had been the artist amongst the Impressionists, along with Renoir, who looked most sincerely to the past and sought to create an art of permanence that might one day take its place alongside the work of those Old Masters he revered. On some level, he continued to believe in a conventional route towards that goal, submitting paintings to the Salon in most years until 1884, and on most of those occasions being rejected despite the vigorous intervention of his friend Guillemet, by then a jury member. But on another level, Cézanne knew that the route he had chosen – as he once put it to a friend, 'to be a classical painter, to become classical through nature' – led to a way of seeing that the majority of the jury, wedded to the tradition of academic painting they had been taught and were now charged with upholding, would never take the time to understand.

The Structure of Feeling

Cézanne spoke also of 'redoing Poussin from nature', a remark that encapsulated his belief that, although it was essential to study and to learn from the great tradition of art, it was worthless without contact with the raw material of picture-making, as the vast majority of spiritless

paintings exhibited at the Salon each year clearly showed. As he put it in a letter towards the end of his life, 'after seeing the great masters … one must hasten to leave and revivify oneself through contact with nature, with the instincts and with the artistic sensations within us'.

And though when it came to the human body he became increasingly averse to painting *sur le motif*, where landscapes were concerned Cézanne spoke often of trying to realize the 'strong feeling' he experienced before nature. His use of the word 'feeling' marks a critical difference with the Impressionists, whose principal aim was to render the world through the momentary play of light upon its surfaces, the colours of objects and the atmosphere surrounding them radically different at different times of the day, as would be demonstrated so vividly by Monet's series paintings of the 1890s. In this regard, Cézanne once described the master of Giverny as 'just an eye, but what an eye!', a comment as dismissive as it is laudatory. For Cézanne, the vision of the world we receive through the

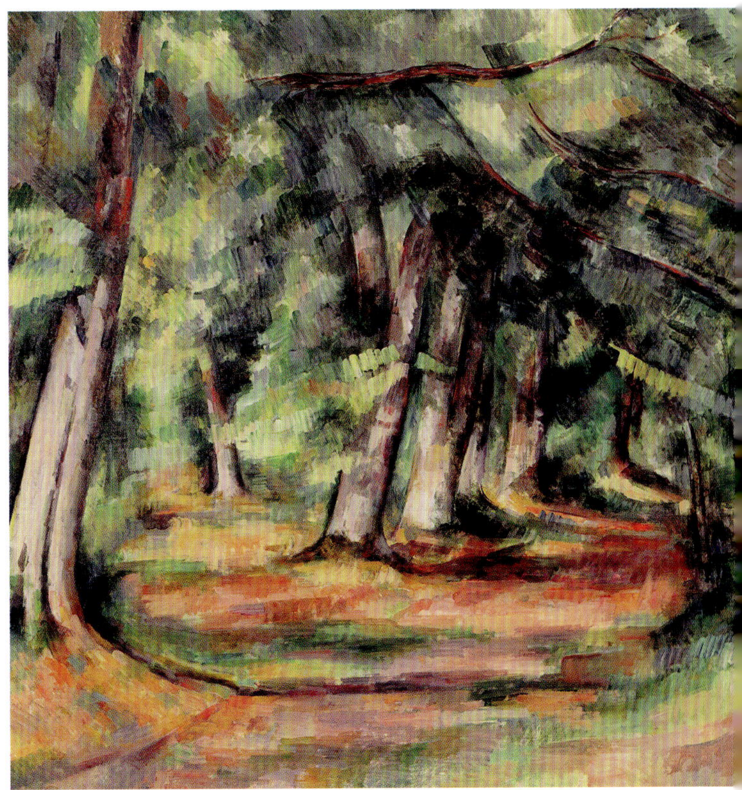

eyes could never be *more* than an impression; what mattered to him was his total experience of what he saw – 'the eye and the brain', as he put it – with painting a way to both understand that experience and intensify it through that same understanding; in his own words, 'to know, the better to feel; to feel, the better to know'.

Zola the Critic

As a young painter, Cézanne had felt intensely, while lacking the ability to convey what he felt, but thanks to Pissarro he learned to discipline his feelings through strict observation and analysis, a process which within a few years had taken him beyond what he saw as the limitations of Impressionism. He still spent long periods at Pontoise with 'God the father', as he often referred to Pissarro, and made listless visits to Zola's increasingly sumptuous mansion at Médan nearby. But Cézanne, who

unlike Zola was privately affluent but temperamentally ascetic, was as put off by these bourgeois trappings of success as the celebrated writer, a judgmental friend since childhood, was pitying of what he saw as the painter's failure to realize his evident genius. To Zola, worldly success was what mattered.

Cézanne increasingly turned in on himself, spending more and more time in the south, either at Aix, painting motifs he found in the garden and grounds of the Jas de Bouffan, or at L'Estaque. He developed a new friendship with Adolphe Monticelli (1824–86), a highly distinctive Romantic painter from Marseille of the older generation, going on painting trips with him in the countryside around Aix. In January 1882, he was paid a visit by Renoir as the Parisian painter was on his way back to the capital from Italy and North Africa. The two of them worked alongside each other, and Renoir returned with

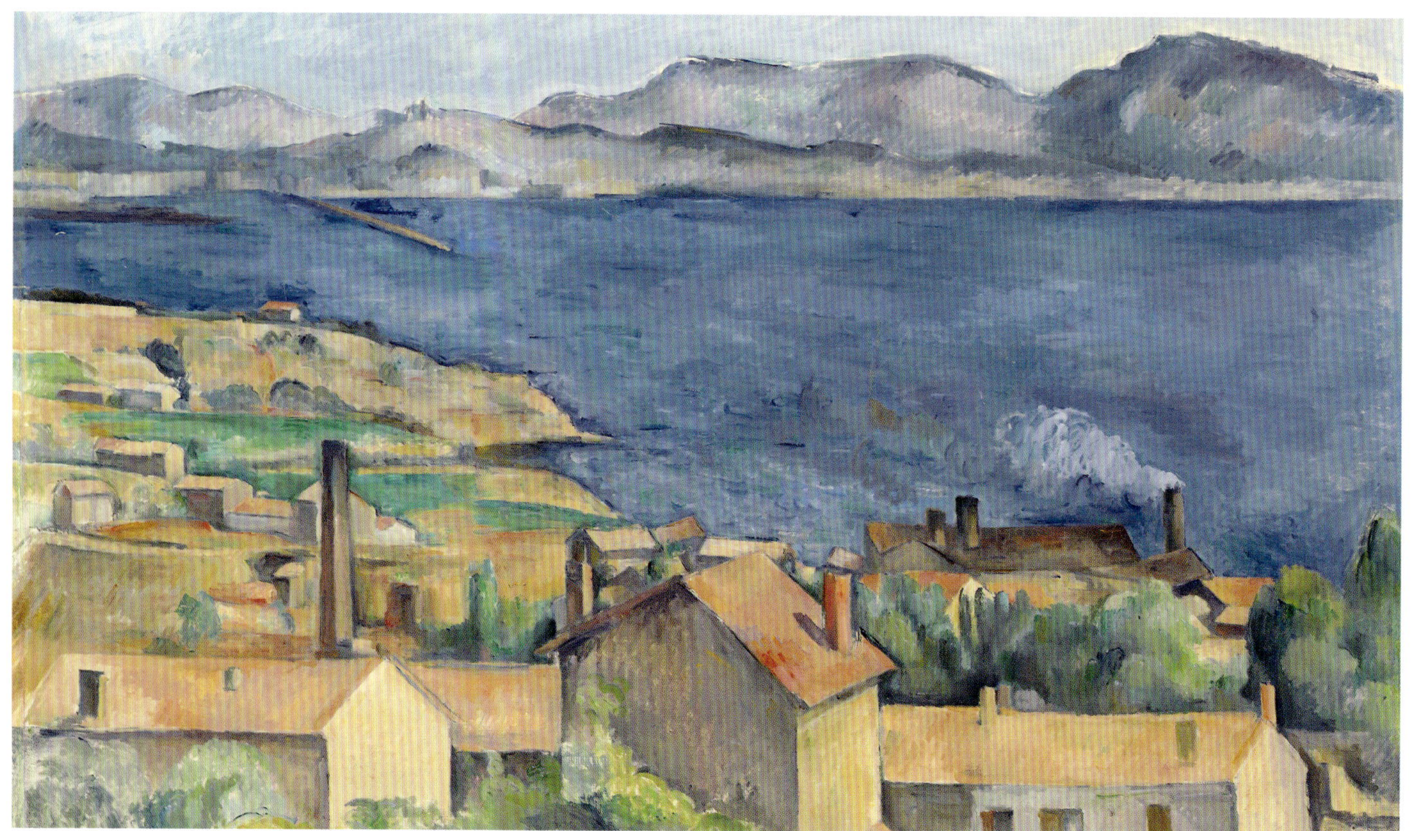

Monet at the end of the following year. Cézanne would pay visits to them both in the north a couple of years later, but the length of these trips was getting shorter, as his obsession with the coast and with the landscapes of his childhood deepened over time.

L'Estaque

The familiarity of these places was central to Cézanne's growing sense of purpose. With no need to accustom himself to motifs he already knew so well, it was a natural thing to look beyond the visual impression to a more fundamental reality, the ideal which even at the end of his life he felt he had still not attained. Nonetheless, his paintings of the Bay of Marseille, painted at L'Estaque throughout the 1880s, were a significant step towards it. These pictures of distant buildings with terracotta-coloured roofs in harsh, bright sunlight are rendered with increasing precision, the straight lines of the roofs and the simplified forms of the buildings appearing as solid planes in a way that differed hugely from the blurred outlines and light-inflected surfaces of similar features in paintings by Monet, for example. The effect Cézanne achieved was closer to earlier French landscape painters of the Roman Campagna – the most classical landscape of all – such as the simplified buildings that are often central to the landscapes of Pierre-Henri de Valenciennes (1750–1819), a pioneer of painting *en plein air* whose work he would have known from the Louvre. There are similarities, too, with the distant structures that appear in the background of certain classical landscapes by Nicolas Poussin (1594–1665), another of Cézanne's tutelary gods. We know that a picture such as *The Bay of Marseille Seen from L'Estaque* (*c.* 1885, *see* left and page 60) depicts its subject in broad daylight, but this is not the specific quality of light associated with a particular moment in time, as an Impressionist painting would seek to depict, but an aggregate of similar moments for which the image might stand as a summation, an almost classical idea of how the same scene ought to appear in broadly equivalent conditions on any given day.

Gardanne

The sharp differentiation in this painting between the red of the foreground roofs, the yellow of the fields beyond them, the cobalt blue

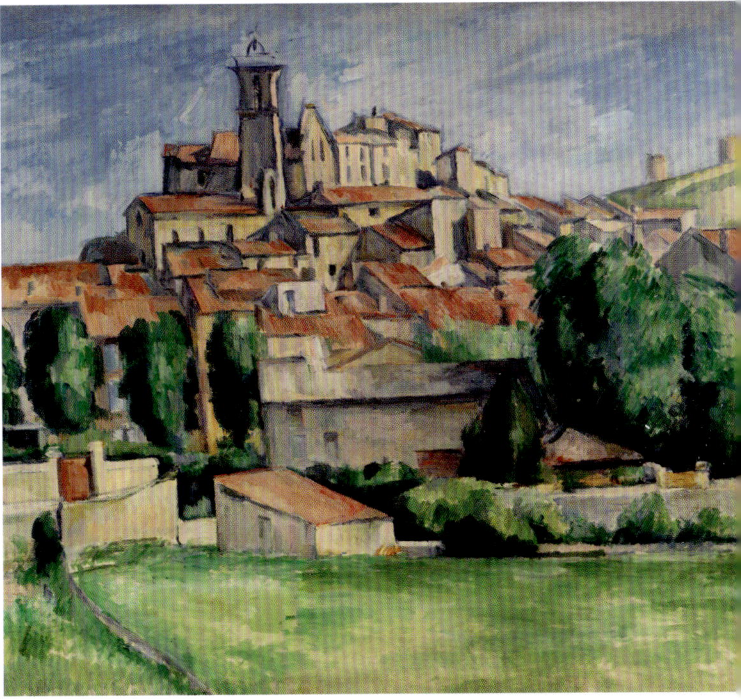

of the sea, the distant grey hills and the lighter blue of the sky divides the painting into several distinct planes. Within each of these, detail is eliminated as far as possible, the distant roofs and walls rendered as strict geometric planes, the trees and faraway mountains as small masses or volumes of colour. Cézanne is inching towards an understanding of the world not as the eye sees it, but as the mind comprehends it, in conceptual shorthand. This geometric method of depicting the world through complex patterns of intersecting planes and coloured volumes was further developed in images he made around the small town of Gardanne, just south of Aix, such as *Gardanne* (*c.* 1885, *see* above and page 58), where he lived and painted for more than a year from August 1885, following the end of what seems to have been a short but passionate affair, possibly with one of the maids at the Jas de Bouffan. Little is known of the liaison, but in any case it seems to have been a one-off, a final eruption of the unbridled passion of his youth. It also seems likely that while his sister Marie knew of the affair, and even dismissed the maid, Hortense was none the wiser when she and son Paul joined Cézanne in his rented apartment in Gardanne later that autumn.

A Fateful Year

Even without the shadow of an affair, the year Cézanne spent at Gardanne would be the most eventful of his life. In April 1886, he was finally persuaded to marry Hortense, after Marie had obtained permission for the union from their father. It was a timely reconciliation, as Louis-Auguste, by now in his late eighties, was to die in October of that year, leaving each of his children a substantial inheritance that would relieve the painter of any financial cares thereafter. But the month before his marriage, the publication of Zola's latest novel and Cézanne's reaction to it after Zola, as usual, had sent him a copy, caused a permanent rupture in a friendship that had once been of the utmost importance to them both.

Entitled *L'Oeuvre* (or *The Masterpiece*), the story's main protagonist was one Claude Lantier, a painter who had featured in previous instalments of Zola's mammoth Rougon-Macquart series depicting the history of a family under the Second Empire of Napoleon III. Zola's friends were used to recognizing themselves in the pages of his works, and Cézanne was already familiar with Lantier from the earlier novels and thus with his own resemblance to the fictional painter. But *L'Oeuvre,* a *roman à clef* following real events in the lives of Zola's painter friends too literally to be mistaken for any kind of fiction, was a step too far not only for Cézanne but also for Monet, Renoir and the other Impressionists who found their struggles exploited in such mercenary fashion and their collective endeavours so witheringly dismissed as a failed enterprise; and just at the point when, as Monet wrote in an angry letter to Zola, they were finally on the cusp of lasting success.

The End of a Friendship

The portrayal of Lantier cut Cézanne to the quick, above all for the crude understanding it showed – what the novel describes as a 'failure of genius' – of what the real-life Lantier was trying to achieve.

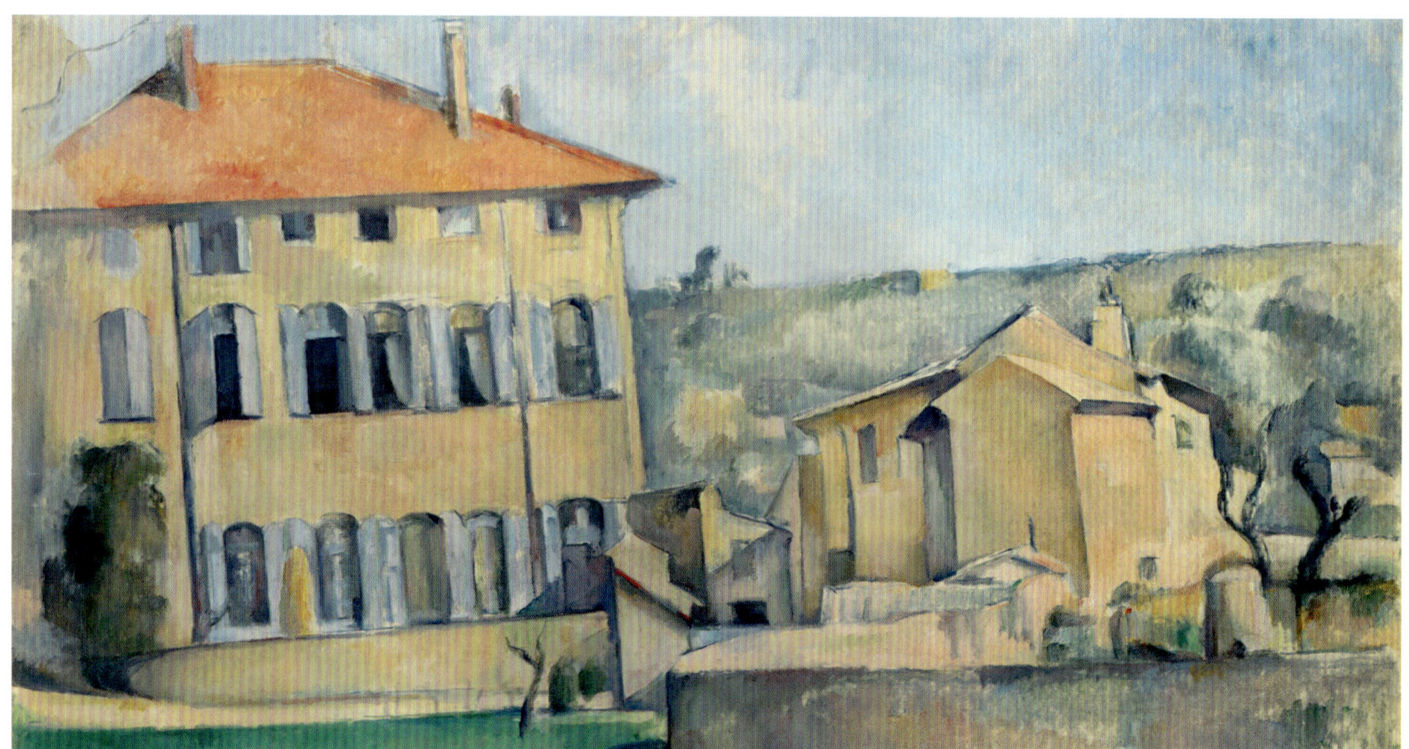

Far from being the tormented figure depicted in the novel, struggling and failing to fulfil an all-consuming need to paint a masterpiece, a failure which finally leads him to take his own life, Cézanne was committed to painting not as a way of producing masterworks but as a way of apprehending the world through thought and feeling symbiotically linked – a new interiority which may have been anathema to the Salon painters of the Belle Époque and even to Zola, but which became central to the future direction of art. The painter's response was to write Zola the coldest imaginable letter of thanks, a missive of caricatured formality that was clearly intended to end the friendship, which it duly did.

Fresh Perspective

With the death of his father, Cézanne now felt able to move into the Jas de Bouffan. Hortense did not see eye-to-eye with either Marie or Cézanne's mother, so she and son Paul moved to an apartment in Aix, continuing the pattern of interrupted family life that had been a consistent feature of the boy's childhood. Cézanne was more than comfortable living with his mother and sister, in preference to his now-wife and child. He spent the whole of 1887 at the Jas, producing images painted with a bracing new clarity, such as *The House in Aix (Jas de Bouffan)* (1887, *see* left), which exhibits the same geometry evident in the pictures of L'Estaque and particularly the more close-up townscape of Gardanne, but with a curious lack of concern for the verticality of the structures depicted, especially the house, as if these are subject to another, more irrational force emerging from beneath the pictorial architecture, a manifestation of what he called his 'feeling before the motif'. In this case, the wonkiness of the house and its slightly unfathomable relationship to the outbuildings in the foreground are exhibiting what one writer has described as Cézanne's 'sensory perspective', which trumps conventional ocular, linear perspective as practised by artists since the Renaissance.

In admitting the emotional truth of this eccentric depiction, Cézanne is surely conveying some essential feeling he had for his childhood home, perhaps the more so given the death of his father the previous year. This infusing of the image with a subjective emotion had also begun to emerge in the growing numbers of portraits he painted from the 1880s onwards, which often reveal a vulnerable humanity in the sitters that is seen only in the work of the very greatest painters. It is a quality we find in the majority of portraits he did of his wife, some 30 in all, for which she would pose patiently for hours on end, often for more than a hundred separate sittings, the more so the more Cézanne grew in experience and subjected every intended mark to rigorous examination before committing it to the canvas.

Model Patience

Among the most remarkable of these images of Hortense is *Madame Cézanne in a Red Dress* (1888–90, *see* page 90), in which not only is there no basic concern for the image's consistent verticality but the

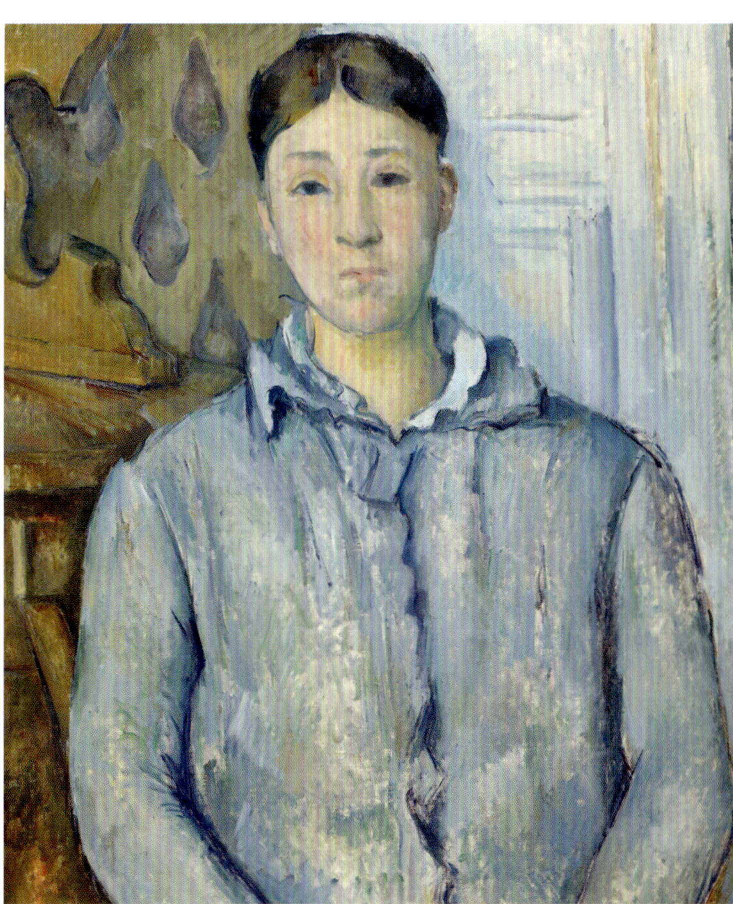

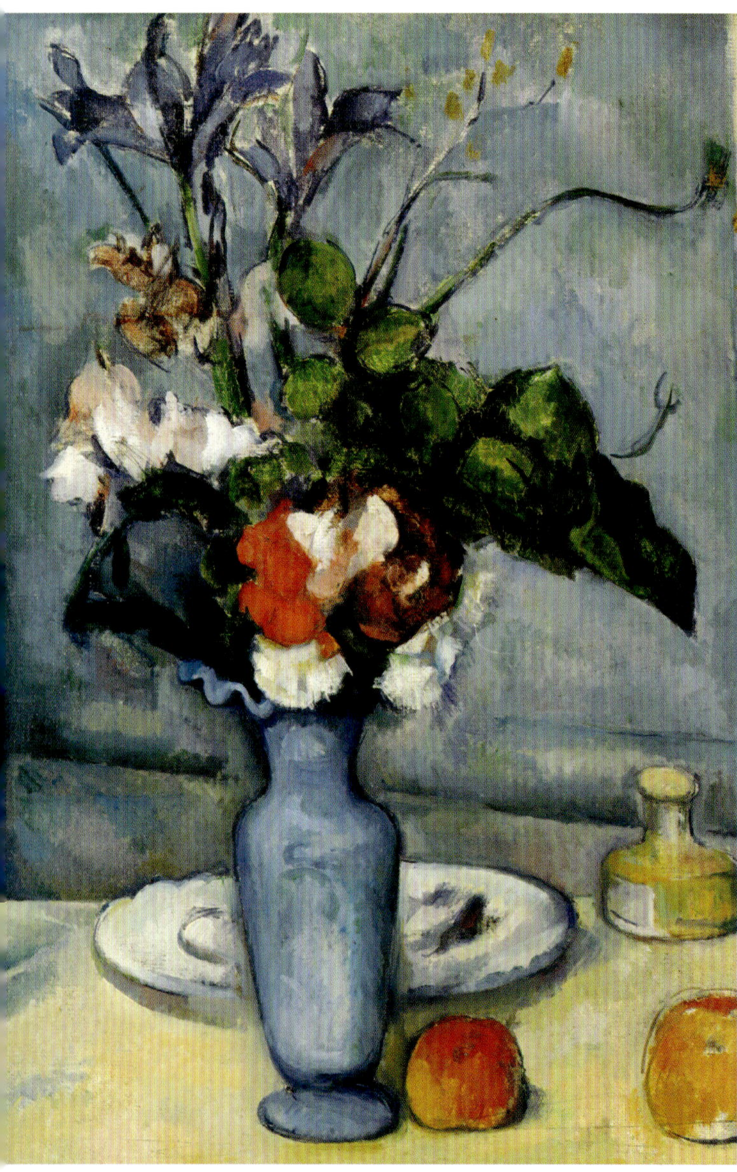

A similar feeling of a world not subject to the normal physical and psychological gravity finds its way into some of the still lifes Cézanne painted during this period, such as *The Blue Vase* (1889–90, *see* left and page 35), whose eponymous subject leans eccentrically one way while the ellipsis of its base tends the other. Cézanne painted still lifes throughout his career – far more than any other painter of his generation – and the increasing slowness and deliberation of his working method presented challenges when the motifs under scrutiny were perishable items such as flowers and fruit. His solution to the problem was not to compromise the longevity of his working methods – it is reasonable to assume from evidence such as the sprouting onions in *Still Life with Onions* (1896–98, *see* page 41), for example, that he continued to take his time – but to turn in later still lifes to paper flowers and artificial fruit.

Critical Attention

In 1888, having spent most of the previous year in Aix, Cézanne returned to live in Paris and again painted at Chantilly. In the same year, he began to attract the attention of writers such as Joris-Karl Huysmans (1848–1907), who a few years earlier had been somewhat dismissive of Cézanne, but now wrote a sympathetic article in the newspaper *La Cravache* and devoted a chapter to the painter in a book he published the following year. By 1889, the tide had begun to turn in favour of the middle-aged generation of one-time Impressionist painters, and even Cézanne had a picture selected for the Exposition Universelle held in Paris that year (albeit with a bit of string-pulling from Victor Chocquet) – the early Impressionist landscape *The Hanged Man's House, Auvers-sur-Oise* (1873, *see* page 50).

Most enthusiastic were the younger generation, including the Belgian group Les Vingts, who invited Cézanne to exhibit with them in Brussels the following year, as well as members of Les Nabis, the group of painters around Paul Gauguin (1848–1903), who were particularly inspired by Cézanne's innovative methods and who bought his work. Among these figures, the precocious Émile Bernard (1868–1941), the originator of Cloisonnism, a style of painting thought to have been inspired by Cézanne, was sufficiently enthused

sitter herself appears weightless, as if barely seated in the yellow chair; as if in fact she were a doll. It is an air of insubstantiality that to differing degrees extends to the personhood of the sitter in so many portraits of his wife, such as *Madame Cézanne in Blue* (1888–90, *see* page 17) and others he did in the years of his maturity, which are similarly unconcerned with individual personality but instead convey something more archetypal and thus more universal about the human condition.

not only to write and publish a pamphlet on the Provençal painter in 1892, but a decade later was still so fascinated with his work that he persuaded the artist to divulge aspects of his approach to painting in a series of letters on which all subsequent understanding of his work has been partly based.

Fear of Influence

This was not an insignificant achievement as, throughout his life, Cézanne had been reluctant to the point of hostility to engage in talk about art, fearing that others would, as he put it, 'get their hooks' into him, influencing his own methods and undermining the integrity of his work. At the same time, he was also acutely paranoid about other painters, on one occasion declaring of his peers that 'they think I've got a secret formula, and they want to steal it from me'. But even praise was something he found almost impossible to accept. On a visit to Monet at Giverny in 1894, when the big-hearted Impressionist delivered an impromptu encomium to his friend from Aix in front of a group including Renoir, the sculptor Auguste Rodin (1840–1917) and the writer Gustave Geffroy (1855–1926), Cézanne accused Monet of making fun of him and departed Giverny with such haste that he left behind at the inn where he was staying several of the canvases he had been working on.

It was partly for these reasons, as much as from mistrust after so many years of ridicule and rejection, that Cézanne was ambivalent about the new levels of attention and respect he began to garner in the early 1890s. Moreover, with no longer any financial need to sell his paintings and keenly aware of his own mortality since the death of his father, the more so with the onset of diabetes in 1890, he regarded the attention as a distraction from the only thing that mattered – his work.

A Change of Scenery

It was also in 1890 that Hortense persuaded him to accompany her and son Paul on a five-month tour to neighbouring

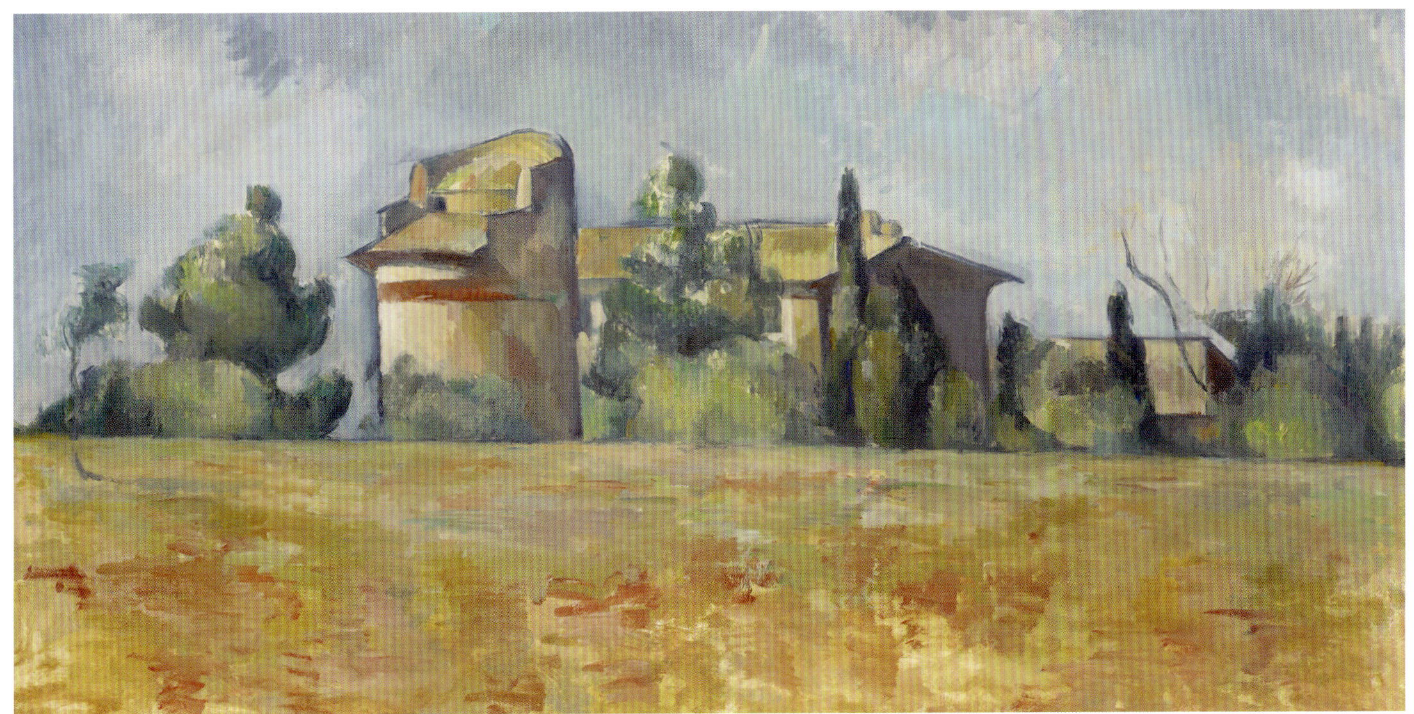

Switzerland, the only trip outside France Cézanne ever made. The new sights made no impression whatsoever on his painting, and it was only when he returned to Aix, among familiar surroundings, that he went back to painting on the range of different themes he pursued over the following few years. These included a remarkable series of landscapes of the house at Bellevue, the property just south of Aix that belonged to his much-younger sister Rose (b. 1854) and her lawyer husband Maxime Conil. These include *The Dovecote at Bellevue* (1888–92, *see* pages 19 and 63), a classically composed subject again reminiscent of de Valenciennes, with detail reduced to a bare minimum of planes and masses, a simplification which somehow makes the image more not less vivid; and *House and Dovecote at Bellevue* (1890–92, *see* page 64), in which his use of colour alone to suggest volume is pushing him towards abstraction, while the areas of bare canvas visible through the foliage are both evidence of the increasing hesitancy with which he worked and an intentional effect that becomes an integral aspect of his late method. He also began the first of four paintings entitled *The Card Players* (1890–92, *see* page 95), which posed peasants from the family estate engaged not in the noble toil for which they were employed, as Jean-François Millet (1814–75) might have had them, but in a kind of communal meditation, inviting us into the conscious quietude not of peasant life but of ordinary men at their leisure. Given the amount of time it took him to finish a picture – these images each took several years to complete – it is fair to say that Cézanne must have taken them away from the work they were supposed to be doing on a fairly regular basis throughout the early to mid-1890s.

Ambroise Vollard

By early 1892, Cézanne had managed to persuade his wife to live permanently in Aix, even if not at the Jas de Bouffan, though she disliked

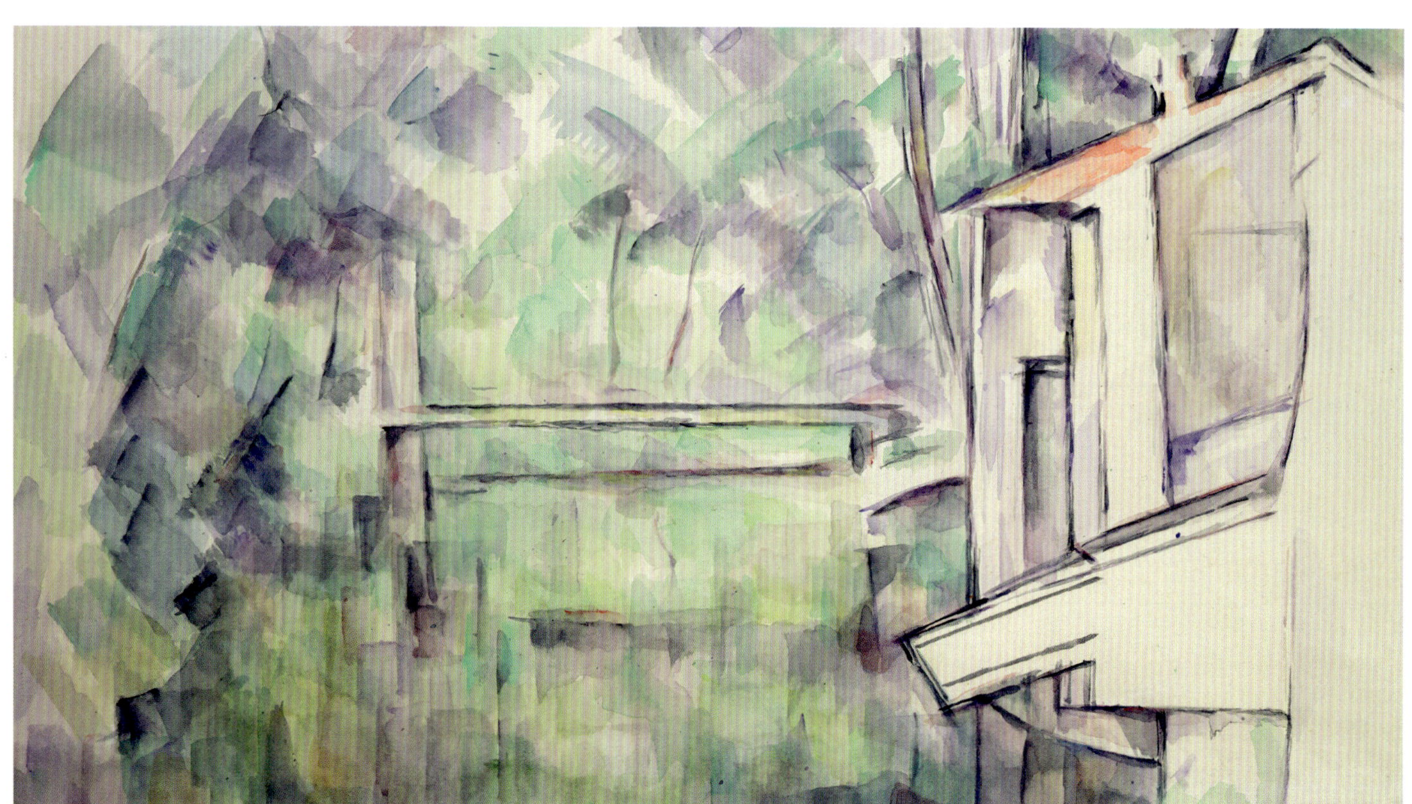

the south in general as much as she did the family home and its female inhabitants. Following what had been the pattern of their relationship over more than 20 years, it would not be long before she left again for Paris. Cézanne was continuing to spend time in the capital himself, though in a sign of his increasing introversion, he had started to cross the street or to use other tactics of avoidance whenever he saw anyone he knew. In fact, though he again rented a place in the city, his reason for returning to Paris in this and subsequent years seems to have been his desire to paint landscapes with which he was already familiar, such as those around Pontoise but especially in the Forest of Fontainebleau, as in the tenebrous canvas *Rocks in the Forest* (*c.* 1893). It was here in 1892 that he bought a cottage in the village of Bourron-Marlotte on the southern perimeter of the old royal hunting forest, which he continued to visit until the year before his death, as we can see from the watercolour *Mill at the River (The Bridge of Maincy)* (1904–05, *see* left).

It was during the early 1890s that a series of deaths of collectors who had bought or acquired Cézanne's work – Chocquet in 1891, and then both Caillebotte and paint dealer Julien-François (a.k.a. *père*) Tanguy (1825–94) in 1894 – dealt his cause a mix of fortunes. On the one hand, he had lost some key supporters, and on the other, a number of his works entered the public domain, in the first instance when Caillebotte's will bequeathed his entire collection, including several paintings by Cézanne, to the Musée du Luxembourg and the Louvre. His work was still being bought by his fellow painters – Gauguin, Monet and Degas in particular – but that same year, 1894, a young dealer called Ambroise Vollard (1866–1939) became acquainted with his painting after a recommendation from Pissarro. Over the next few months, with the help of Cézanne's son Paul, Vollard persuaded the painter to send him some 150 canvases – more than he had room to exhibit – to mount a show at his gallery in Paris the following year.

Quarry Man

At the same time, Cézanne was discovering new motifs in the Bibémus quarry, the old stone quarry just outside of Aix to which he was repeatedly drawn back over the next few years. Worked continuously from Roman times until being abandoned in 1885, the atmospheric

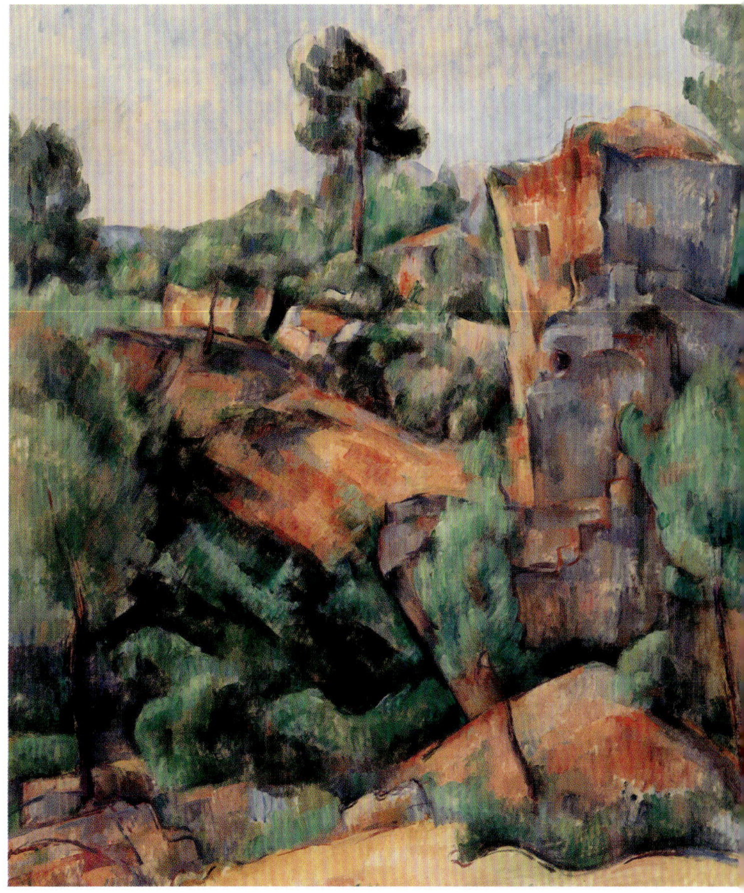

galleries of limestone bluffs, cut on the overhang to protect the distinctive ochre colour of the remaining rock from the weather, had provided the stone used in the buildings of his home city. He rented an old stone *cabanon*, or cottage, originally built for olive pickers, where he would stay for long periods at a time while working on motifs within the quarry. Here Cézanne found in the sharp intersections of the cut surfaces of rocks patterns of coloured planes infinitely more irregular than any he had encountered in his images of the roofs, buildings and fields of L'Estaque and Gardanne in the previous decade, as we can see in *Bibémus Quarry* (1895, *see* above) or *Mont Sainte-Victoire Seen from the Bibémus Quarry* (*c.* 1897, *see* page 71). This latter painting combined the new motif with another he had been painting for two decades by then, in pictures such as *Mont Sainte-Victoire with Large Pine* (*c.* 1887, *see* page 62): namely, the sentinel mountain which dominates the landscape for miles around Aix-en-Provence and which became an abiding obsession in Cézanne's final years.

Double Vision

It was in his final images of the mountain that Cézanne would later apply with radical freedom the discoveries already evident in these images of the quarry. Cézanne often talked about needing to understand the geological structure of a motif before he was able to paint it. In the literal geology of these multifaceted rocks we can see what this meant not only for his own painting but in the challenge it laid down to every painter who came after him. Around this time he remarked to Renoir that it had taken him 40 years 'to find out that painting is not sculpture', by which he meant that the illusion of modelling masked the reality of painting as a two-dimensional object primarily concerned with colour and pattern. His insight was pushing at a door first opened by the Impressionists. In his case, he recognized that in depicting such fragmentary patterns he was disrupting the picture plane, calling attention to the artificial reality of painting itself, which in realizing the motif through colour and pattern created what he called 'a harmony parallel with nature'. Moreover, the complexity of surfaces in these images of Bibémus reveal something about the nature of looking that Cézanne had been inching towards for years: a sense of the image being viewed, and having been painted, from more than one vantage point, as if we were watching a three-dimensional film without the red and green glasses that enable us to assemble the

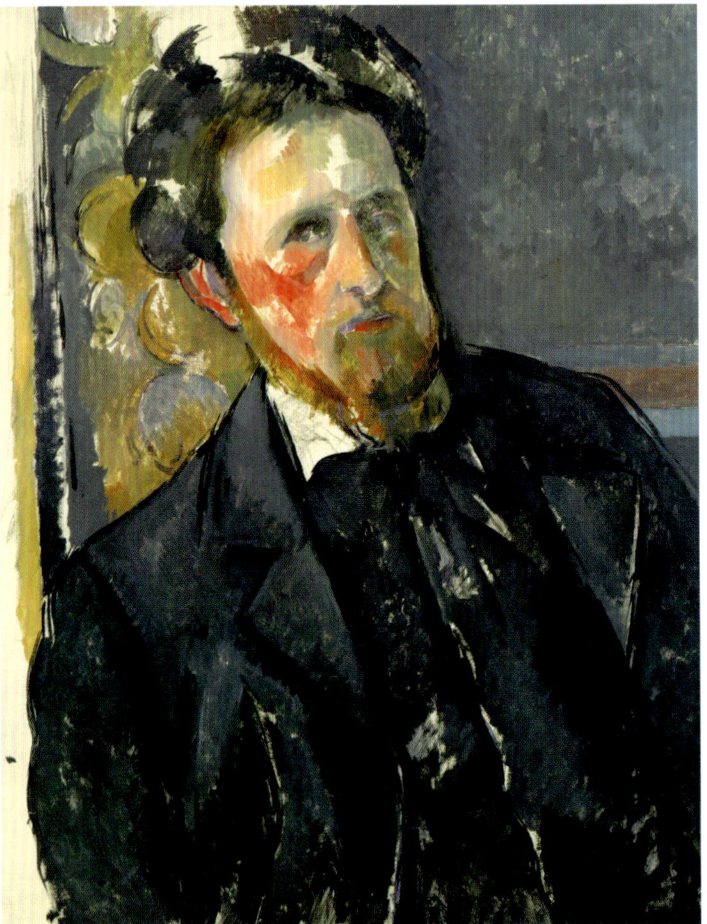

two-dimensional, binocular image into a three-dimensional whole.

This fragmentation or splitting of vision is something Cézanne had already begun to apply to motifs other than the obvious complexity of planes he found in the rocks of Bibémus, in remarkable pictures such as *Underwood (near Jas de Bouffan)* (1890–94, *see* pages 13 and 65), *Great Pine near Aix* (1895–97) and *Lac d'Annecy* (1896, *see* page 69). This last dreamlike image he painted at the resort town of Talloires on Lake Annecy in the foothills of the French Alps, on another holiday Hortense persuaded him to take, this time in July and August 1896. That same year, he met Joachim Gasquet, the son of a former school friend, with whom he kept up a dutiful correspondence in the later 1890s and beyond, and who later wrote one of the many memoirs of Cézanne that appeared in the years after his death. Gasquet, the subject of one of Cézanne's most remarkable, if unfinished late portraits, *Portrait of Joachim Gasquet* (1896–97, *see* above), was at the centre of a group of younger writers and painters from the south who were doing their military service in Aix and who looked upon Cézanne's work with awe.

Château Noir

The following year, 1897, Cézanne spent the later months in Aix, again painting in the quarry and also around the village of Le Tholonet close by. It was here that he found more new motifs, especially around the Château Noir, a mid-nineteenth-century Neo-Gothic building which, being unfinished, had about it the air of a ruin. With money no object, he rented a room there and from the terrace that surrounds the property on three sides painted further images over the next decade of what became his favourite motif, Mont Sainte-Victoire. These include *Mont Sainte-Victoire and Château Noir* (c. 1904–06, *see* below and page 76), an astonishing picture in which the almost amorphous volume of blues, greens and pinks – rendered in his characteristic short strokes – depicting the sky, mountain and foreground forest is broken only by the geometric projection of the château, jutting out from the hillside like a yellow apparition of human separateness from nature.

Room with a View

In October 1897, Cézanne's beloved mother died, and two years later, in November 1899, the Jas de Bouffan was sold and the proceeds divided amongst Cézanne and his siblings. With the painter unable to look after himself, and with his wife and son now permanently back in her native Paris, his sister Marie found him an apartment at 23 Rue Boulegon in the centre of Aix and engaged a housekeeper, Madame Brémond, to cook his meals and manage the household. He lived simply, as had always been his wont, though despite this his physical condition continued to deteriorate as the diabetes progressed. Increasingly aware of his mortality, he had returned to the Catholic faith some 10 years earlier and now went every day to Mass at the Cathedral of Saint Sauveur, a short walk from his apartment.

Then, with the money he made from the sale of the Jas, towards the end of 1901, Cézanne purchased a plot of land in an area called Les Lauves on a hillside just to the north of Aix. He commissioned a building on the plot, which included a 50-square-metre studio, the last

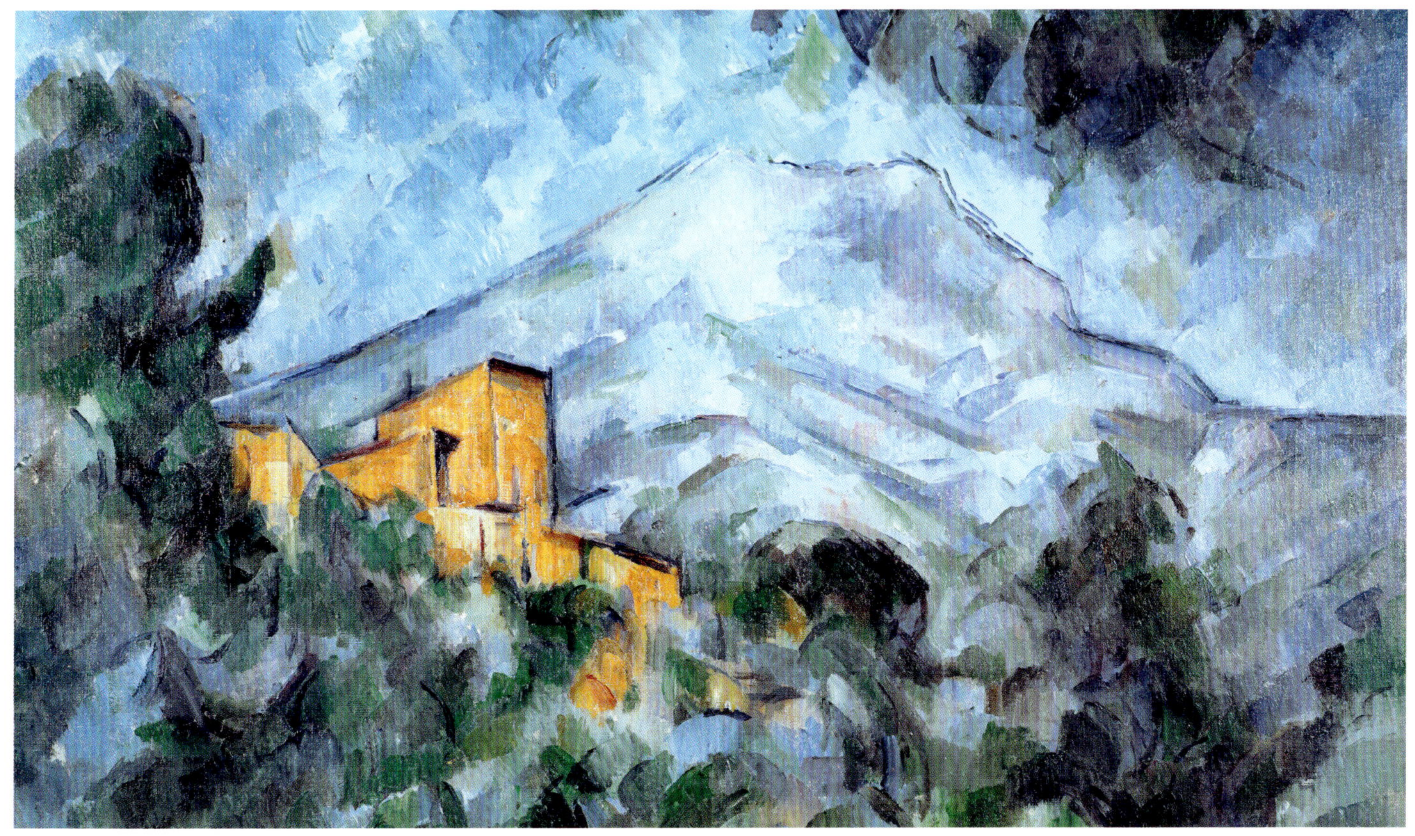

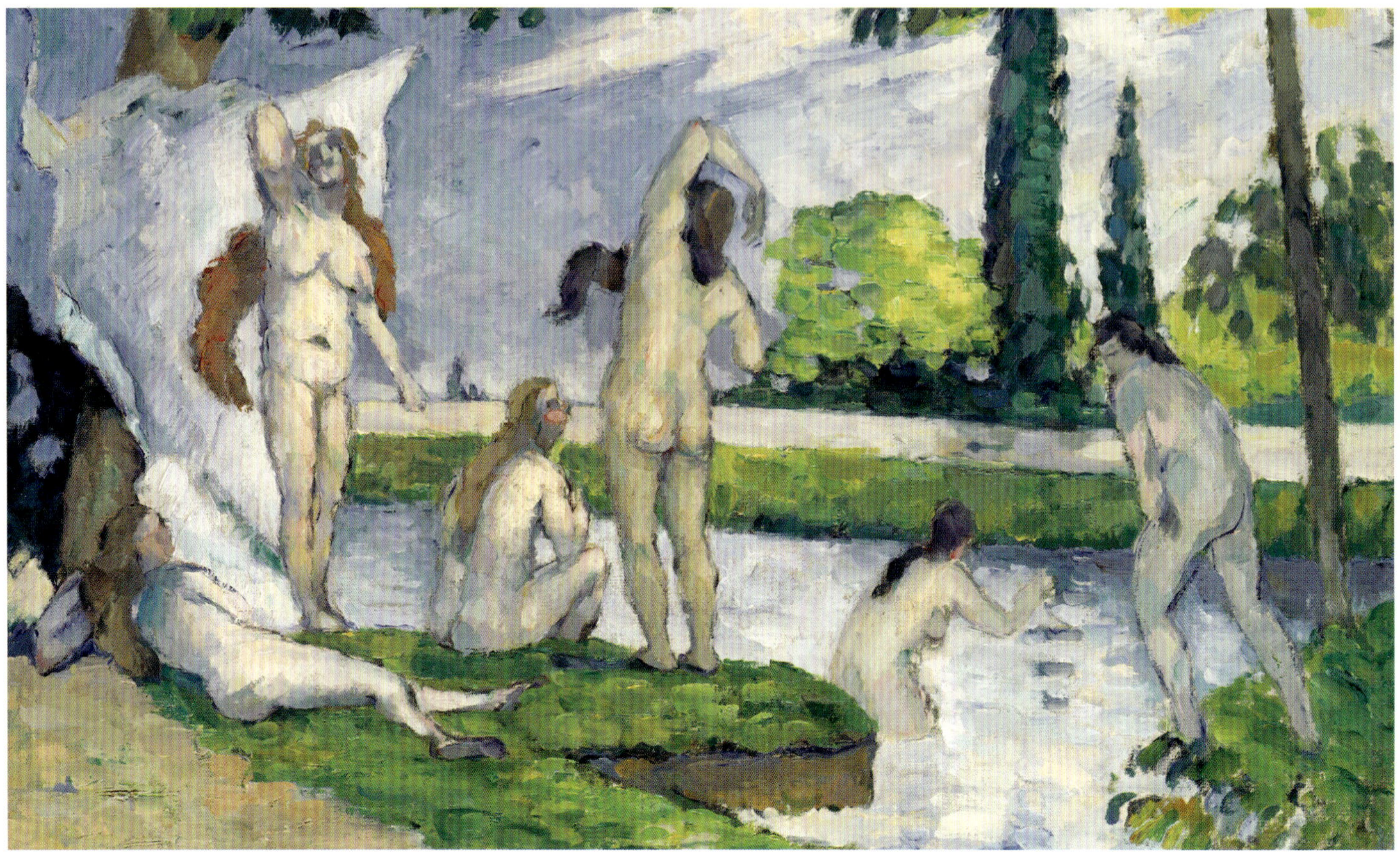

and the largest of the 26 this restless hermit had used in the course of his career. This giant room was on the upper floor of the new building, its walls painted a special shade of grey that Cézanne himself had created to provide him with optimal conditions of light. In addition to massive windows, the room, which was five metres high, had a large opening in one wall, through which he could take outside the giant canvases for which he had needed to build a workspace of this size – the paintings we know as *The Large Bathers* – so that he could paint the background landscapes, as he had always done, *sur le motif*.

The Death of Zola

In late September the following year, a matter of days after Cézanne had moved into his new studio, his gardener, Vallier, brought him news of the sudden and wholly unexpected death of Zola, his former friend. The shock of it broke through the wall of indifference he had affected to maintain since his abrupt ending of the friendship some 16 years earlier. Ashen with grief, he shut himself away in his studio for the rest of the day, seeing no one until later that evening when he sought out Solari, the Aixois sculptor and a childhood friend to them both, and the only person in his home city whom he felt he could trust. Now that his work was being seen in Paris at the Salon des Indépendants and later at the Salon d'Automne, as well as in cities as far away as Vienna and Berlin, the more hostile critics in the French press had turned on him again. This provoked anger among the respectable bourgeois of Aix arising from the shame they felt he was bringing on the city. What before had been an attitude of indifference towards the ascetic visionary in their midst suddenly acidified into anonymous hate mail shoved under his door suggesting he should think of leaving town.

Cézanne was too old, too ailing, too affluent and too naturally antisocial to pay them any mind. Aware that he was running out of time, he kept up a prodigious work rate, above all on the three great paintings of bathers he had begun working on in the 1890s at the Jas de Bouffan. It was a theme he had tackled as early as the 1860s, during his Romantic, *couillarde* period. He had returned to it over the next two decades, in canvases such as *Bathers* (1874–75, *see* left and page 113) and *Five Bathers* (1885–87, *see* below and page 115), though he had also painted other, smaller pictures, such as the later version of *The Temptation of St Anthony* (*c.* 1877, *see* right and page 111) or *Bathsheba* (1885–90, *see* overleaf and page 116). In these he was attempting to integrate the naked body, which he found so bewildering, within the physical landscape – the living Arcadia from which he conjured the 'parallel harmonies' of his landscape paintings.

Fantasy and Reality

These late pictorial fantasies of bathers, whose figures were based on photographic nudes Cézanne asked his young acolytes to procure for

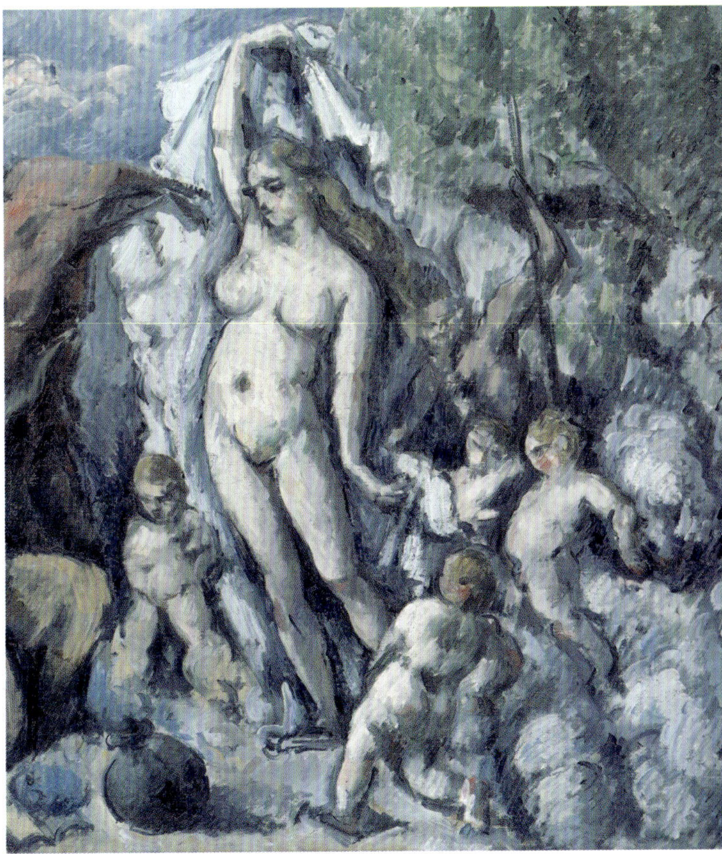

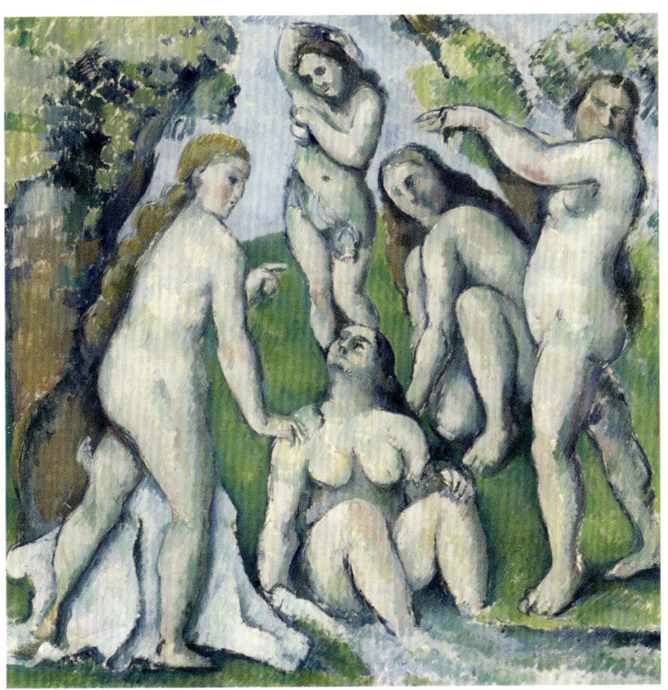

him, bring to final realization a theme he had struggled with since those turbulent visions of the 1860s; the period before he had brightened his palette – and his outlook – through contact with Impressionism and had learned to discipline his passion through diligent observation of the motif. Over time, he had internalized this process of looking to such an extent that what he observed and attempted to commit to canvas was increasingly his emotional response to the motif. Now, at the end of his life, the strain of fantasy that still lurked within him re-emerged in the final monumental canvases of bathers, tempered – though not tamed – in paintings that married the long-established habit of observed reality with the vividness of a sensual imagination which had broadened over decades through contact with nature.

The monumental bathers preoccupied Cézanne throughout his last decade, as he finally found the means to realize them. But there

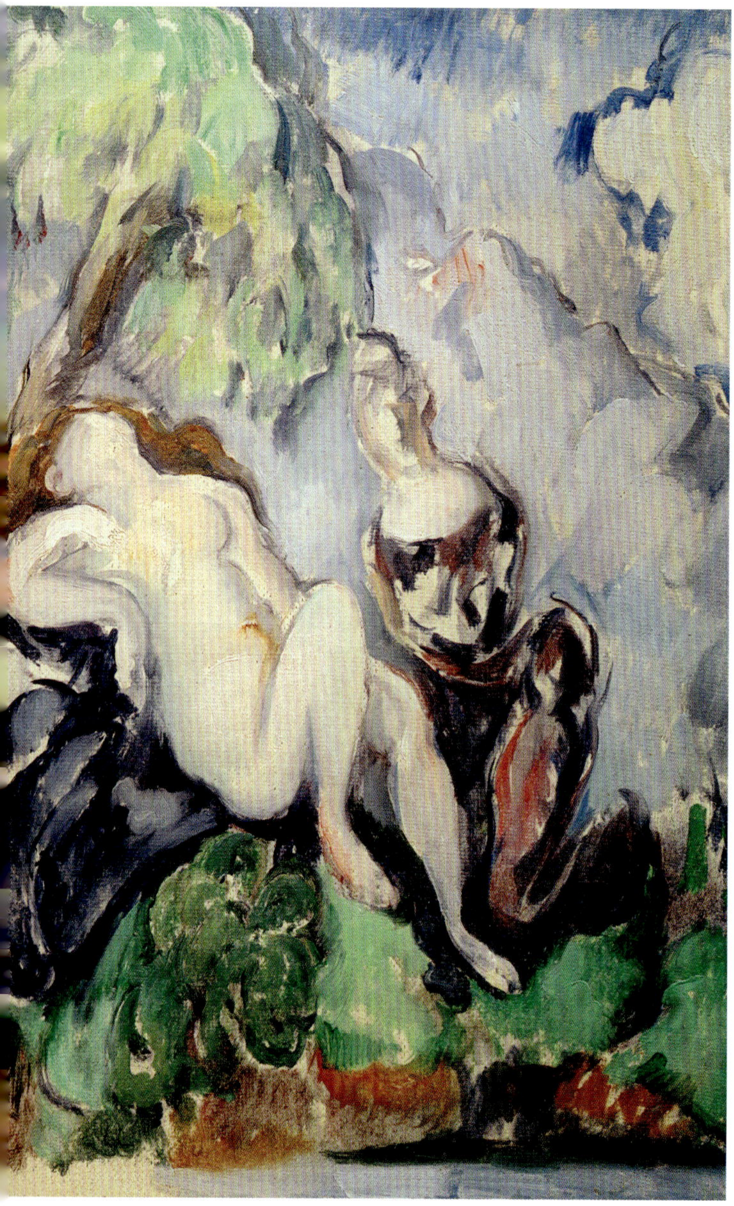

was another motif which obsessed him during these last years, as it had done for decades: the mountain which had loomed over his neighbourhood, his childhood, his life, and which he could see every morning as he trudged up the hill from his apartment to his studio at Les Lauves. In all, Cézanne made 87 separate paintings of Mont Sainte-Victoire throughout his career, with 11 significant images

during his last decade. He found the ideal view of it he had perhaps been looking for his entire life, just up the hill from the studio, from where it is hard not to be awestruck by the way it dominates the wide, fertile valley that lies between mountain and city. It is in the paintings he made of the mountain, such as *View of Mont Sainte-Victoire from Les Lauves* (1904–06, *see* opposite), that the development of his vision is easiest to trace. And it is in these almost mystical final images, which he continued to paint throughout the summer of 1906, that he comes closest to pure abstraction, pure pattern, the 'harmony parallel with nature' achieved through colour alone – the imprint the experience of nature makes on the soul.

The Promised Land

On 15 October, Cézanne was again engaged on this indispensable subject, painting at the same superb vantage point a 15-minute walk up the hill from his studio, when a storm blew up. Immersed in his seemingly inexhaustible feelings before this most essential of all his motifs, he carried on painting in the rain for several hours and, according to some accounts, was found later that afternoon by two laundrymen, unconscious by the side of the road. The men brought him back to the Rue Boulegon, carried him upstairs and put him to bed. Cézanne came round later that evening, and the following morning set off again up the hill to his studio, to work on a portrait of Vallier. But he was so weak that even this effort was beyond him. Gravely ill, he returned to the apartment and took to his bed with pneumonia, where a week later, on 22 October, he died.

So had he fulfilled the wish he had divulged a few years earlier, to be able to enter the Promised Land? Despite his timidity and self-doubt, Cézanne also felt himself to be one of the immortals, declaring at one point to Bernard that 'there's only one painter in the world, and that's me'. Given the visionary paintings of his final years, in which the landscape around Aix becomes a land of dreams, we might imagine that he felt he had earned his place in that painters' Olympus, though he was also cautious to the last – in the month before his death, in his final letter to Bernard, he claimed only to be 'making some slow progress' towards his goal. It is true that he never spoke of his works as 'paintings', only as 'studies' or 'experiments', and it is perhaps in this spirit of experimentation that his greatest legacy can be seen.

The Father of Modern Art

Beyond the immediate impact he had on Gauguin, Bernard and the members of Les Nabis, it was Pablo Picasso (1881–1973) who later spoke of him as the 'father of us all'. Certainly, in his fragmentation of motifs and the insight that, based on our experience of them, we might see them inwardly, simultaneously, from more than one viewpoint, Cézanne suggested ways of apprehending objects that led Picasso and Georges Braque (1882–1963) to develop the Analytical Cubism that was one potential outcome of his 'experiments'. On the other hand, his deployment of colour in the creation of structure inspired Les Fauves, the 'wild beasts' led

by Matisse, who as a young artist was so in awe of this 'sensitive savage', as Pissarro once described Cézanne, that he was too timid even to visit him. Nonetheless, Cézanne's courage remained a paragon for Matisse throughout his life, stiffening his own resolve in moments of doubt.

In truth, the resources Cézanne bequeathed to future generations were so bountiful that it is possible to see his influence in any number of different painters and their works, from the quirky Viennese cityscapes of Gustav Klimt (1862–1918) and Egon Schiele (1890–1918) to the colourful wilderness paintings of Canada's Group of Seven. It would have pleased him to know that, on account of his efforts, those who came after him could enter the Promised Land: a vision of the world based on the painter's subjective feeling for it. Cézanne found both vision and the way to express it in the landscapes and people of his beloved region of Aix, and above all, like Moses, in a mountain.

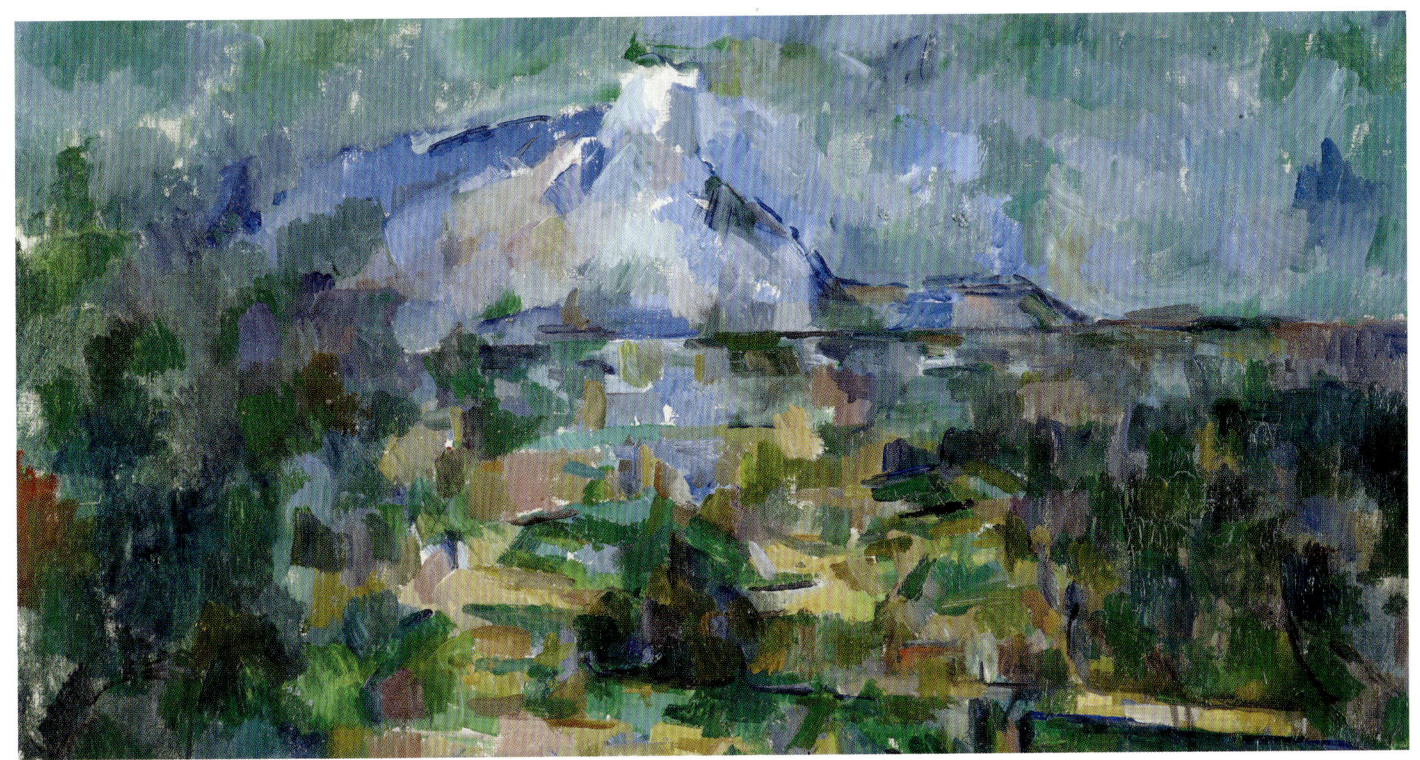

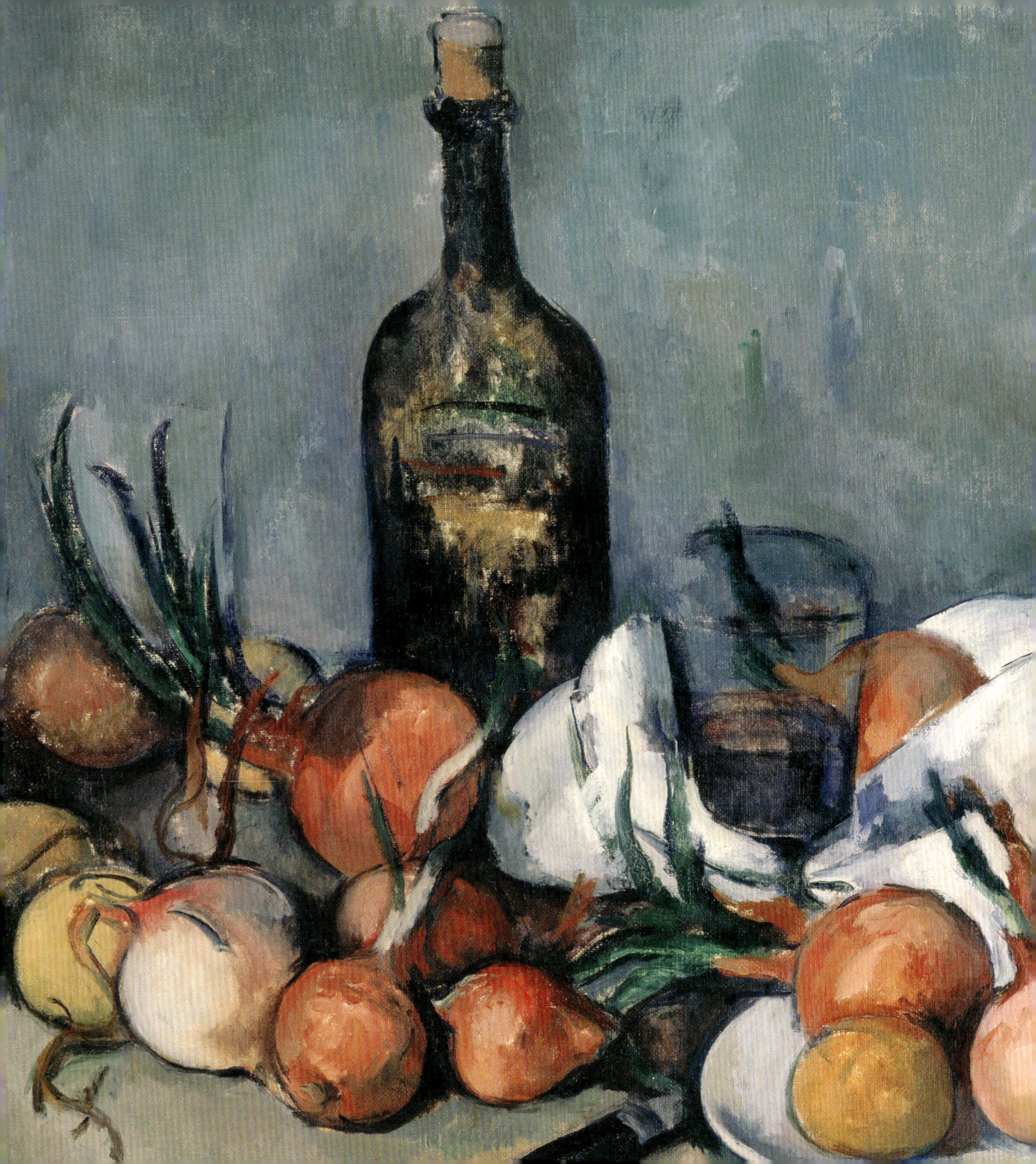

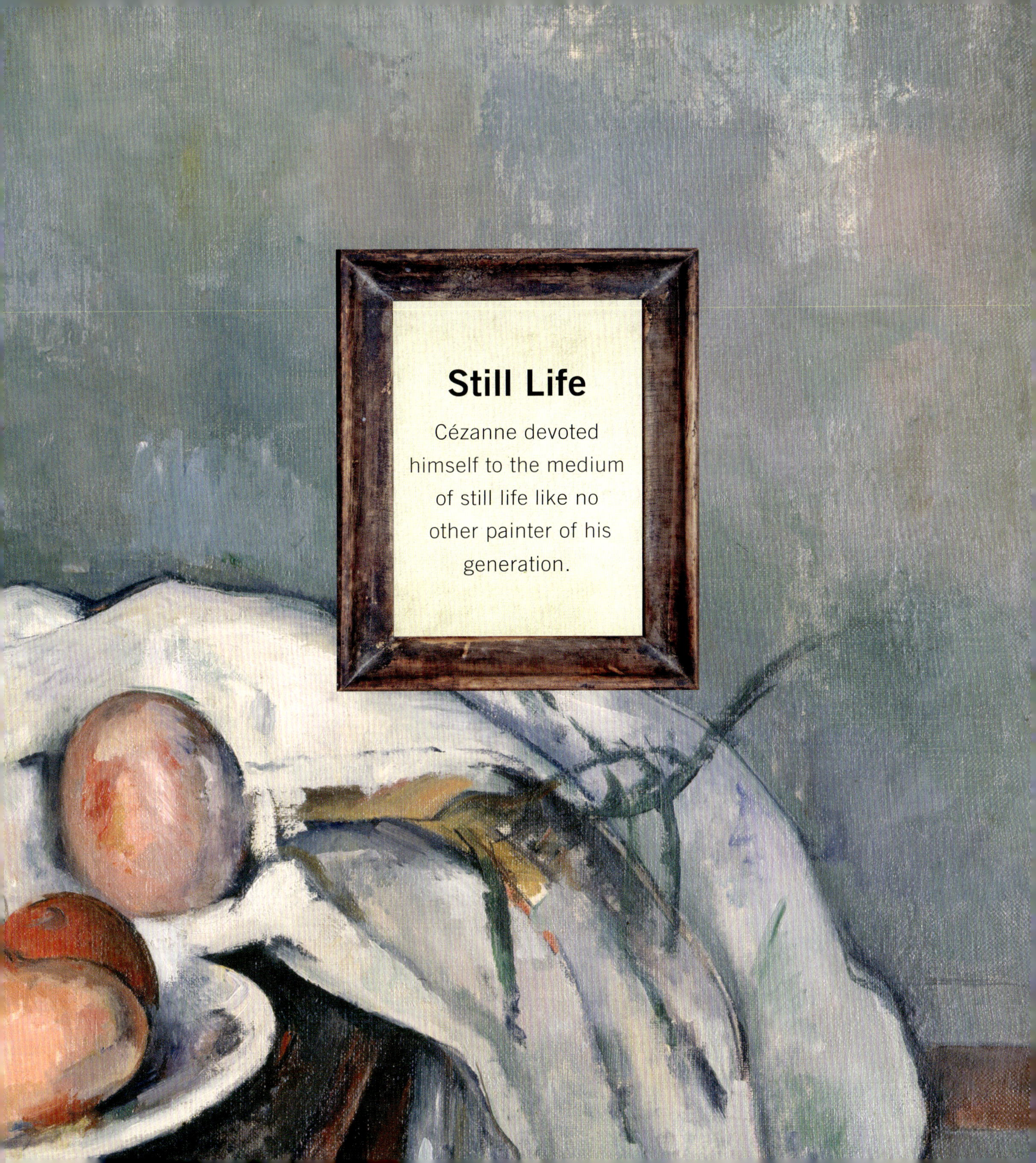

Still Life

Cézanne devoted
himself to the medium
of still life like no
other painter of his
generation.

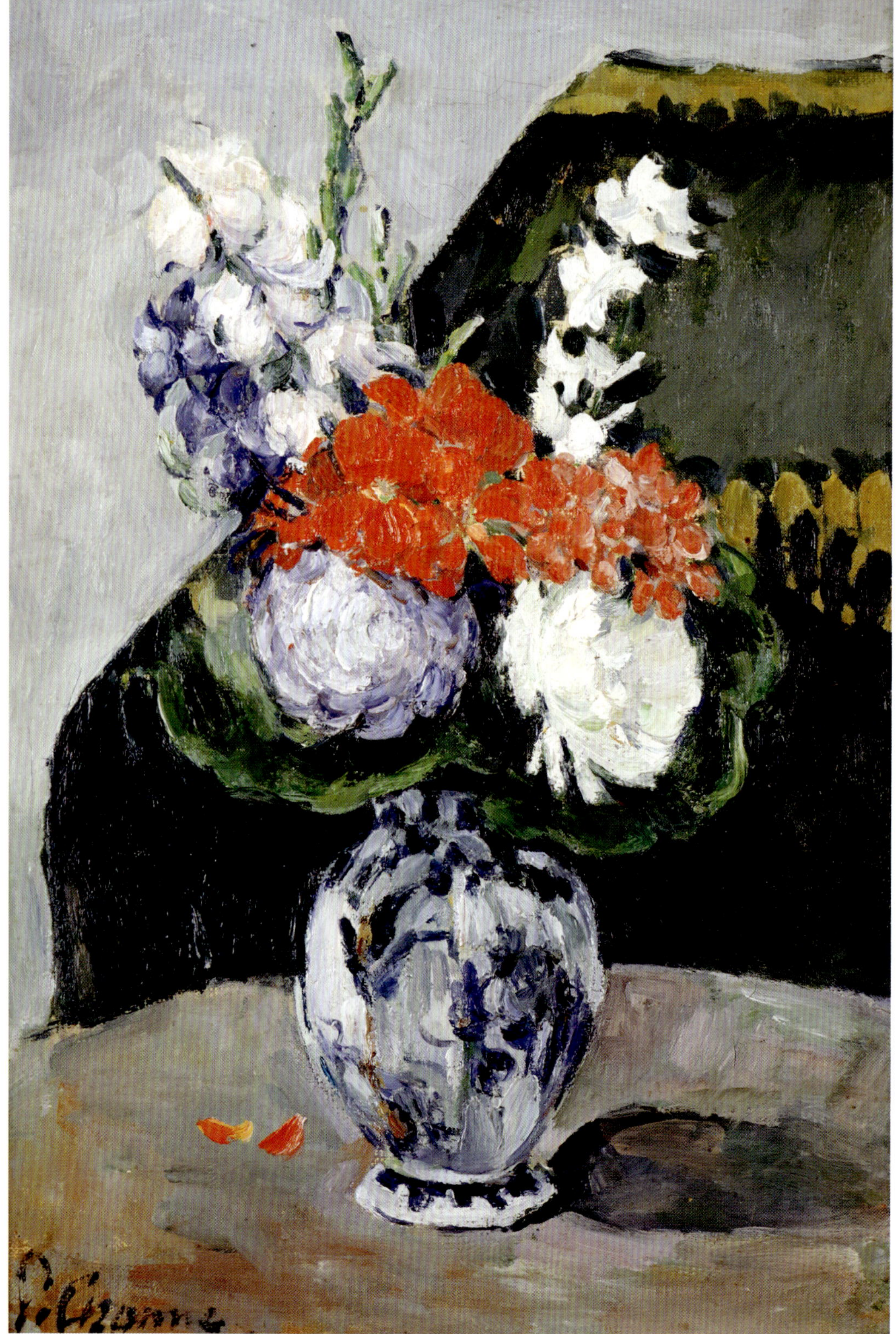

Bouquet in a Small Delft Vase, 1873
Oil on canvas, 41 x 27 cm (16⅛ x 10⅝ in) • Musée d'Orsay, Paris

Living with Dr Paul Gachet in Auvers-sur-Oise in 1873, Cézanne turned to the colourful flowers picked by Madame Gachet from her garden, which helped brighten his palette using the Impressionist technique he had learnt from Pissarro.

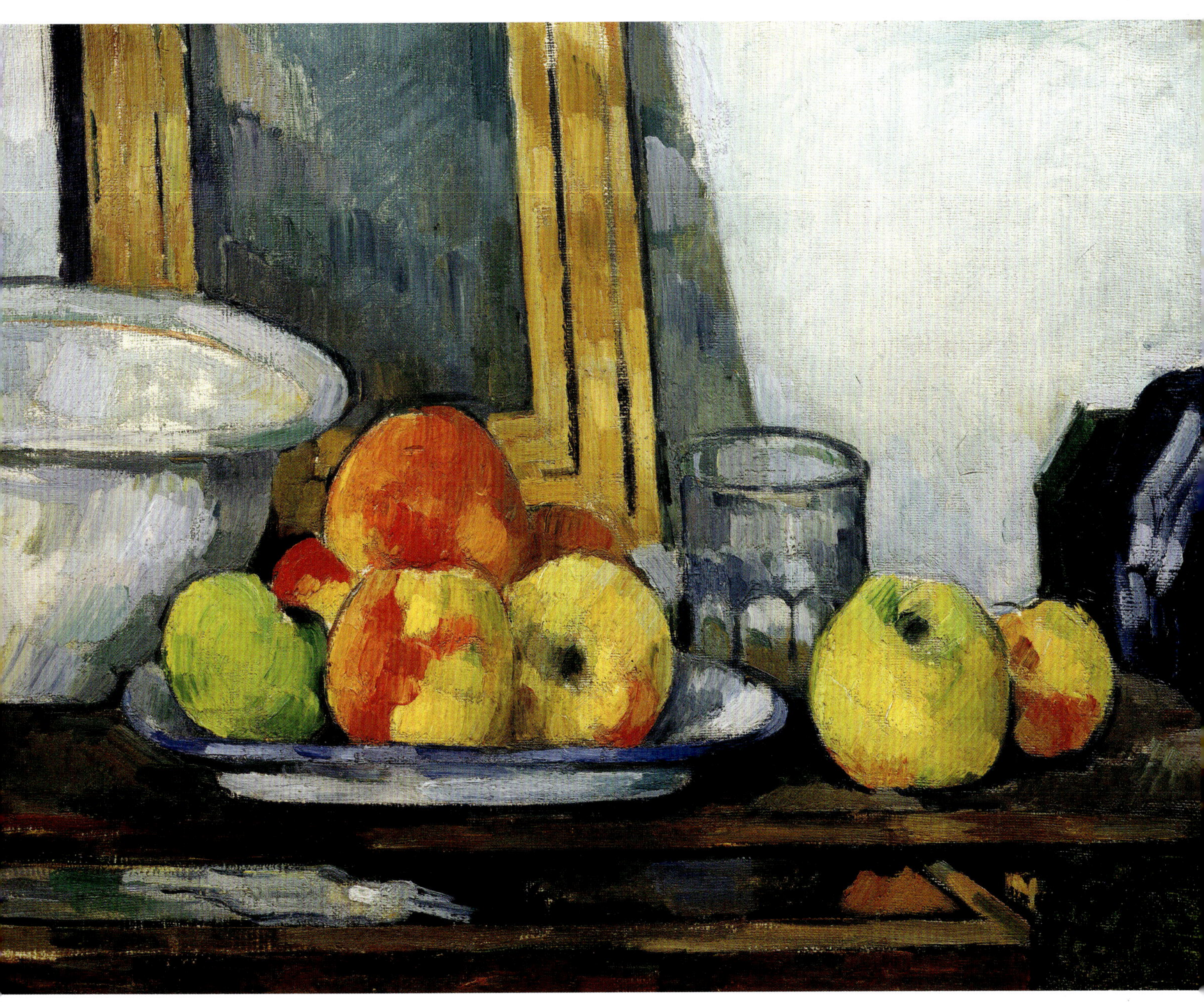

Still Life with Open Drawer, 1877–79
Oil on canvas, 32.5 x 41 cm (12¾ x 16⅛ in) • Musée d'Orsay, Paris

The cut-off composition of this image, as if it had been glimpsed rather than properly looked at, suggests the lingering influence on Cézanne of the fleeting Impressionist gaze, a visual strategy inspired by Japanese woodblock prints.

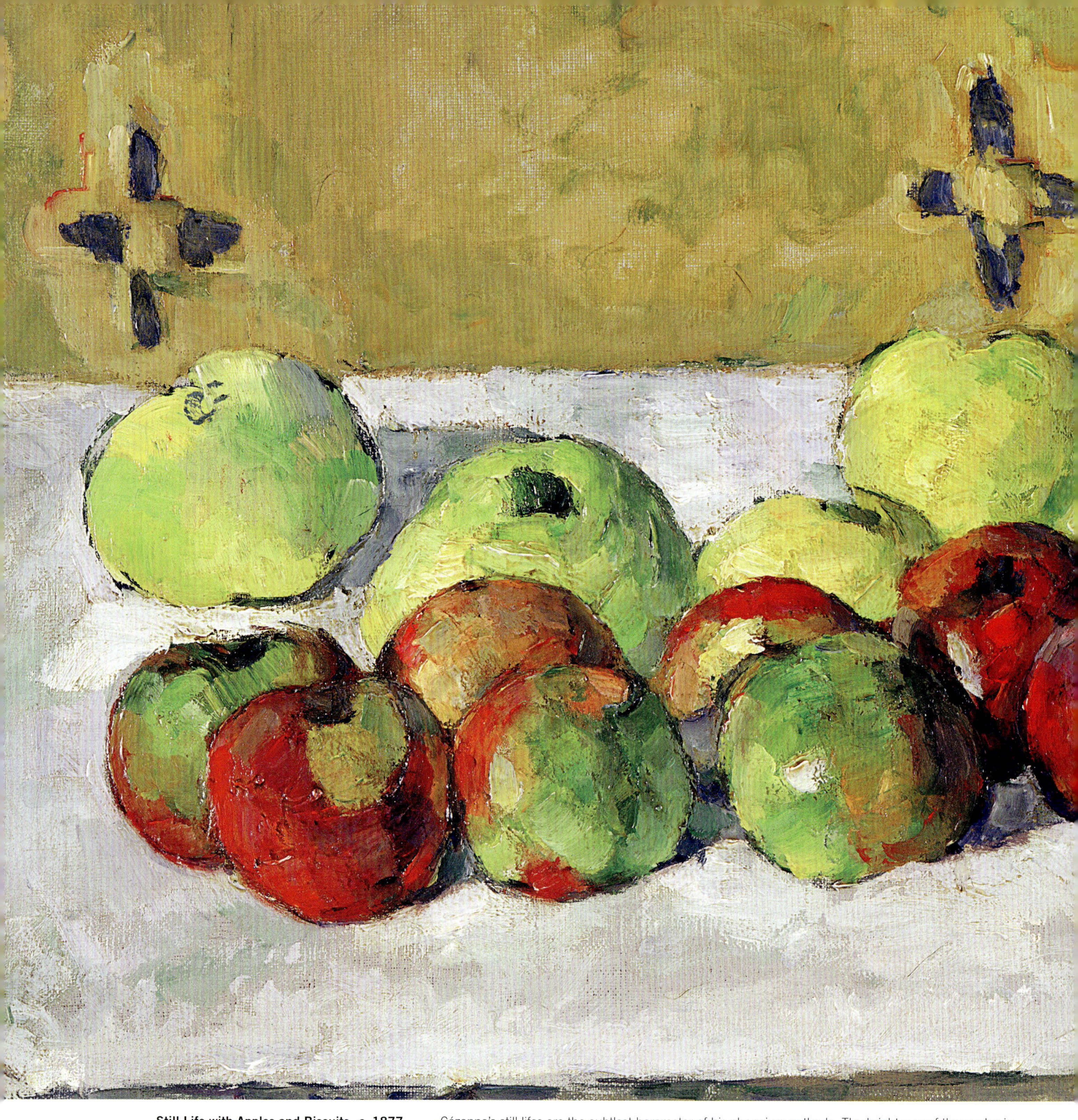

Still Life with Apples and Biscuits, *c.* 1877
Oil on canvas, 38 x 55 cm (15 x 21⅝ in) • Private Collection

Cézanne's still lifes are the subtlest barometer of his changing methods. The brightness of the apples in this image can be compared to the more subdued treatment of the same subject in a canvas done a few years later – *Apples and Biscuits* of *c.* 1879–80 (*see* the work on page 10).

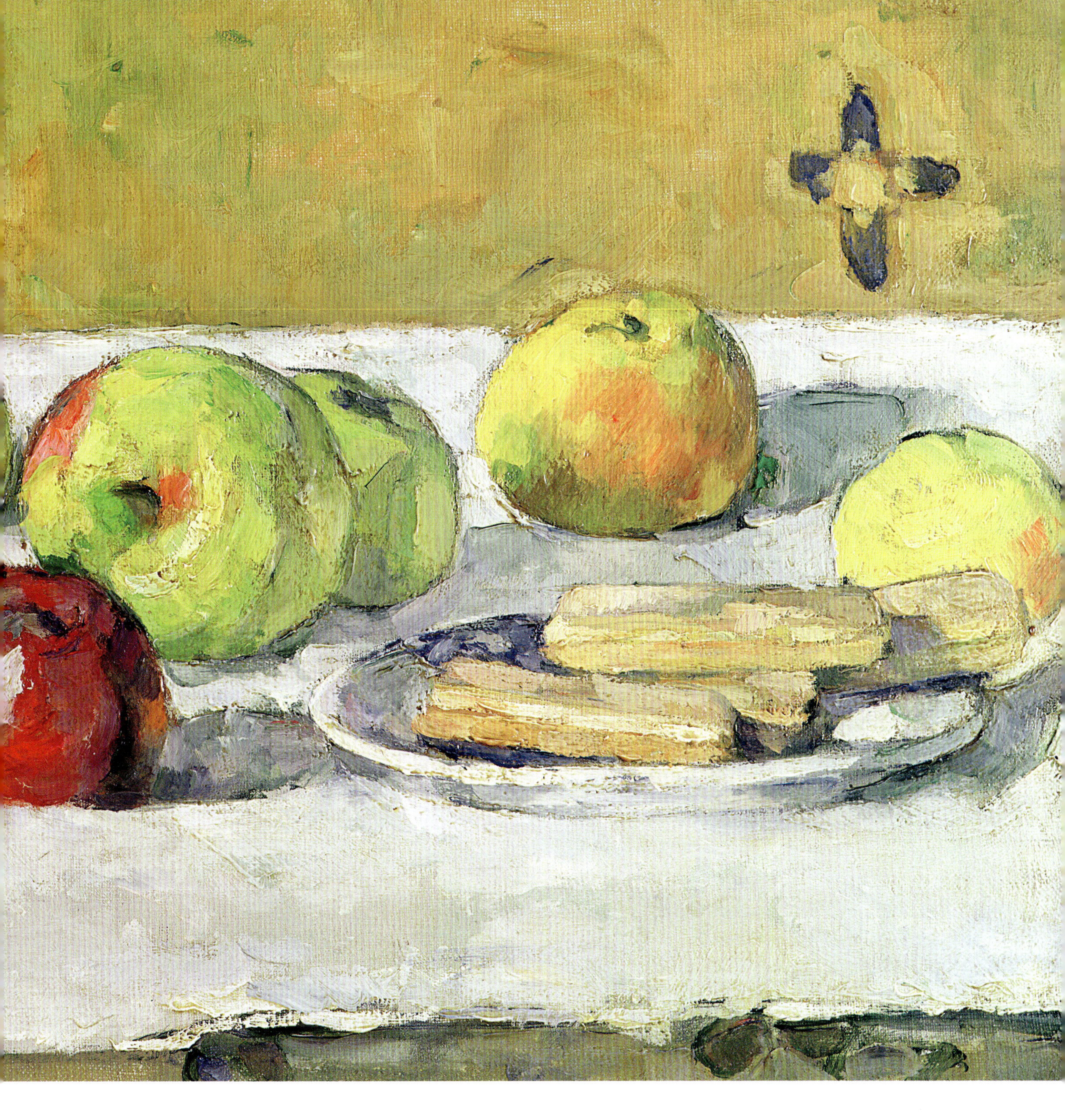

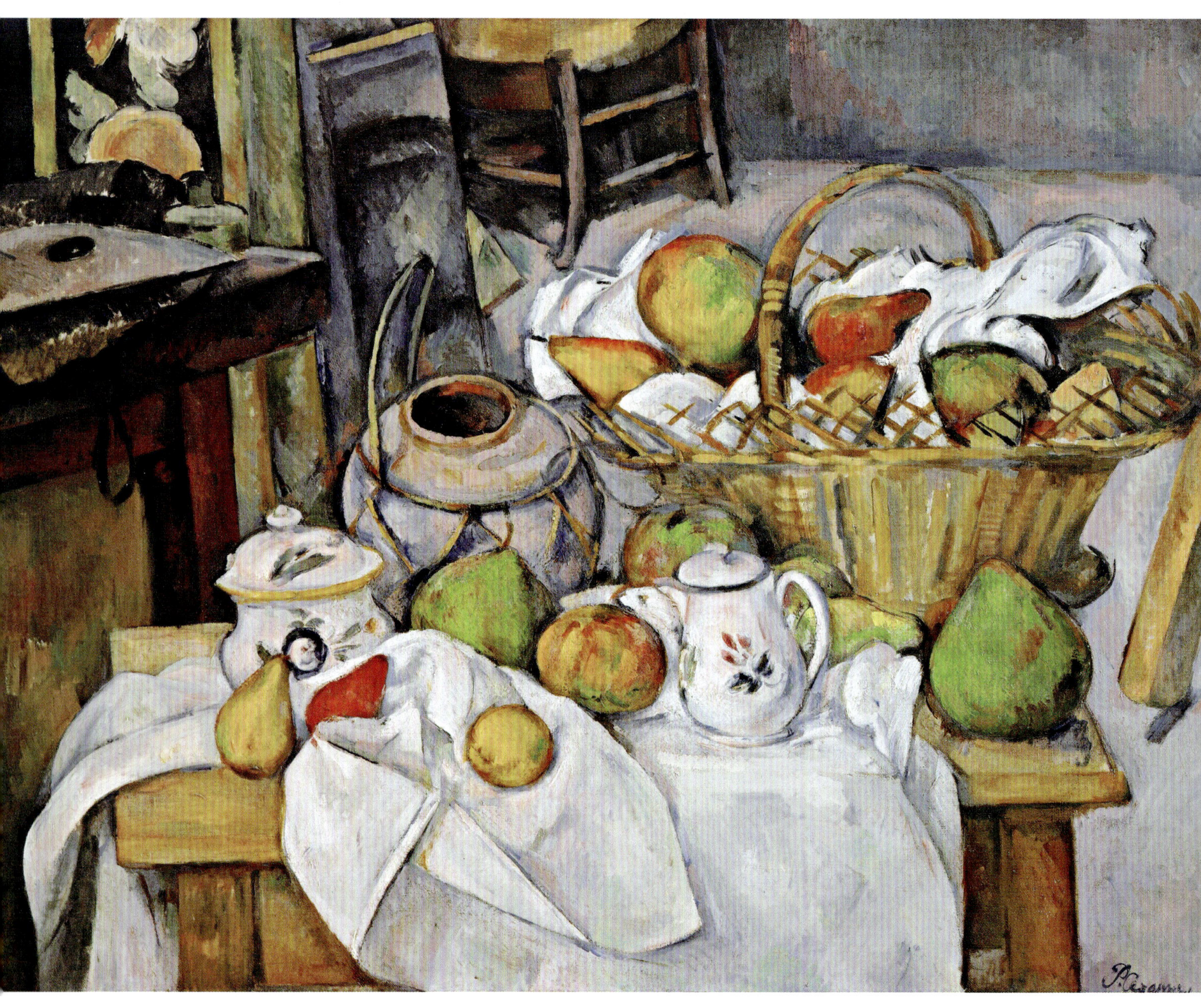

Kitchen Table (Still Life with Basket), 1888–90
Oil on canvas, 65 x 81.5 cm (21⅝ x 32⅛ in) • Musée d'Orsay, Paris

Cézanne's still lifes are marked by perspectival distortions that arise from his feeling for a subject overriding the dictates of conventional one-point perspective. In this image, the pot at the rear is on a different plane to the other pots.

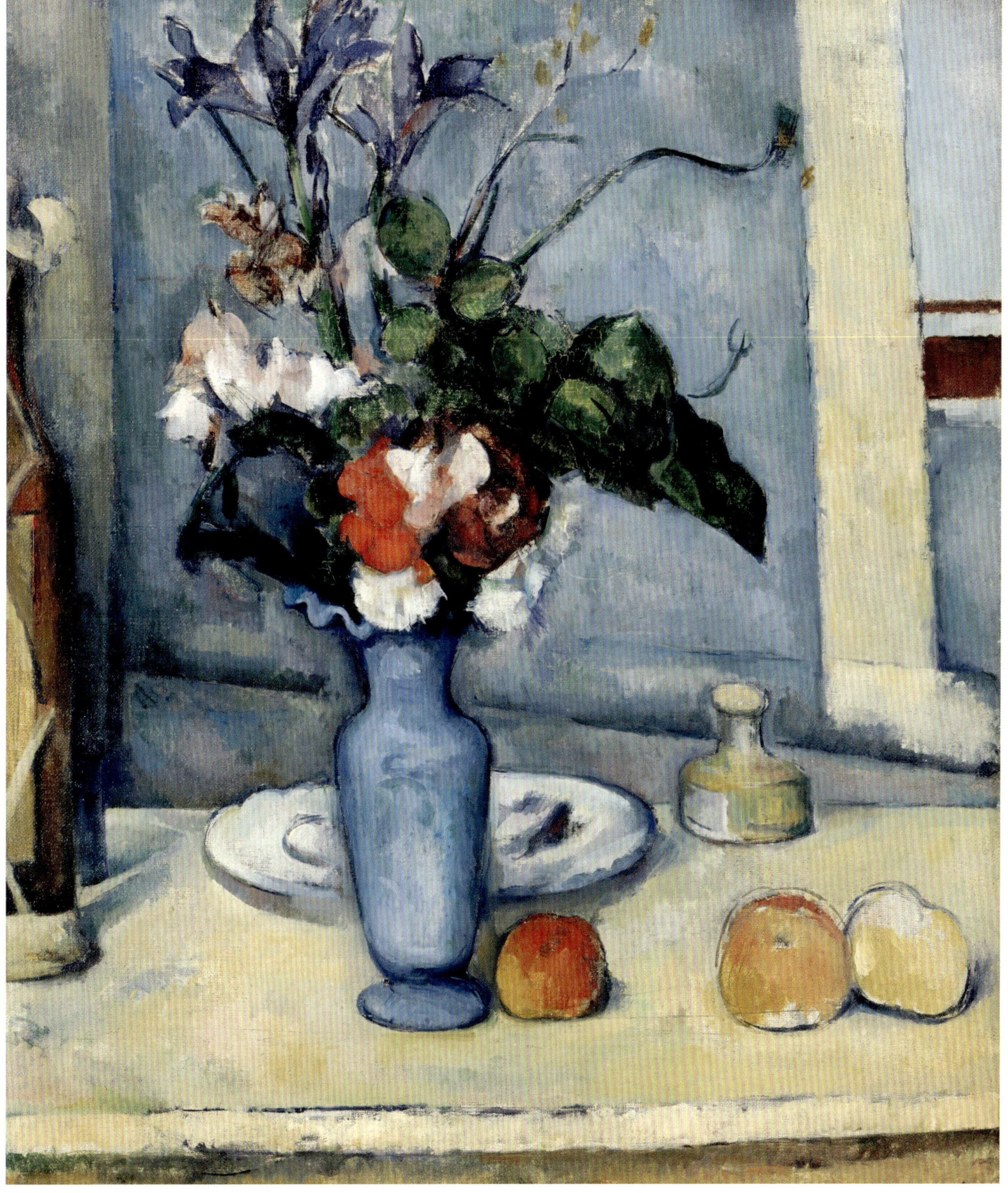

The Blue Vase, 1889–90

Oil on canvas, 61.2 x 50 cm (24⅛ x 19¾ in) • Musée d'Orsay, Paris

By this point in his career, Cézanne was painting with increasing slowness and deliberation, and for this reason he often used paper flowers and artificial fruit in his still lifes, some of which took him months to finish.

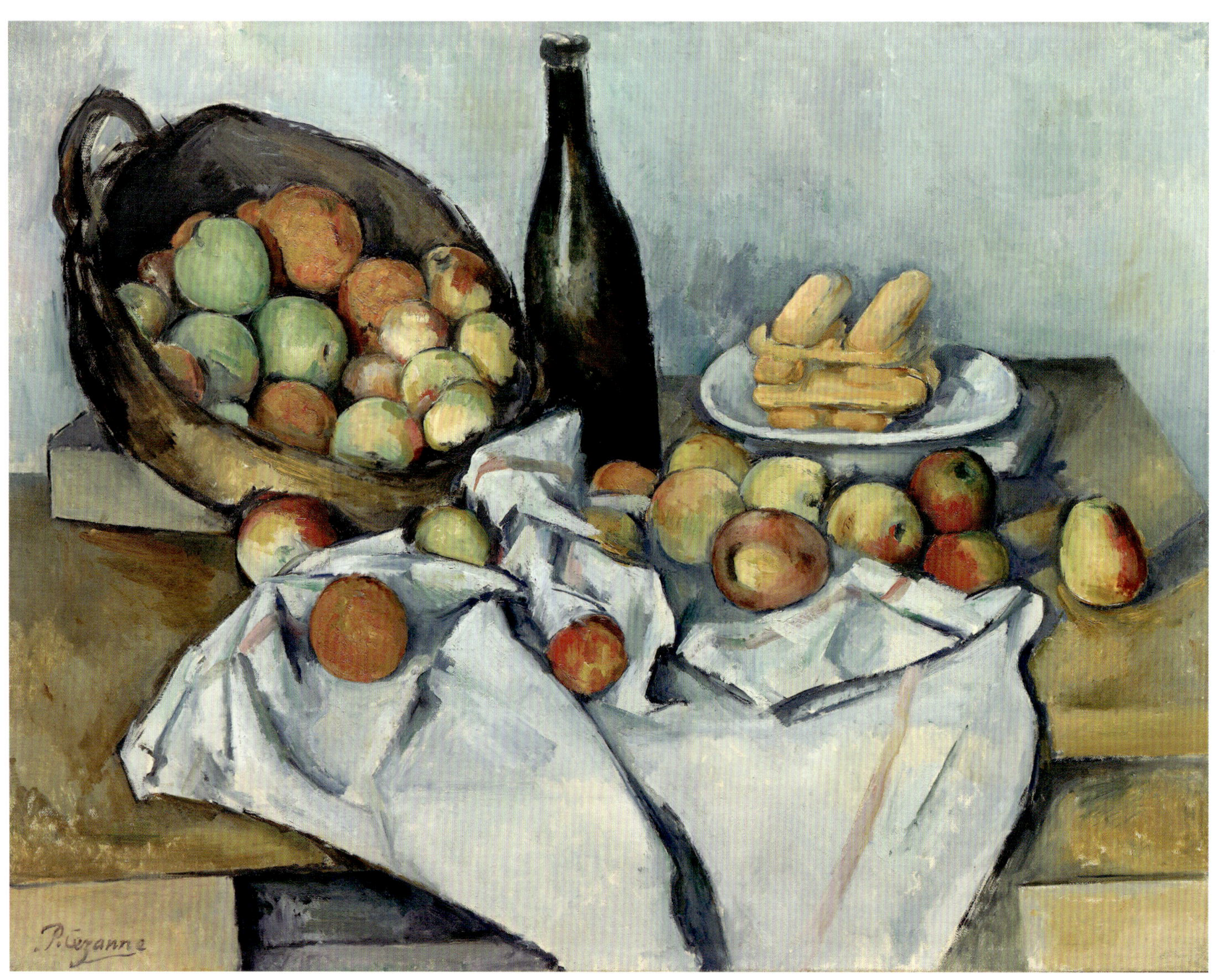

The Basket of Apples, *c.* 1893
Oil on canvas, 65 x 80 cm (25⅝ x 31½ in)
• Art Institute of Chicago, Chicago

Tablecloths or drapery in still lifes were a staple element of the great tradition of still-life painting that began with the painters of the Dutch Golden Age. Unlike Impressionists such as Monet, Cézanne sought to measure himself against the past.

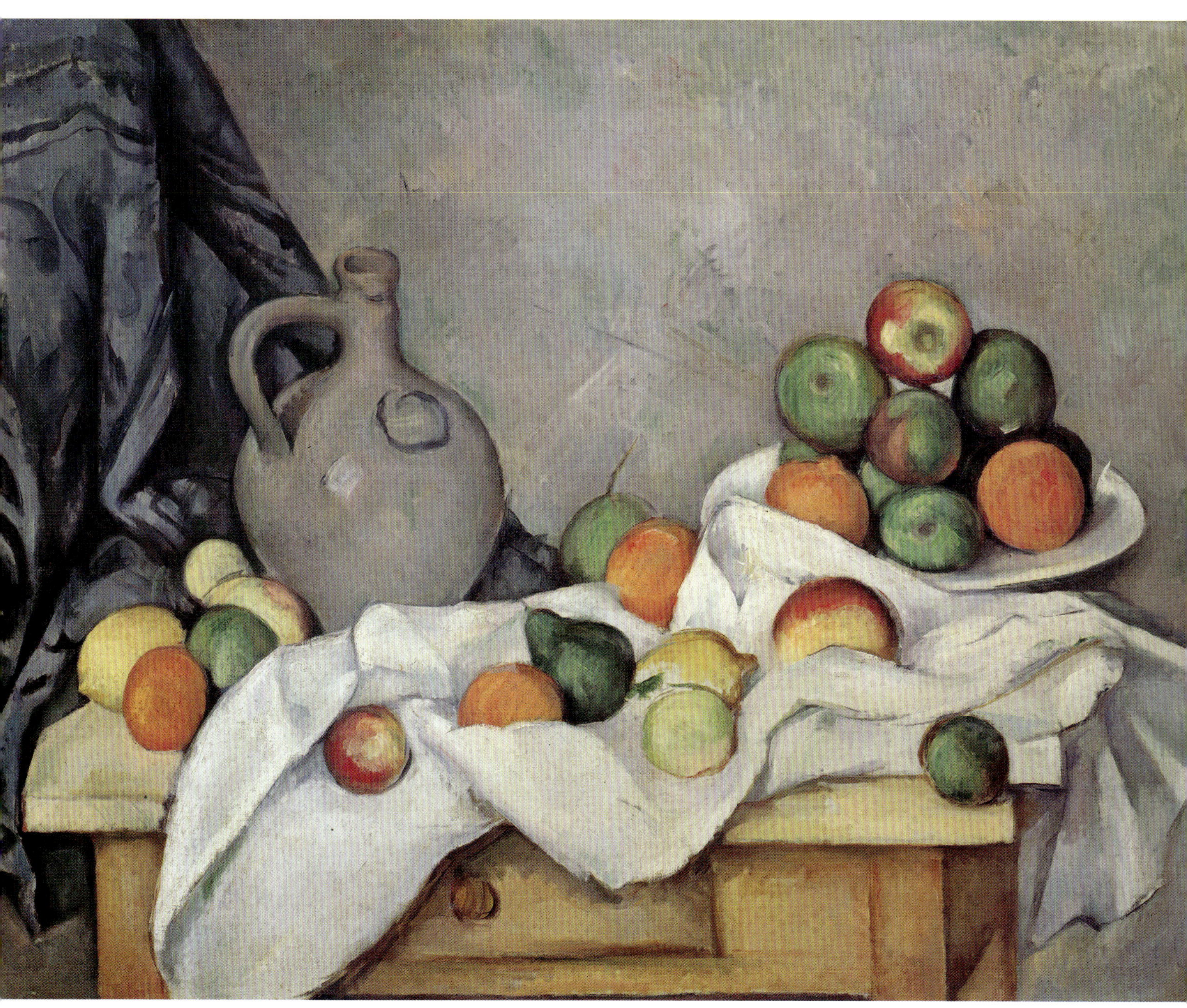

Still Life, Drapery, Pitcher and Fruit Bowl 1893–94
Oil on canvas, 60 x 73 cm (23⅝ x 28¾ in) • Private Collection

Here Cézanne renders the tabletop as a trapezoidal shape, as if seeing the same object from different viewpoints rather than the single-point perspective we might expect. But this is how it felt to him, so this is how it appears.

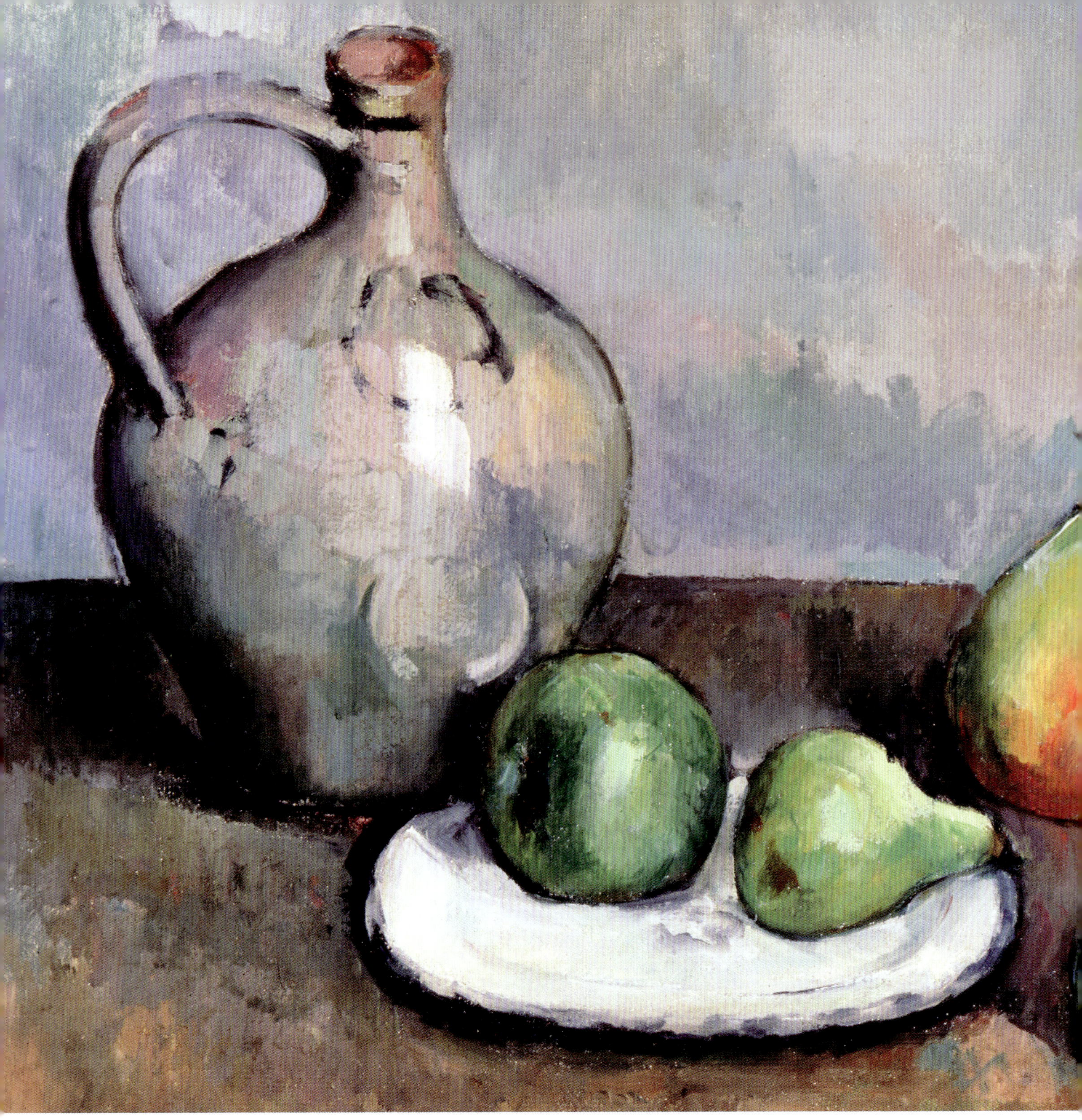

Still Life with Pitcher and Fruit, 1893–94
Oil on canvas, 43 x 63 cm (17 x 24⅘ in) • Private Collection

Cézanne's friend, the painter Louis Le Bail (1866–1929), once observed him in the process of assembling a still life. He noted his great scrupulousness in arranging the composition to achieve a harmonious balance of colours, tones and forms.

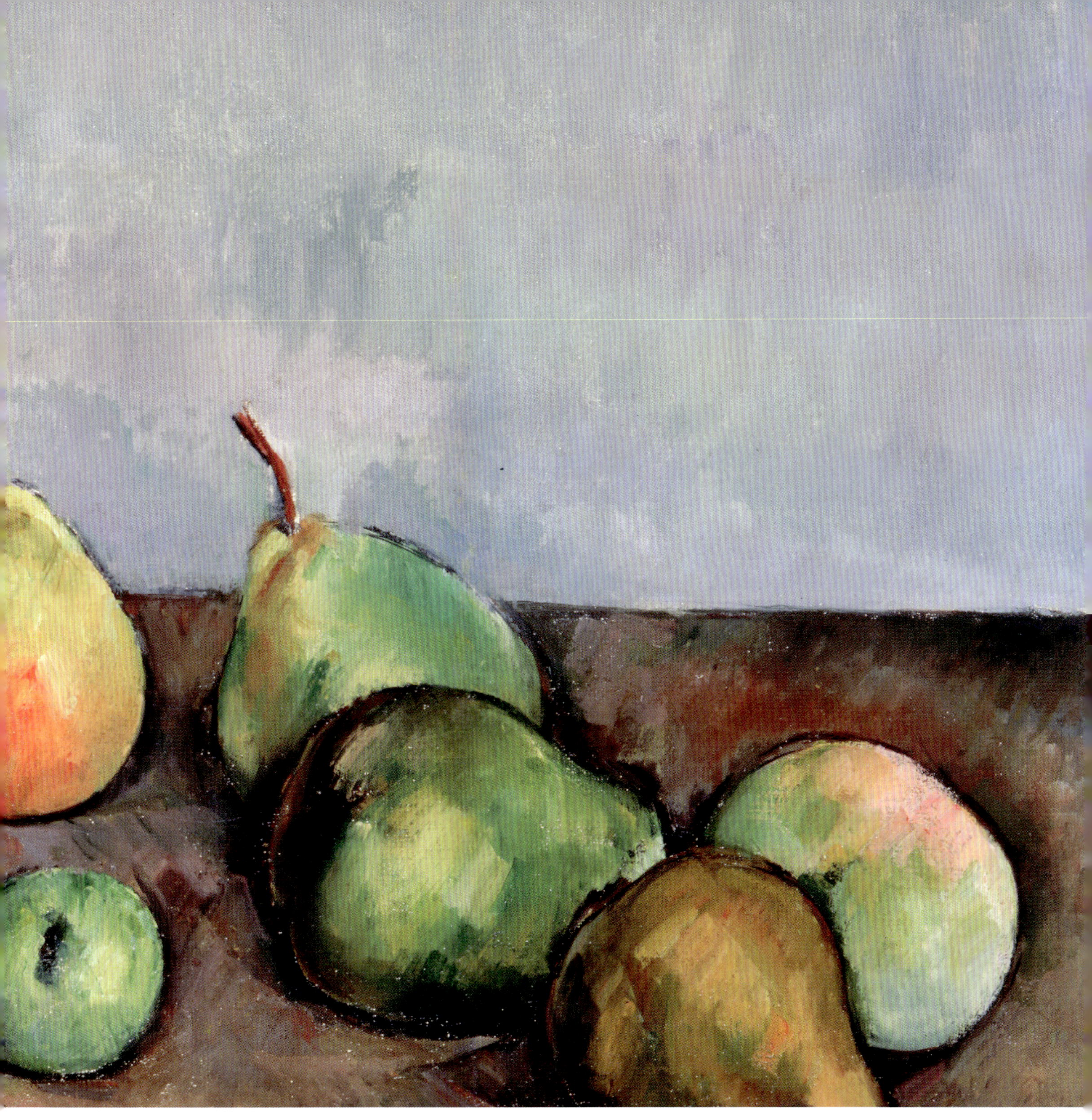

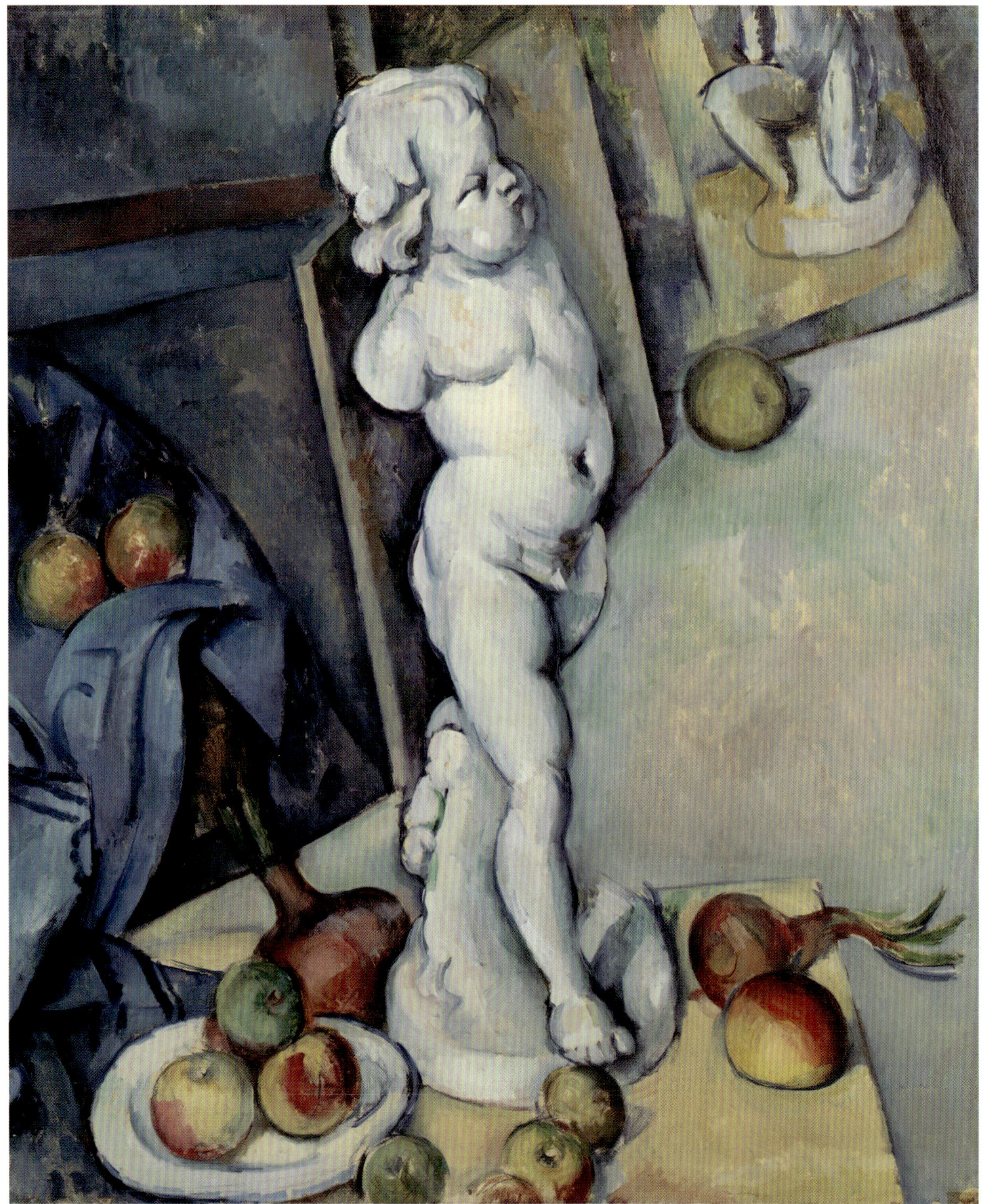

Still Life with Plaster Cupid, *c.* 1894
Oil on paper on board, 57.3 x 70.6 cm (22⅔ x 27¾ in)
• Courtauld Institute of Art, London

Cézanne himself made the plaster cupid in this image. The use of portrait format to accommodate the figure of the putto may have contributed to the unusual and rather giddy vantage point, looking down at the floor from a tilted angle.

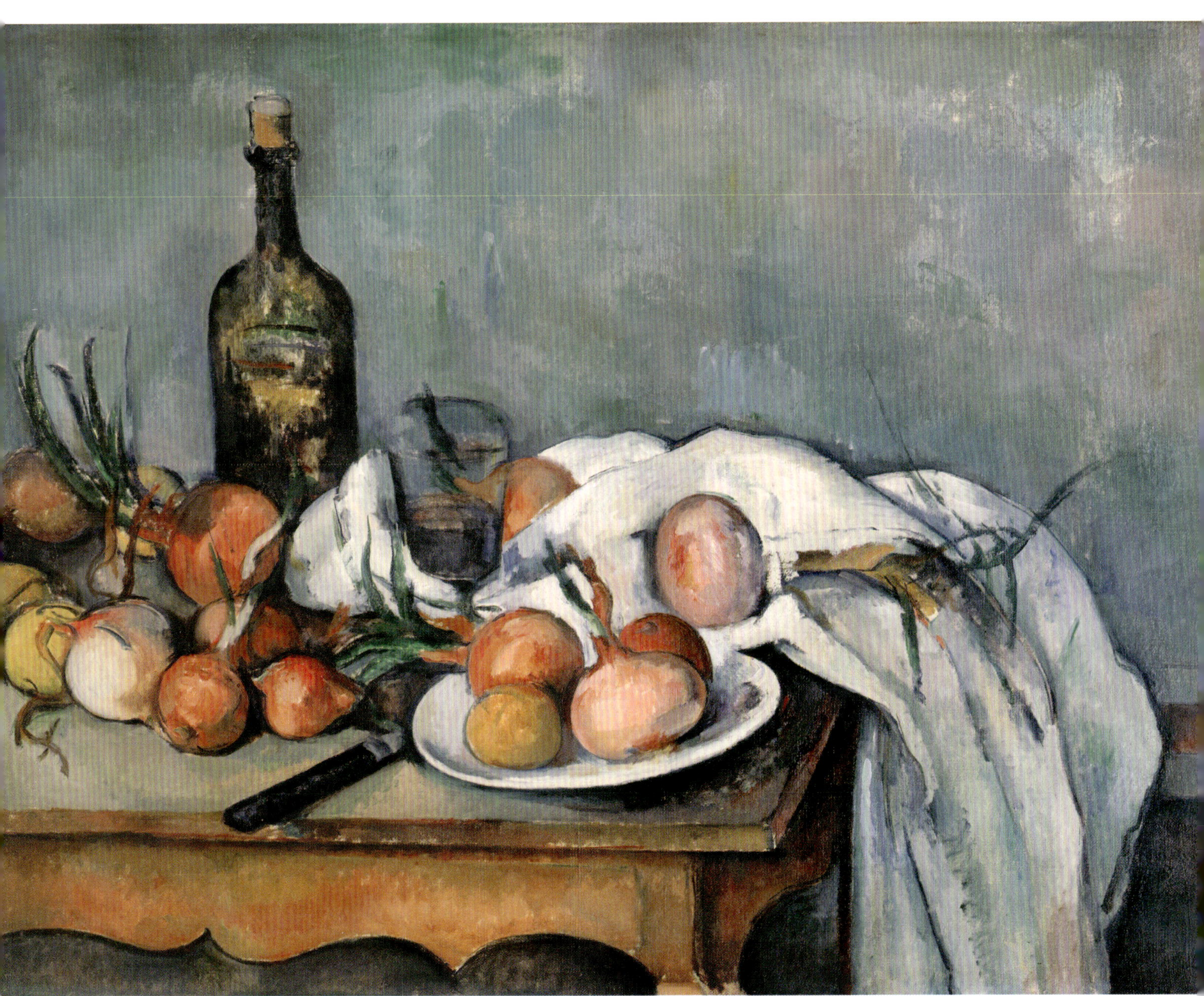

Still Life with Onions, 1896–98
Oil on canvas, 66 x 82 cm (26 x 32¼ in) • Musée d'Orsay, Paris

The plate in this image seems not to lie flat on the table, while some of the onions on the plate are further overbalanced. These were effects Cézanne himself deliberately engineered by placing coins beneath objects.

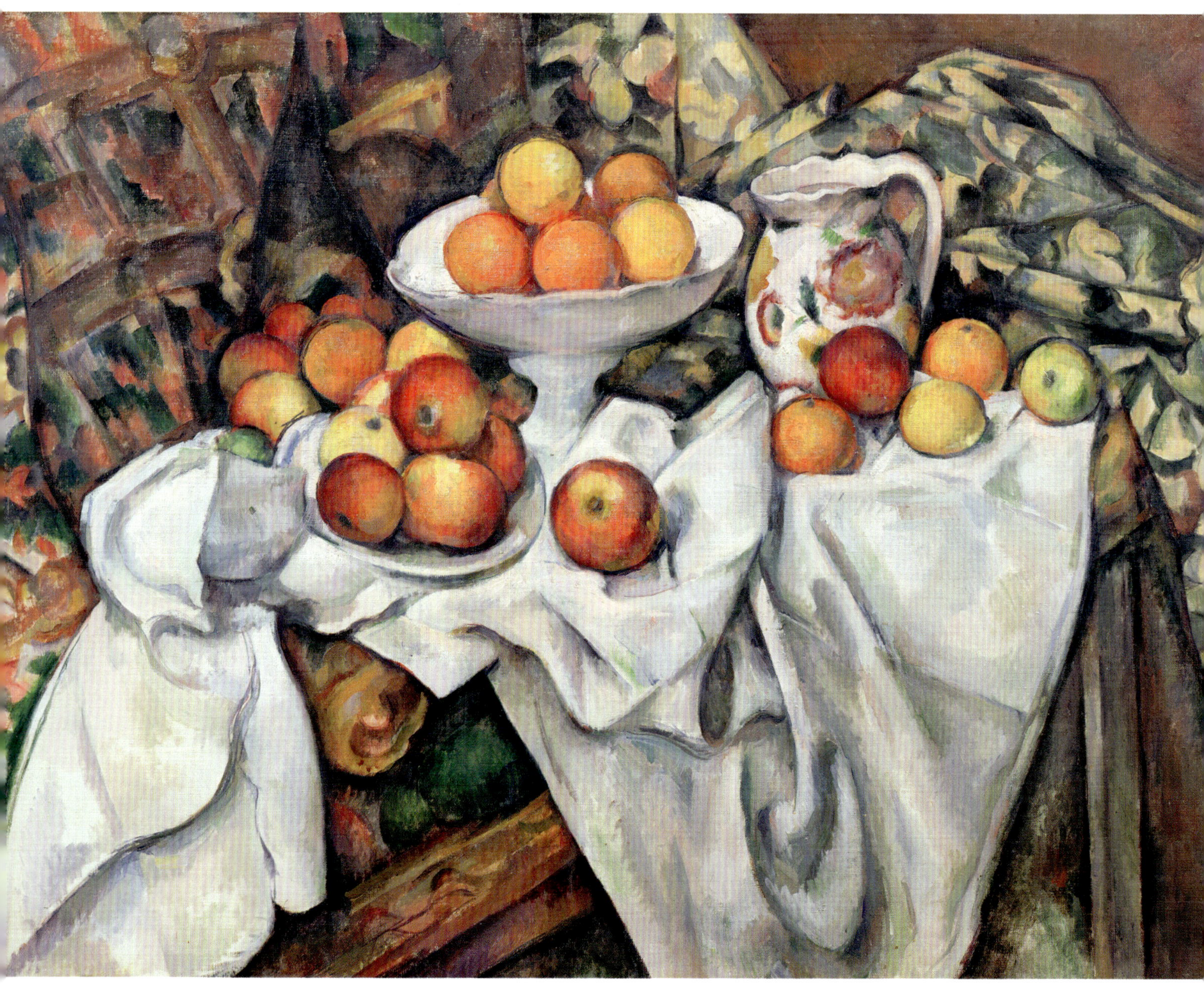

Apples and Oranges, *c.* 1899
Oil on canvas, 74 x 93 cm (29⅛ x 36⅝ in) • Musée d'Orsay, Paris

In Cézanne's later still lifes, as in the other works from his last years, the source of the light is unspecific. Light, he once said, is something that cannot be directly reproduced but must be rendered by something else, such as colour.

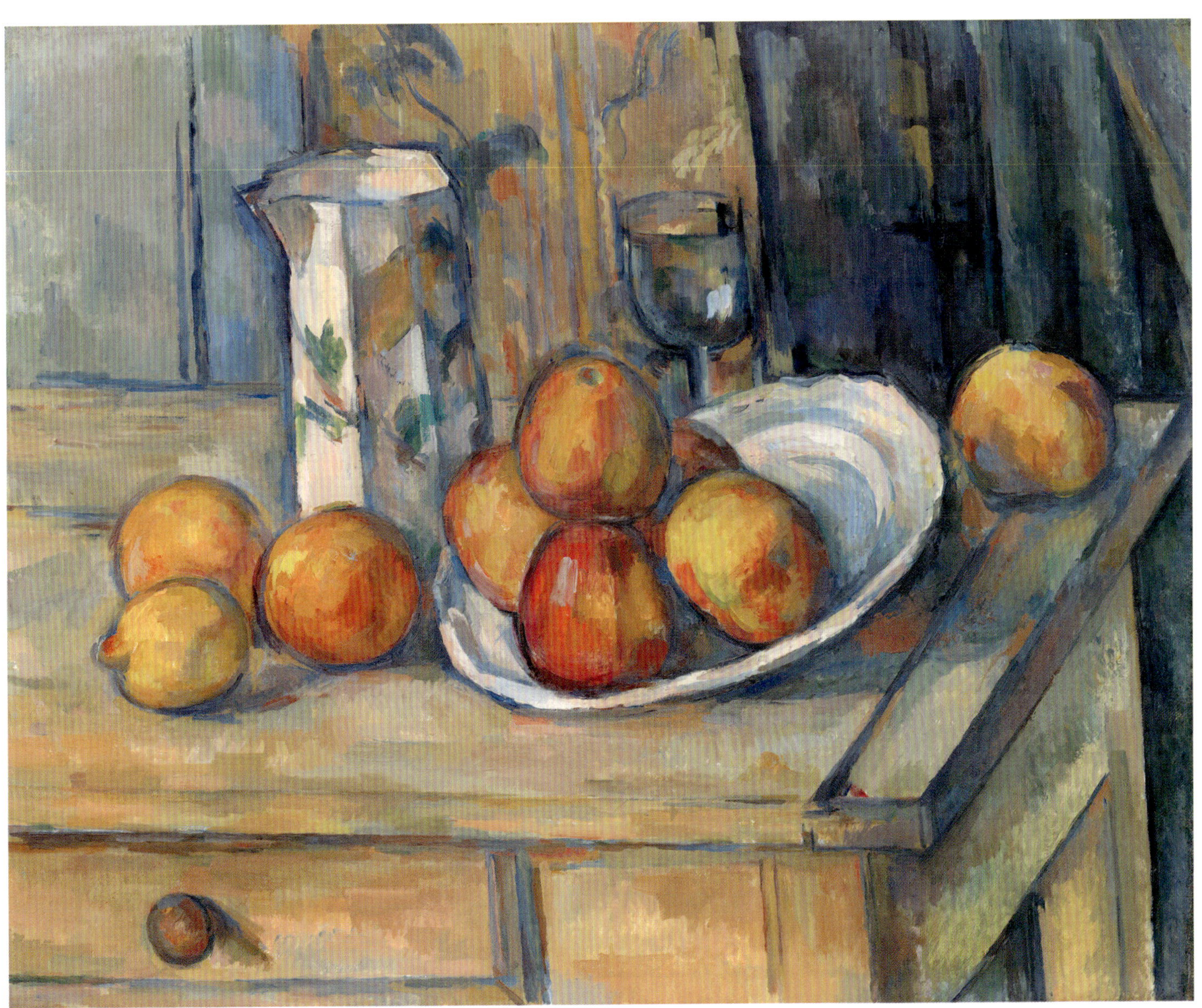

Still Life with Milk Jug and Fruit, *c.* 1900
Oil on canvas, 45.8 x 54.9 cm (18 x 21⅝ in)
• National Gallery of Art, Washington, D.C.

The absurd arrangement in this image is deliberate. Only in the artist's mind could a plate raised so dramatically on one side support a pile of apples without them falling. The precariousness of this arrangement is the picture's focal point.

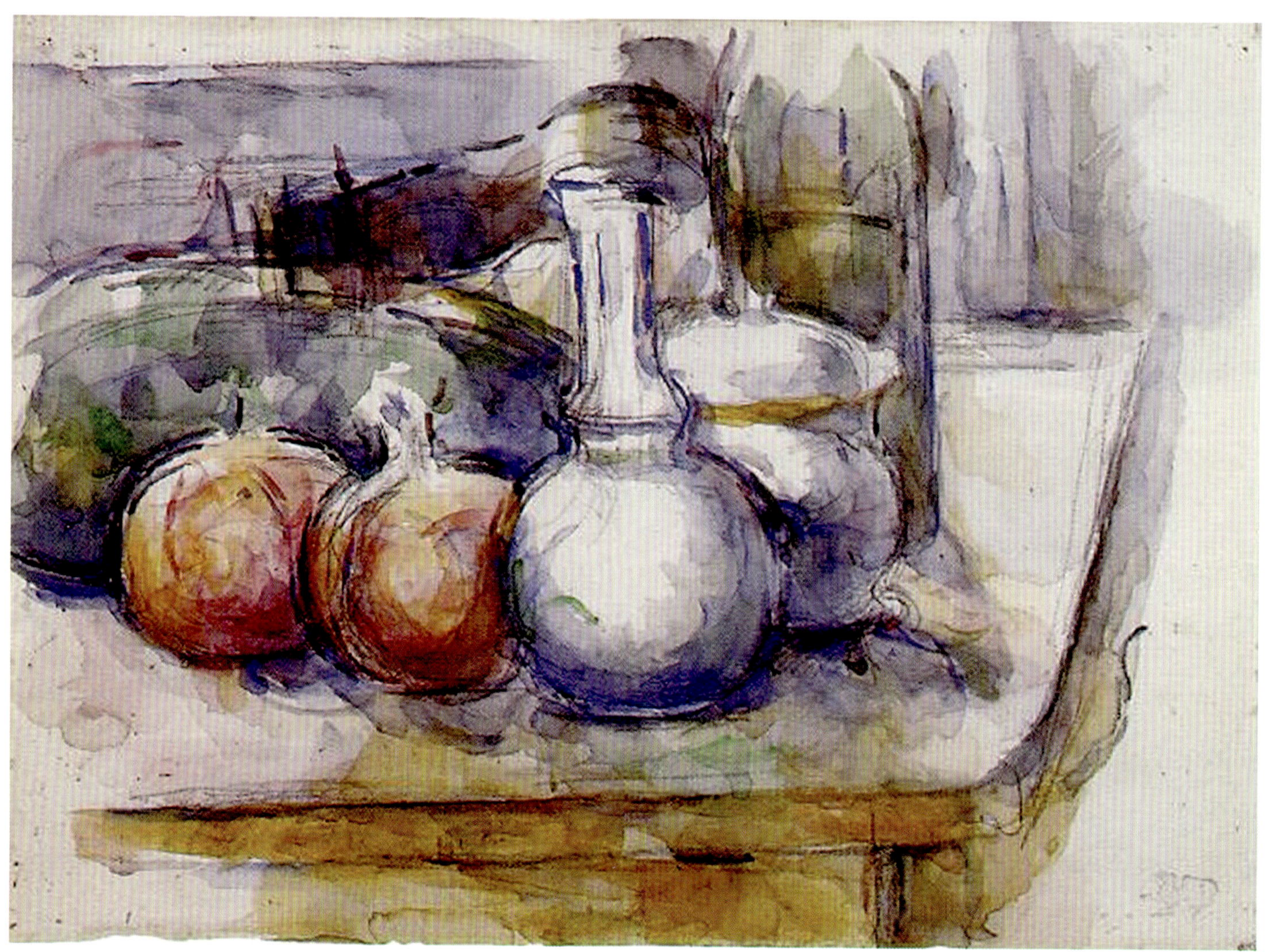

**Still Life with Pomegranates, Carafe, Sugar Bowl,
Bottle and Watermelon, 1900–06**
Watercolour over pencil on paper, 31.7 x 43.2 cm (12½ x 17 in)
• The Louvre, Paris

After 1890, Cézanne turned increasingly to watercolour. The demands of the medium taught him lessons
he would draw on in his oils, as the latter took on some of the improvisational qualities of the former.

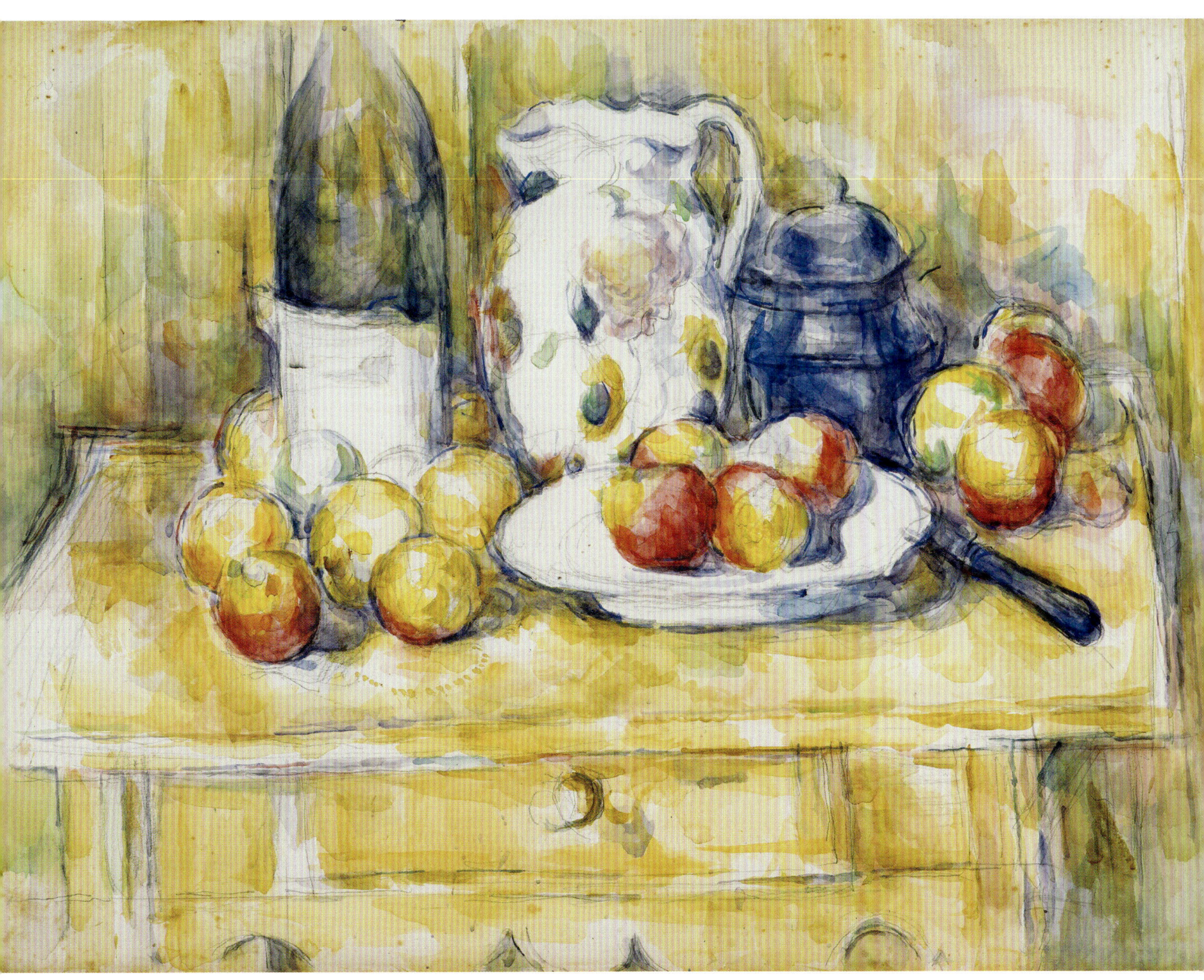

Still Life with Apples on a Sideboard, 1900–06
Watercolour over pencil on paper, 48.6 × 63.2 cm (19⅛ × 24⅞ in)
• Dallas Museum of Art, Texas

The arrangement of objects in this still life is less contrived than in other images from the painter's last two decades, with the interest residing above all in the saturated yellow of table, walls and apples, a radical use of a single colour.

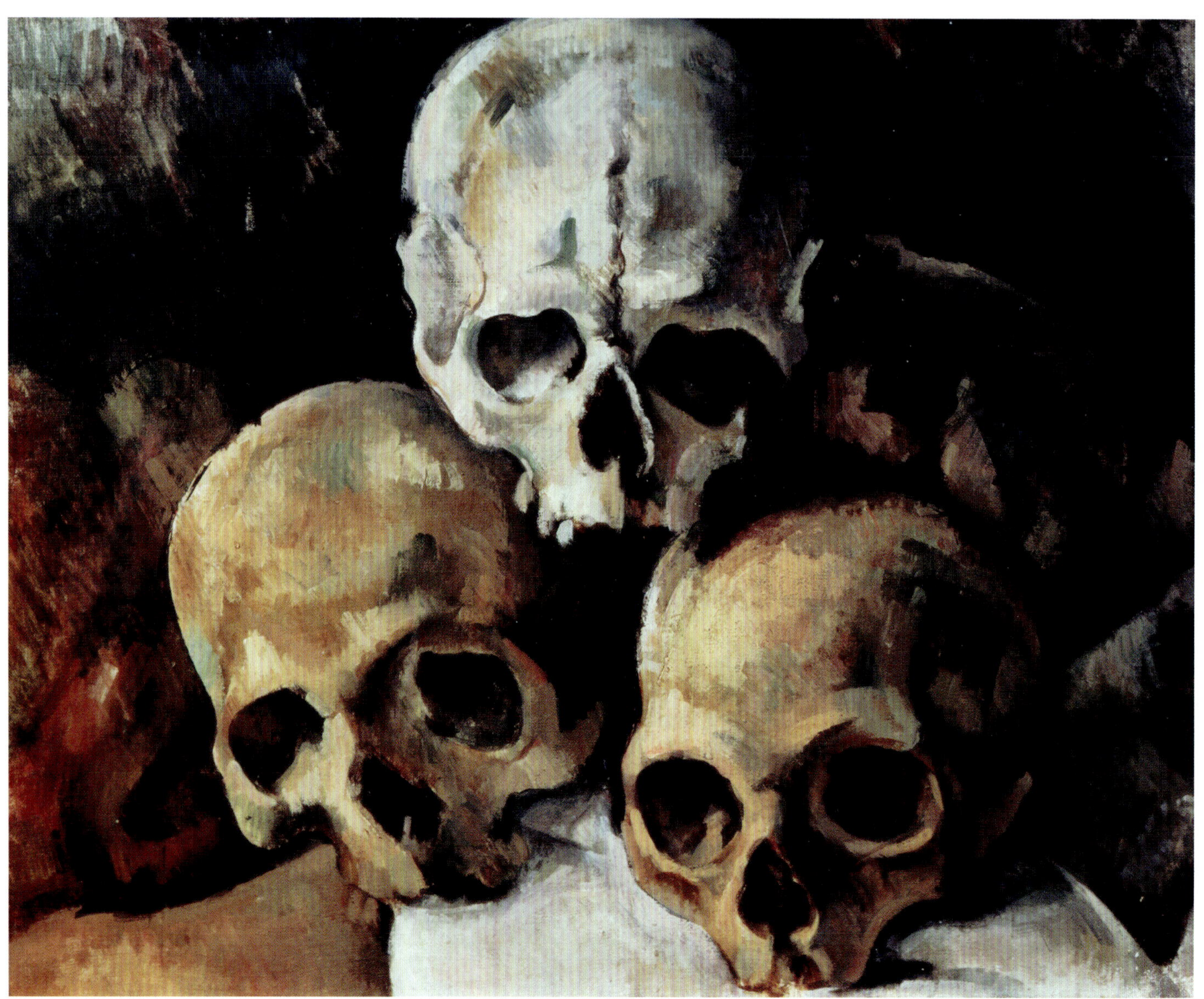

Pyramid of Skulls, 1901
Oil on canvas, 37 x 46 cm (14⅝ x 18⅛ in) • Grand Palais, Paris

After the death of his father in 1886, Cézanne's thoughts turned increasingly towards his own mortality. He did several pictures of skulls, a typical feature of the vanitas images of the Dutch Golden Age that reflected on the transience of life.

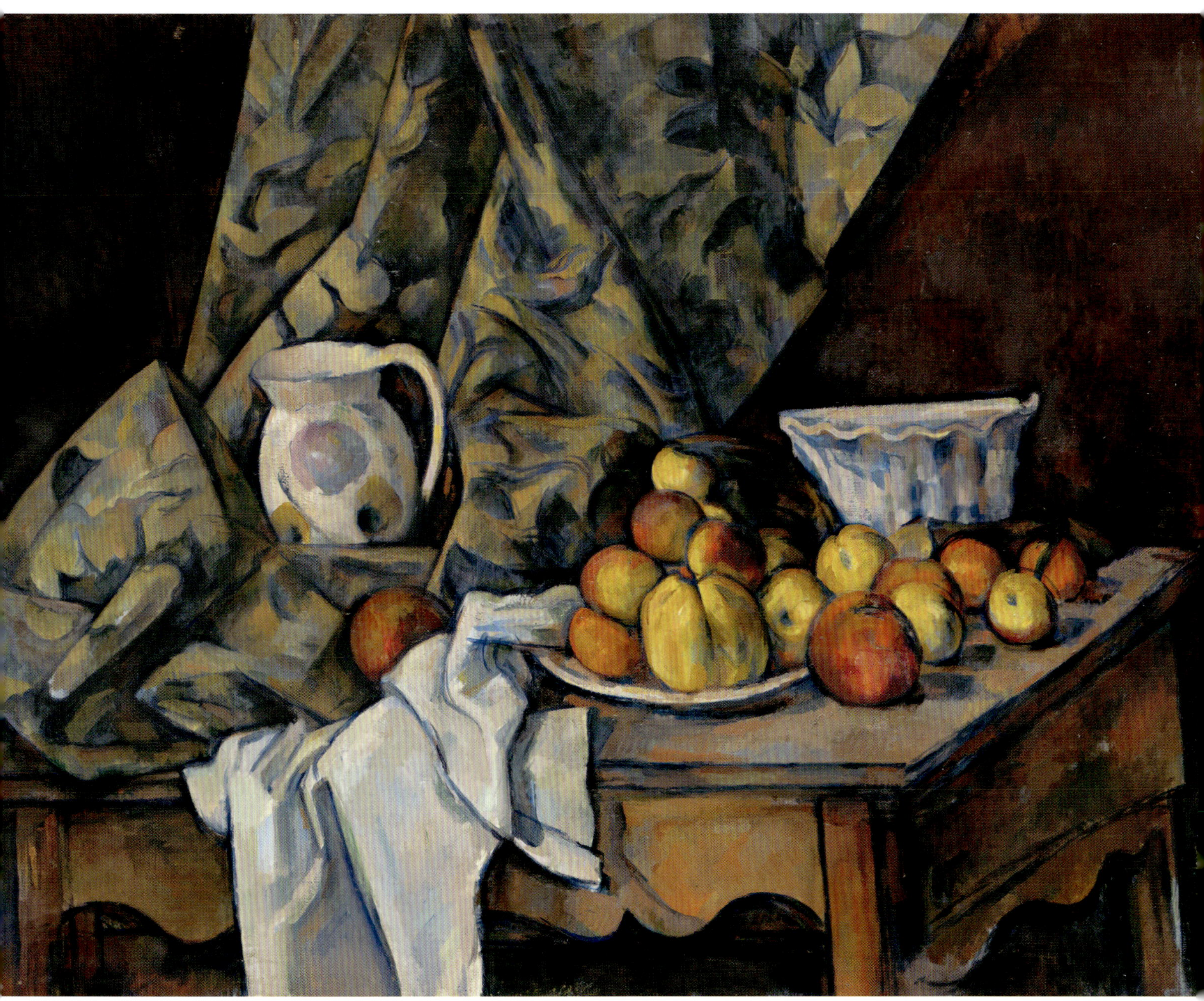

Still Life with Apples and Peaches, *c.* 1905
Oil on canvas, 81 x 100.5 cm (31⅞ x 39⅔ in) • National Gallery of Art,
Washington, D.C.

The painter Émile Bernard said about Cézanne's technique for painting still lifes: 'He started with a shadow and with a brushstroke, then covered it with another, larger one, then a third, until all the spots of tones … modelled the object in colour.'

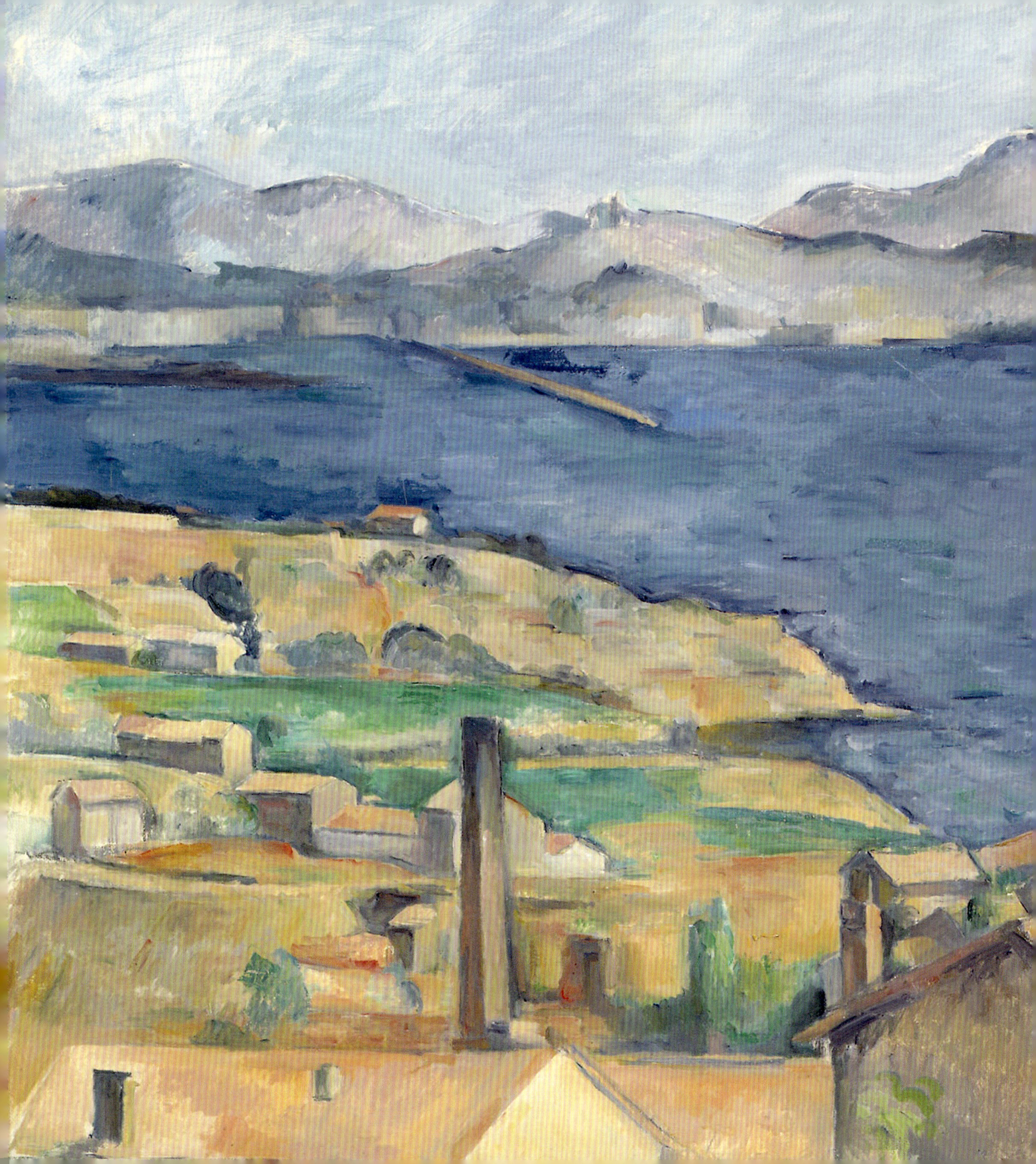

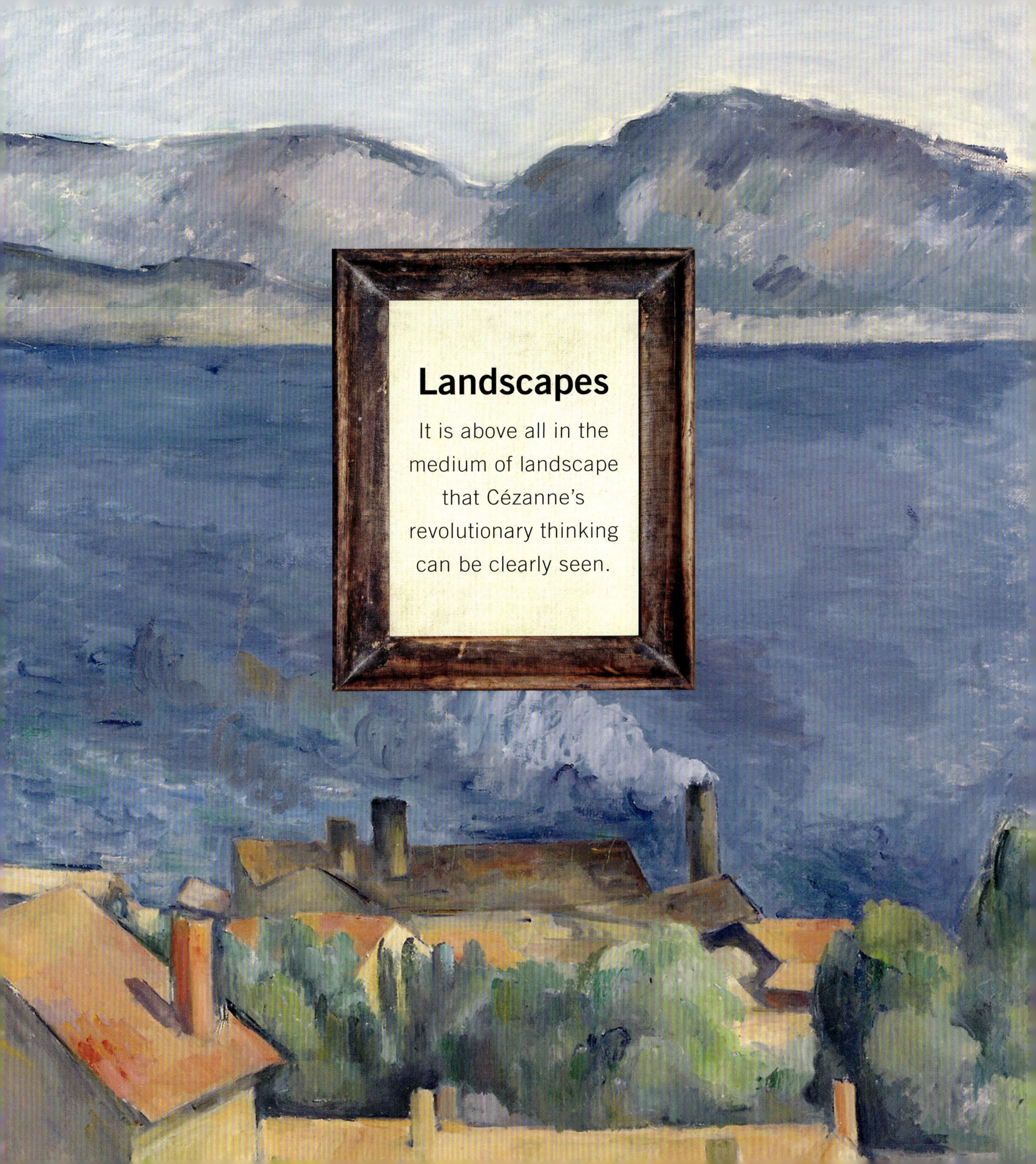

Landscapes

It is above all in the medium of landscape that Cézanne's revolutionary thinking can be clearly seen.

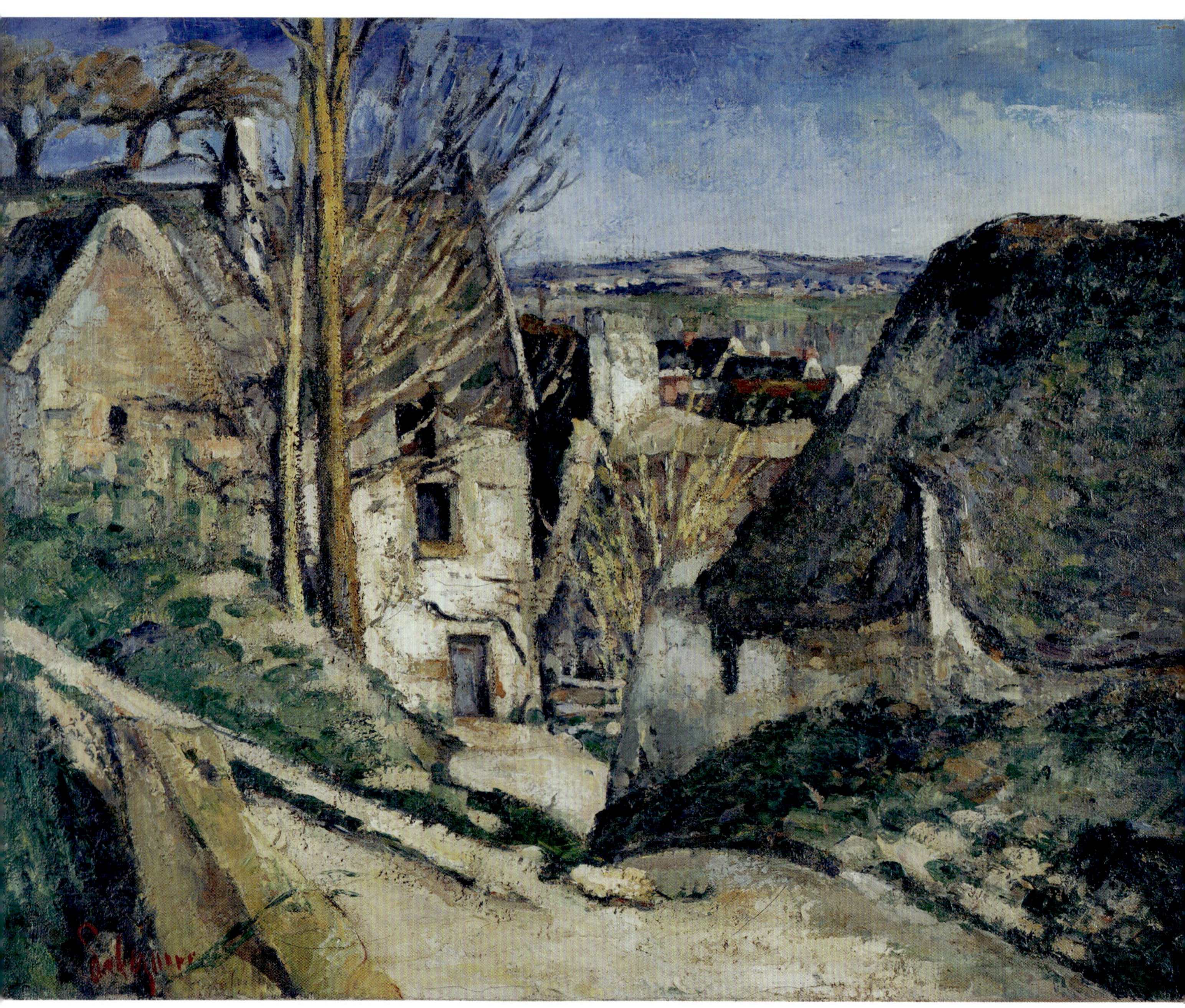

The Hanged Man's House, Auvers-sur-Oise, 1873
Oil on canvas, 55.5 x 66.3 cm (21⅞ x 26⅛ in) • Musée d'Orsay, Paris

This landscape shows how drastically Cézanne's style had changed since the landscapes he had painted at L'Estaque just three years earlier (*see* page 8). Under Pissarro's tutelage, not only his technique but also his whole way of seeing had evolved.

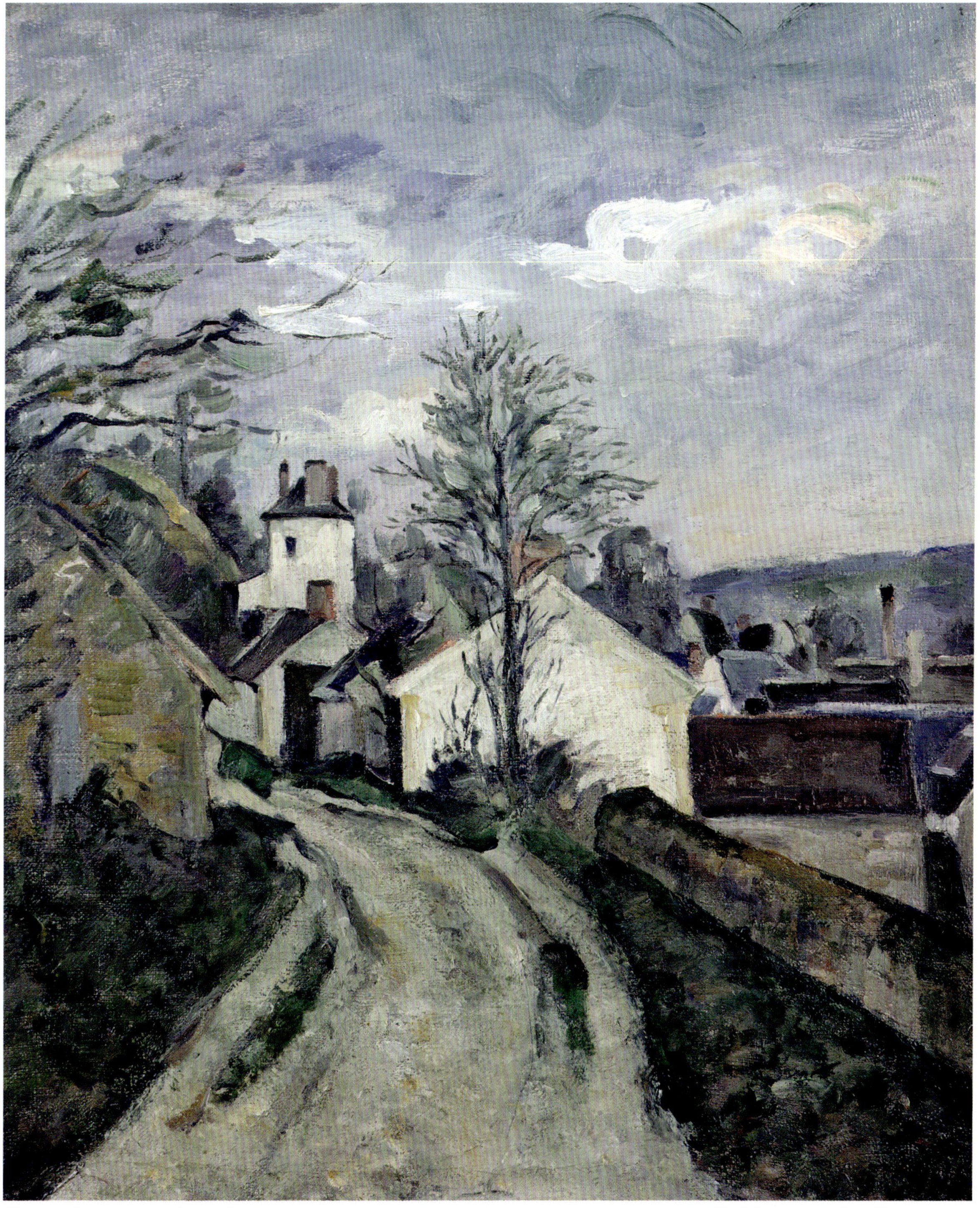

The House of Doctor Gachet in Auvers, *c.* **1873**
Oil on canvas, 46 x 38 cm (18⅛ x 15 in) • Musée d'Orsay, Paris

Dr Paul Gachet was an important early supporter of the Impressionists and hosted Cézanne, Hortense and their infant son for extended stays at his house in Auvers-sur-Oise, which the painter has depicted in this wintry Impressionist canvas.

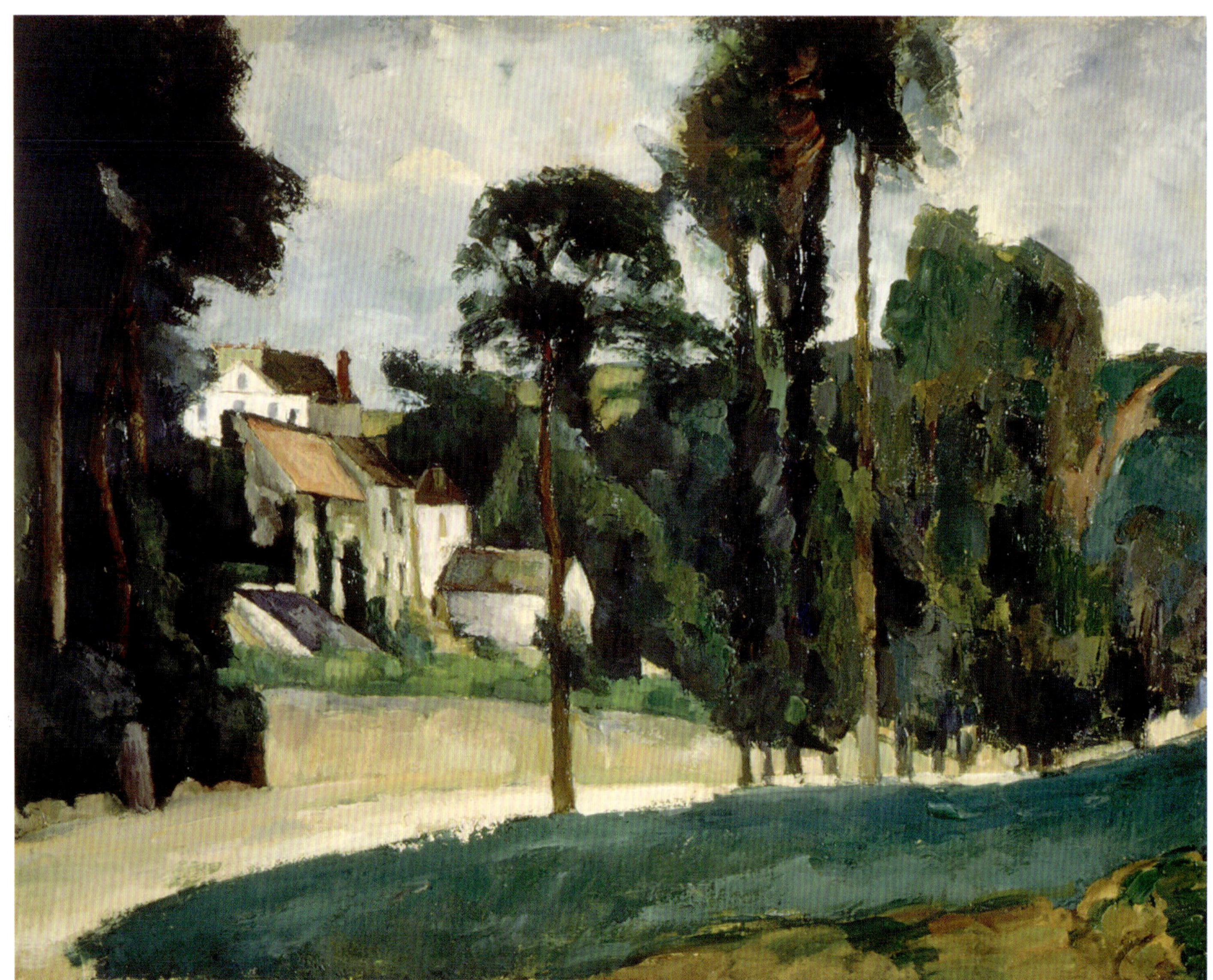

The Road at Pontoise, 1875–77
Oil on canvas, 58 x 71 cm (22⅞ x 28 in) • Pushkin Museum, Moscow

Though in 1877 he exhibited work in the third Impressionist exhibition, in this image of the Trinitarian monastery at Pontoise, Cézanne is already moving beyond Impressionism to a more solid sense of structure and a simpler use of colour.

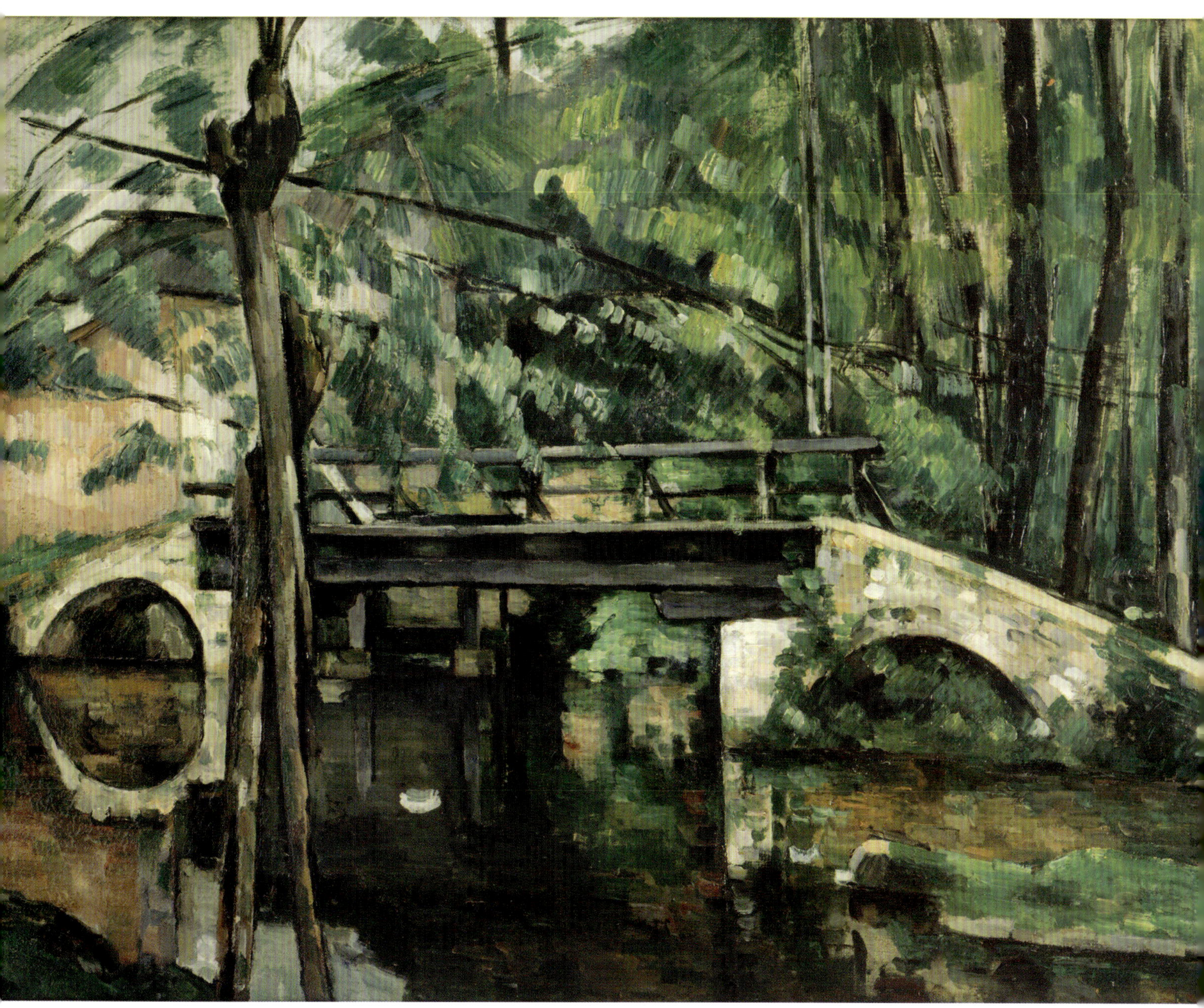

The Bridge at Maincy, *c.* 1879
Oil on canvas, 58.4 x 72.4 cm (23 x 28½ in) • Musée d'Orsay, Paris

The intimate atmosphere of this painting, one of Cézanne's most celebrated landscapes, is intensified by the intersecting verticals and horizontals that give it such a clear structure. It marked the start of a new phase in his thinking.

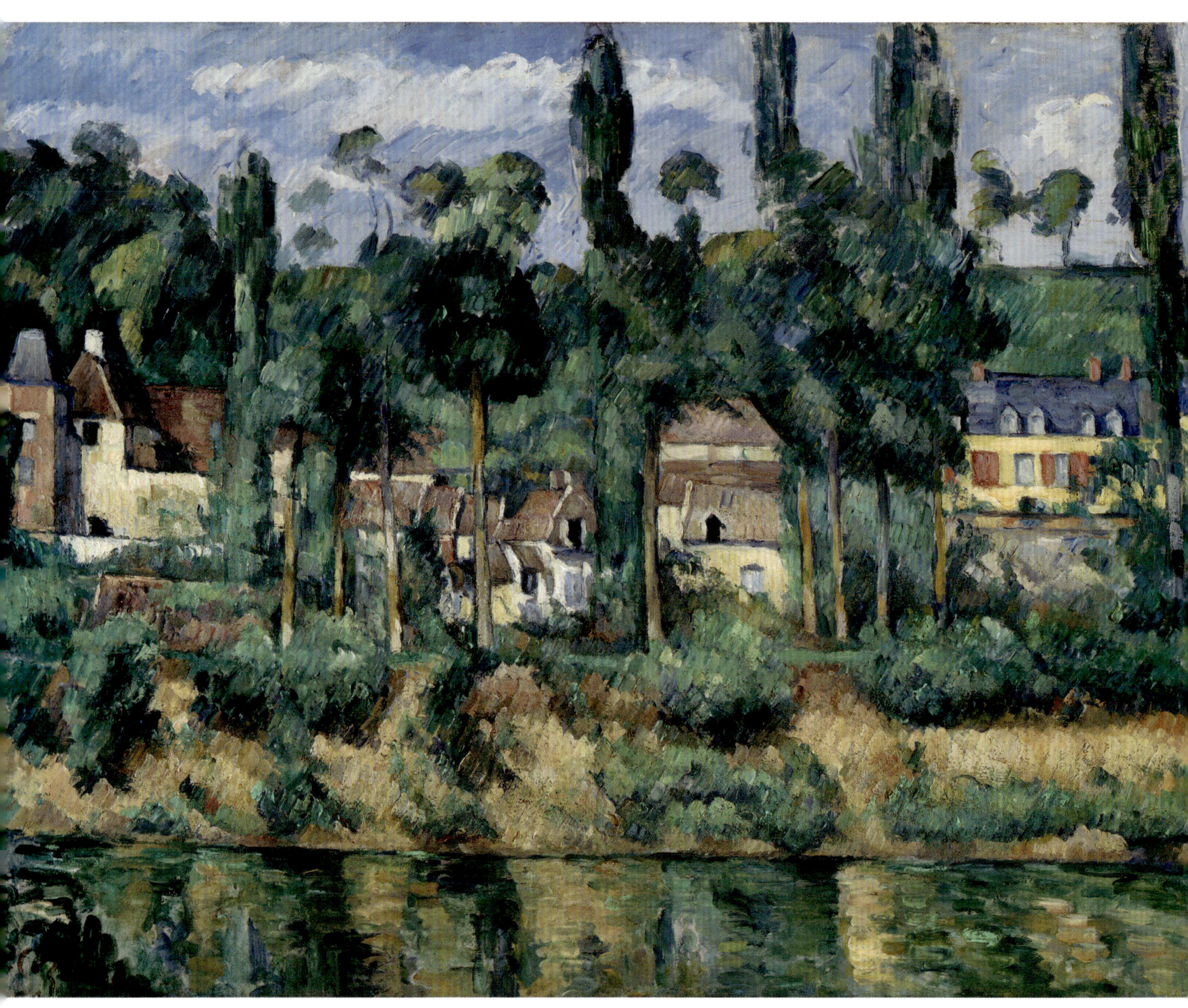

The Château of Médan, *c.* **1879–80**
Oil on canvas, 59.1 x 72.4 cm (23¼ x 28½ in)
• The Burrell Collection, Glasgow

This view, which includes Zola's mansion at Médan, was painted from an island in the River Seine. Cézanne reached it using Zola's boat, called *Nana* after the novel of the same name that his friend was writing during the time this was painted.

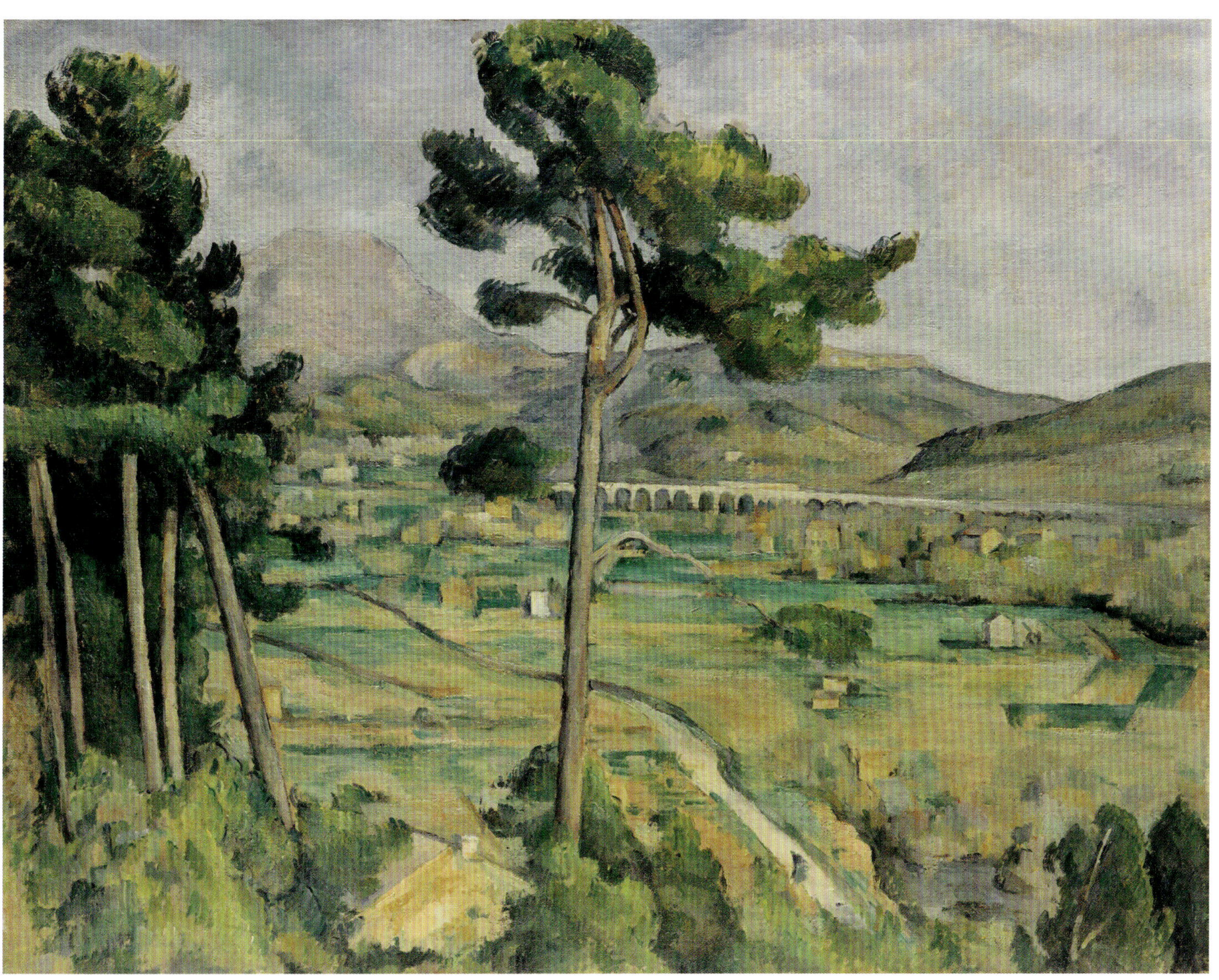

**Mont Sainte-Victoire and the Viaduct of the
Arc River Valley, 1882–85**

Oil on canvas, 65.4 x 81.6 cm (25¾ x 32⅛ in)

• Metropolitan Museum of Art, New York

This is Cézanne's first significant image of the mountain he would depict more than 80 times in all,
though here the valley, the viaduct and, above all, the pine tree in the foreground are as much the
subjects as Mont Sainte-Victoire.

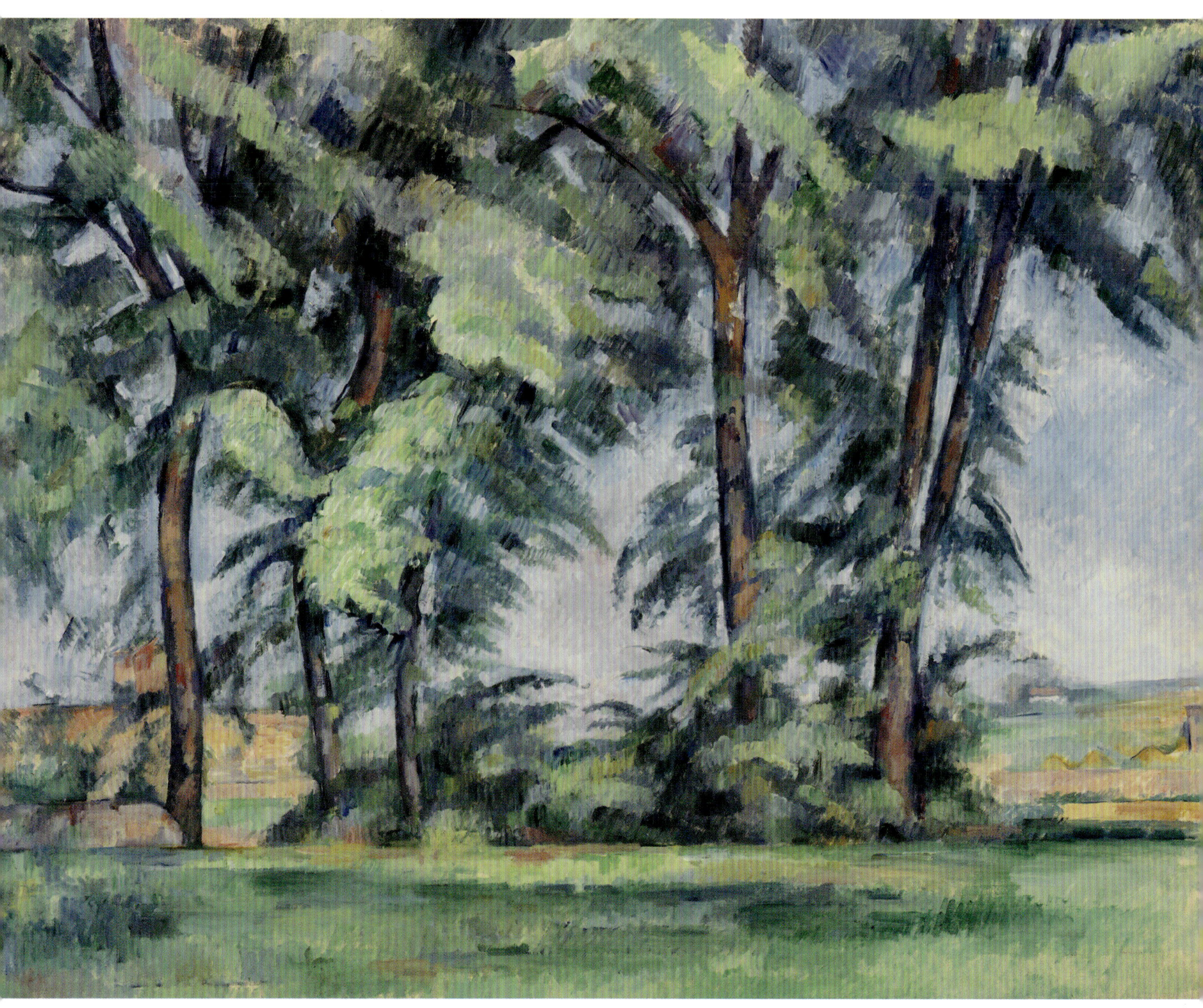

Tall Trees at the Jas de Bouffan, c. 1883
Oil on canvas, 65 x 81 cm (25⅝ x 31⅞ in)
• Courtauld Institute of Art, London

Cézanne loved to paint in the grounds of the family home a mile or so to the west of Aix-en-Provence. As with *The Bridge at Maincy* (*see* page 53), the short parallel brushstrokes he used for the foliage suggest the swish of leaves in the breeze.

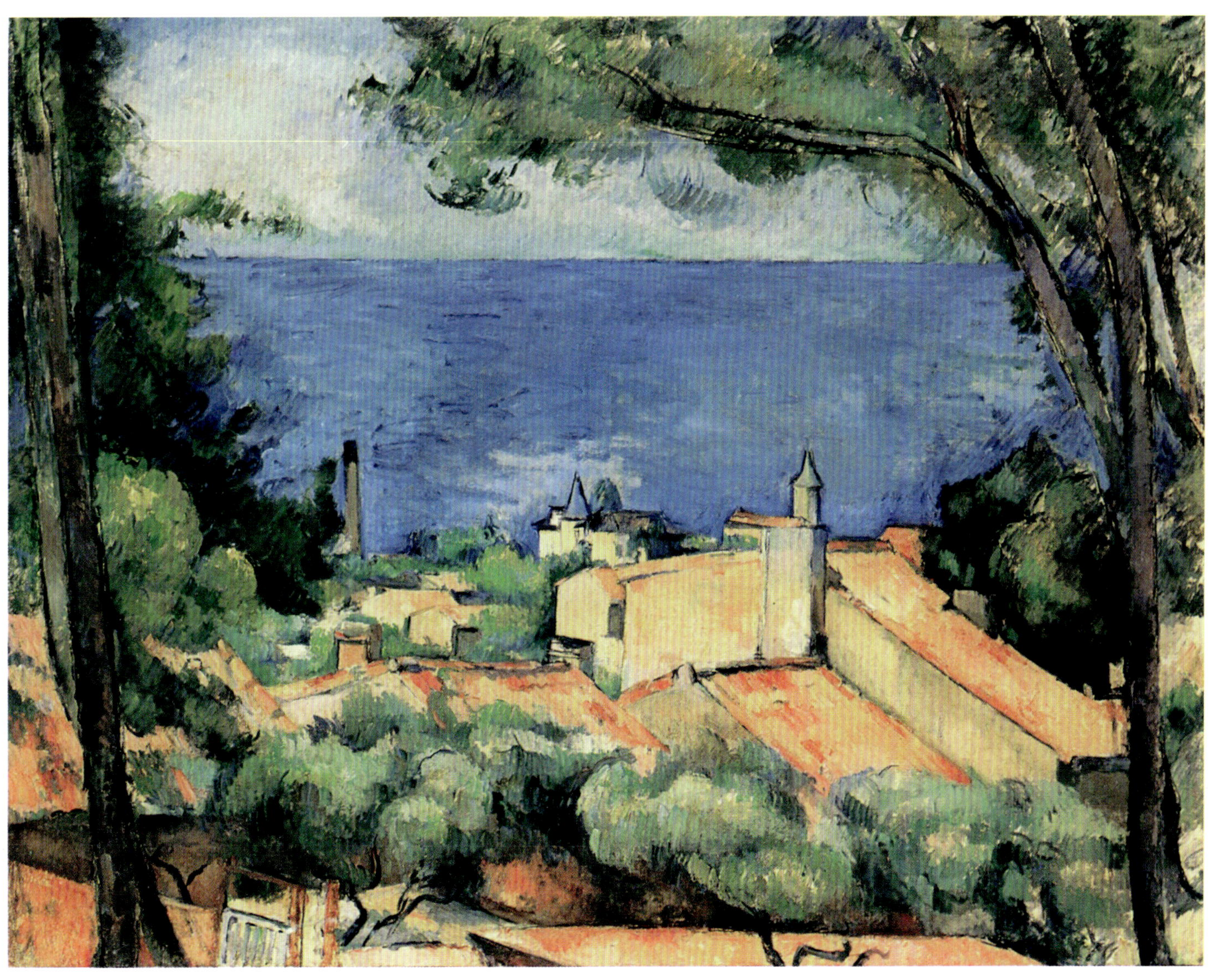

L'Estaque with Red Roofs, 1883–85
Oil on canvas, 65 x 81 cm (25⅝ x 31⅞ in)
• Private Collection

By the time he painted this image, Cézanne had been visiting the village of L'Estaque overlooking the Bay of Marseille for some 15 years. During this period, he painted various views looking over the roofs of the village to the sea.

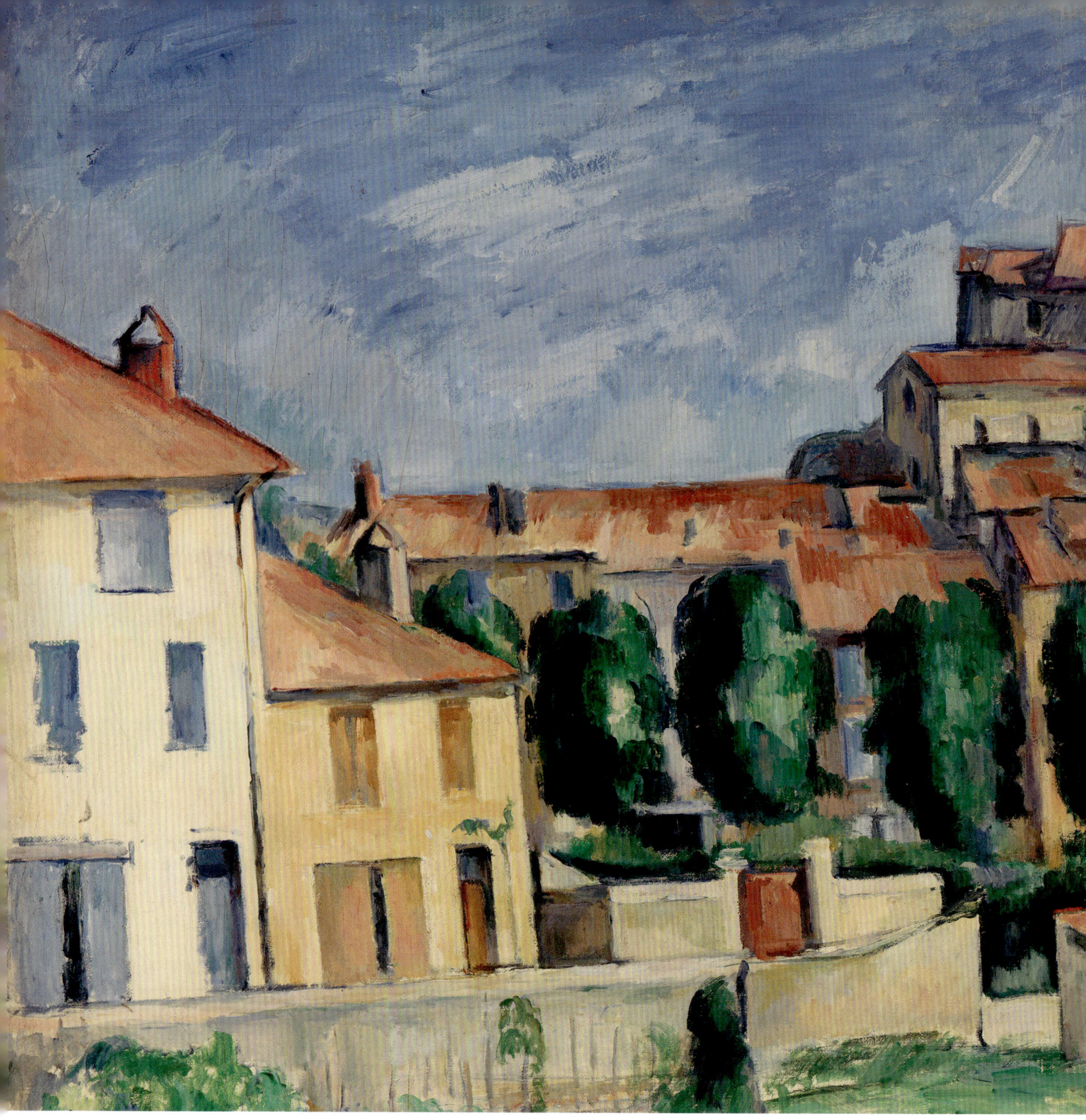

Gardanne, *c.* 1885
Oil on canvas, 65 × 100.3 cm (25⅔ × 39½ in)
• Barnes Foundation, Merion, Pennsylvania

Cézanne moved Hortense and their son Paul to the little town of Gardanne in late summer 1885. He found numerous motifs in the town and surrounding landscape during his time there, before marrying Hortense the following spring.

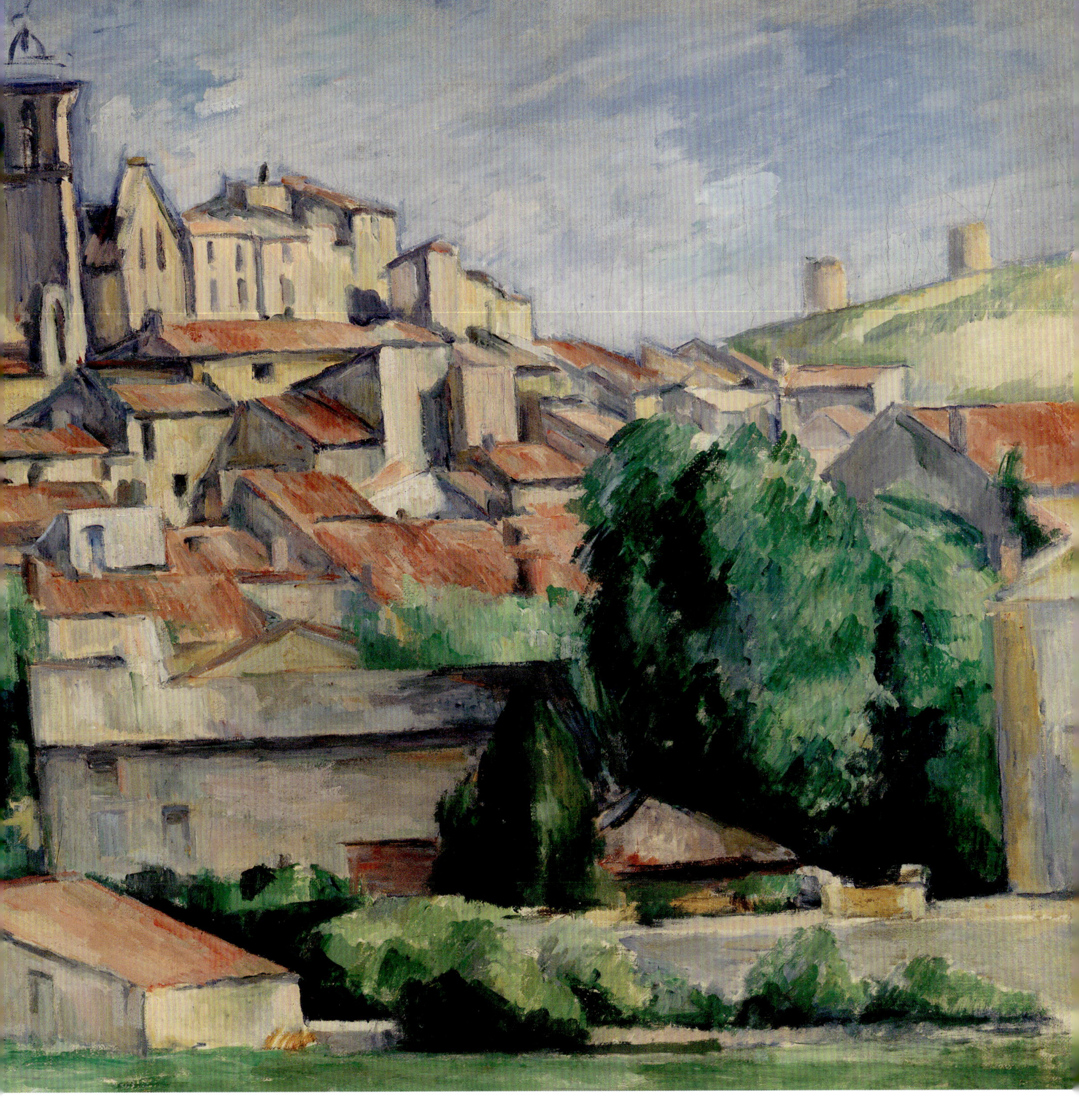

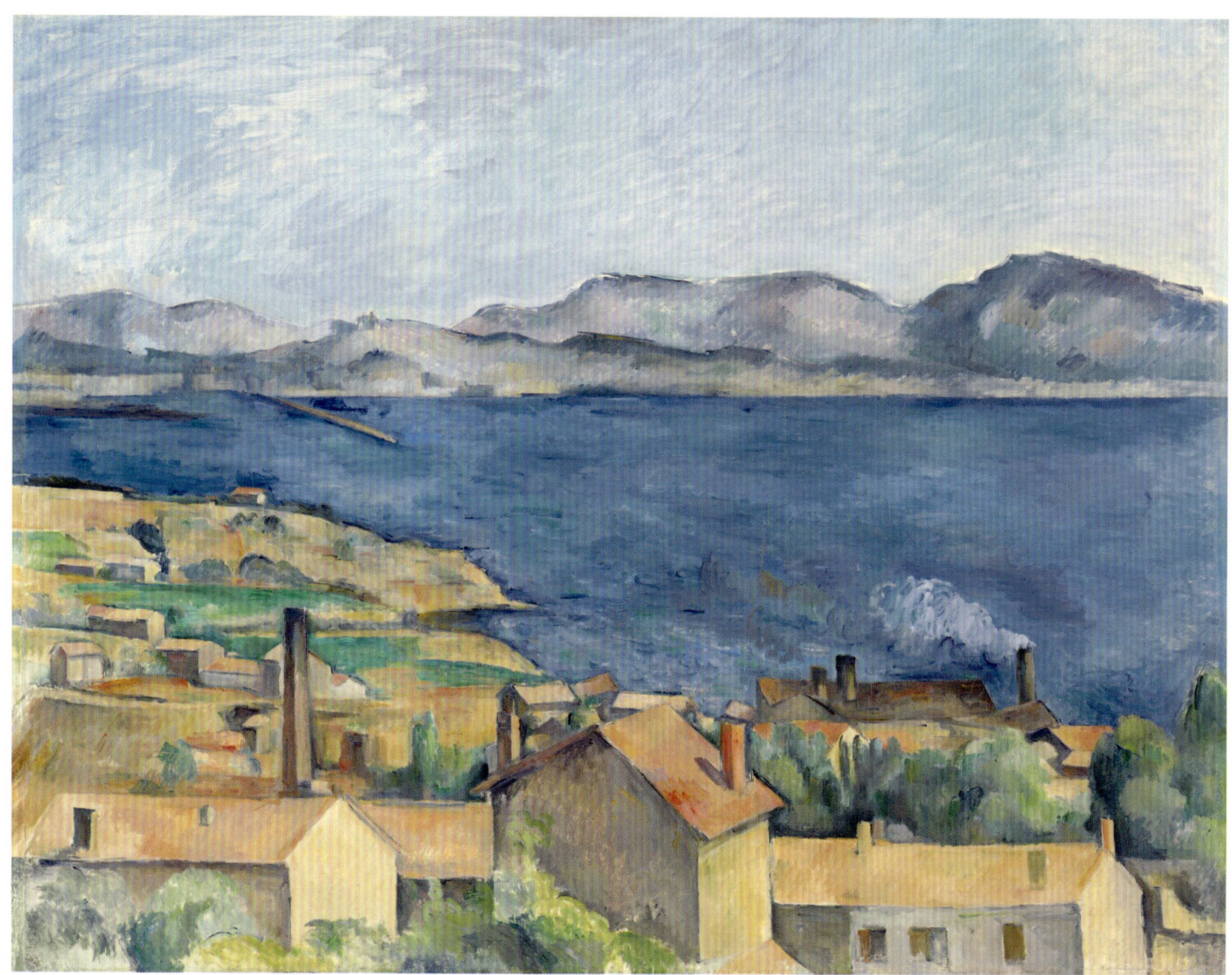

The Bay of Marseille, Seen from L'Estaque, *c.* 1885
Oil on canvas, 80.2 × 100.6 cm (31⅛ × 39⅝ in)
• Art Institute of Chicago, Chicago

Cézanne believed that light in a painting could be represented through colour alone. The striking colour contrasts between the different zones in this picture suggest the intensity of the southern sun, which the painter himself found oppressive.

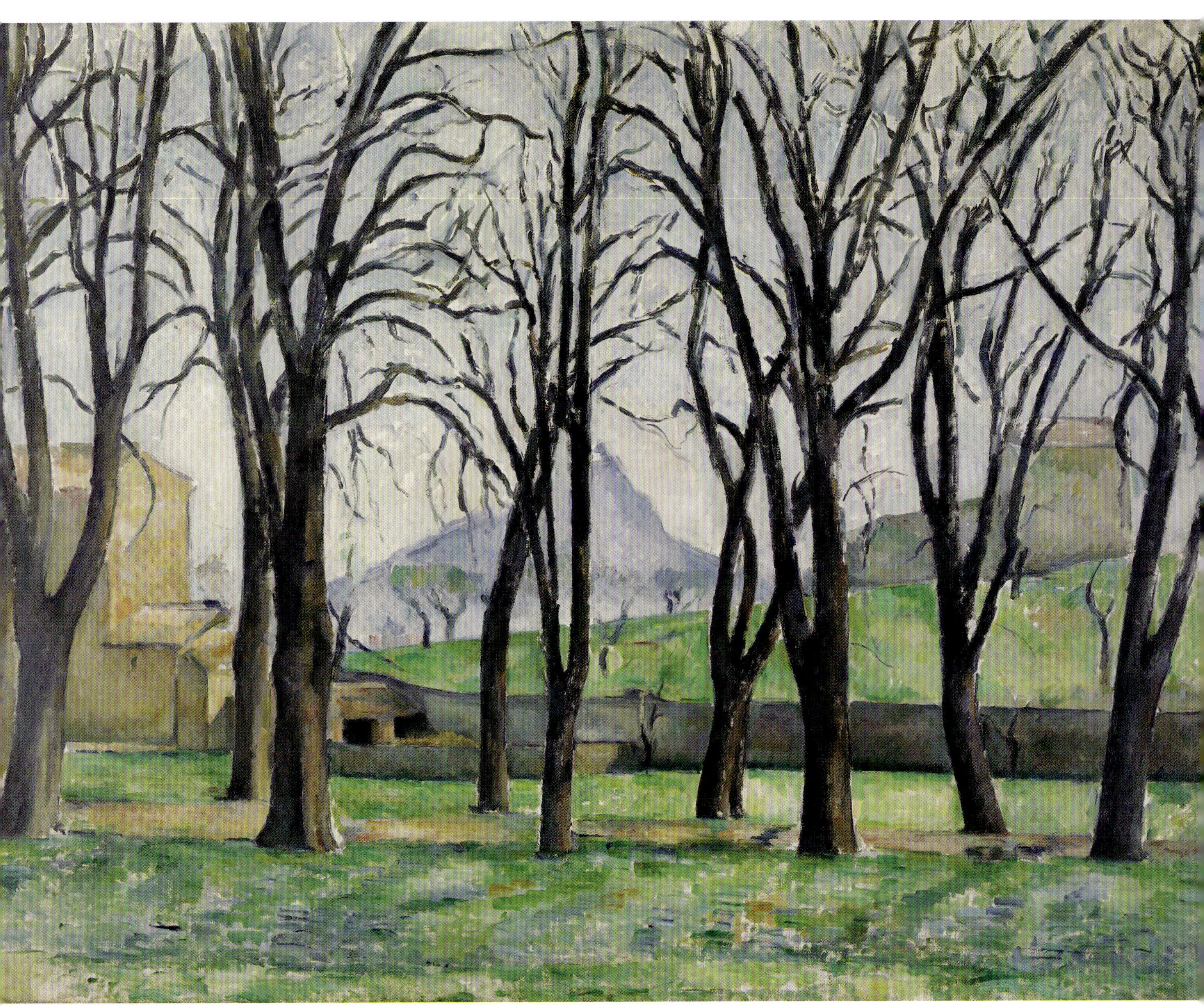

Chestnut Trees at Jas de Bouffan, *c.* 1885–86
Oil on canvas, 71.1 x 90.2 cm (28 x 35½ in)
• Minneapolis Institute of Arts, Minnesota

The trees in this wintry image are a screen for what lies behind them: various buildings on his father's estate, the Jas de Bouffan, and in the distance the Mont Sainte-Victoire, a presence here as it is almost everywhere around Aix.

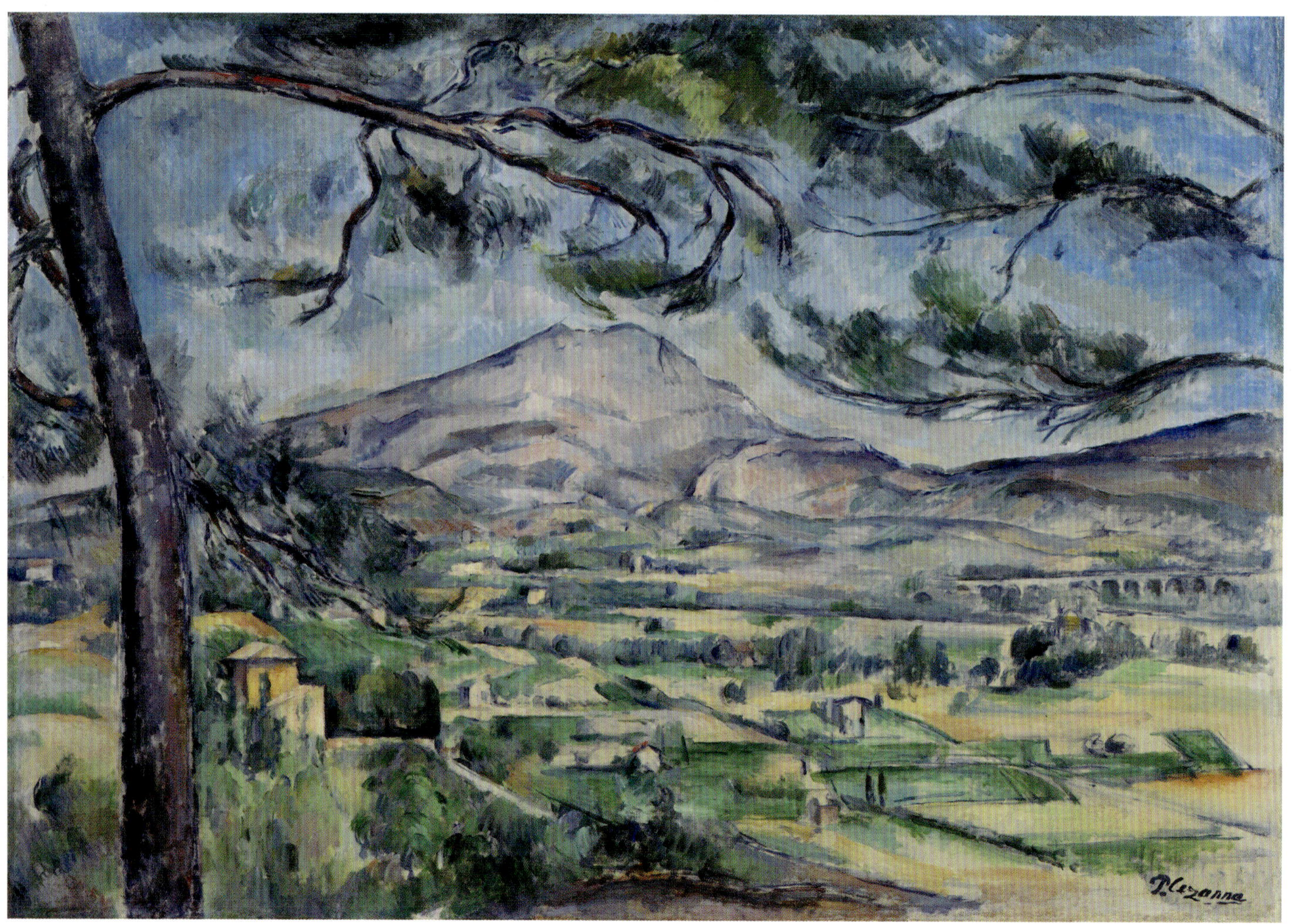

Mont Sainte-Victoire with Large Pine, *c.* 1887

Oil on canvas, 66.8 x 92.3 cm (26¼ x 36⅜ in)

• Courtauld Institute of Art, London

Like the images of Mount Fuji by the Japanese artist Katsushika Hokusai (1760–1849), who had so influenced Impressionism, this image is one of the many different views Cézanne depicted of his own sacred mountain, Mont Sainte-Victoire.

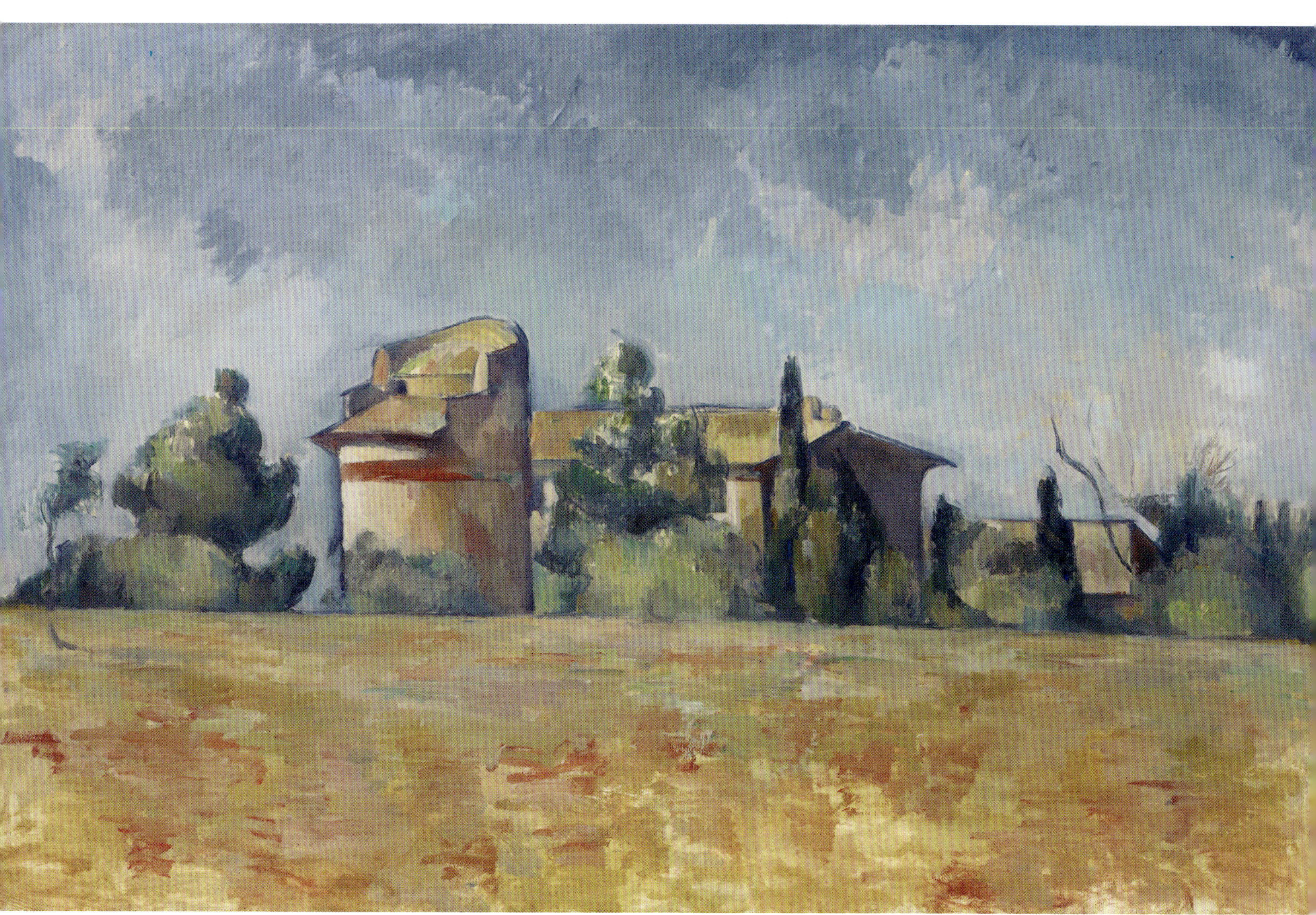

The Dovecote at Bellevue, 1888–92
Oil on canvas, 54.2 x 81.2 cm (21⅜ x 32 in) • Kunstmuseum, Basel

The arresting stillness of this image is a quality common to most of the pictures of Bellevue, the property of his sister and brother-in-law that Cézanne painted several times in the late 1880s and early 1890s, before it was sold.

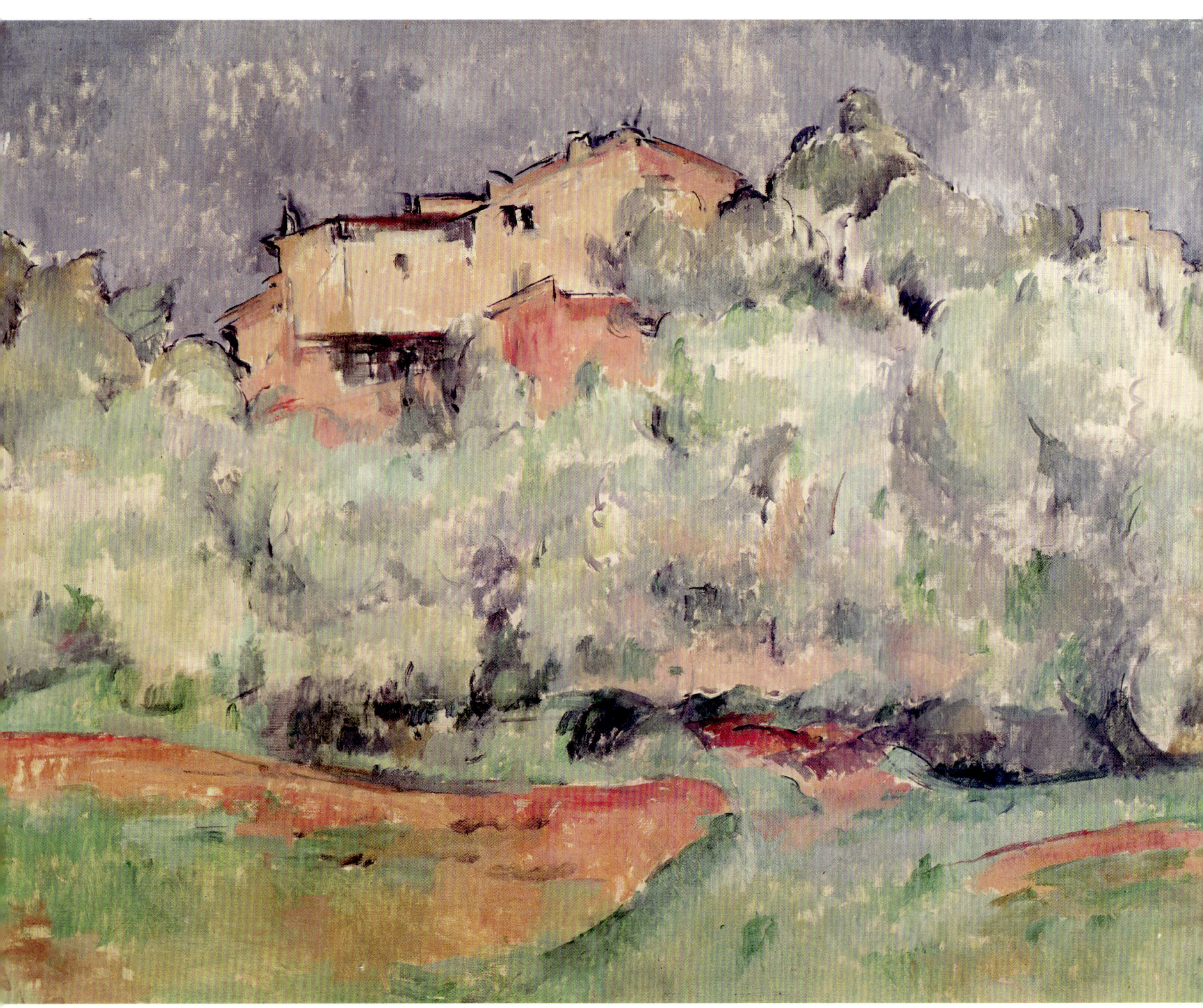

House and Dovecote at Bellevue, 1890–92
Oil on canvas, 65 x 81.2 cm (25⅝ x 32 in) • Museum Folkwang, Essen

This painting uses just a few colours to convey a series of planes while unifying these by anchoring each of the colours in more than one of the planes. The result is a depth of perspective achieved almost wholly by colour alone.

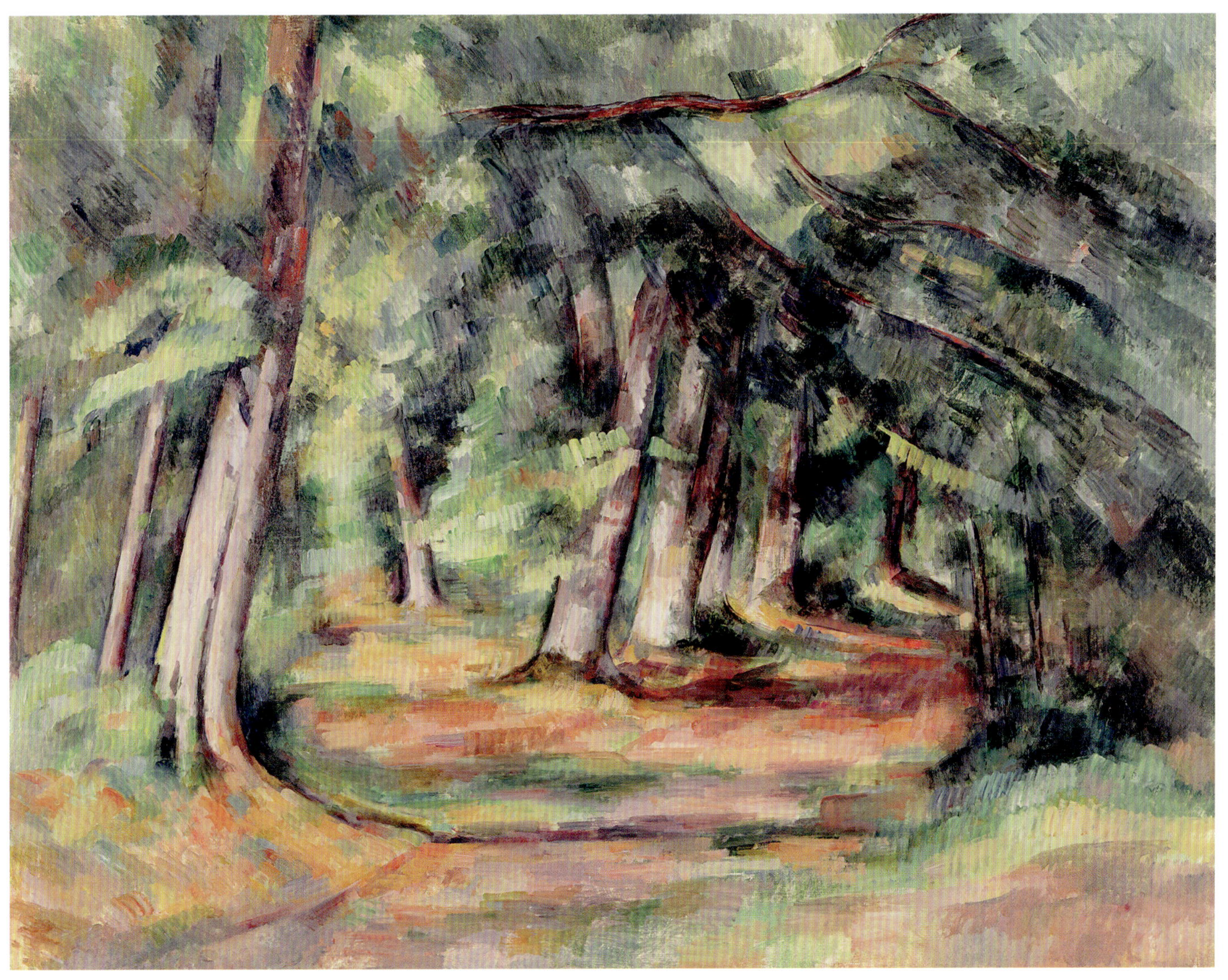

Underwood (near Jas de Bouffan), 1890–94
Oil on canvas, 65 x 92 cm (25⅝ x 36¼ in) • Private Collection

Every part of this remarkable picture seems to be in flux. Cézanne has managed to suggest through colour alone both the agitation of the branches in the breeze and the prismatic flickering of light and shadow on the forest floor.

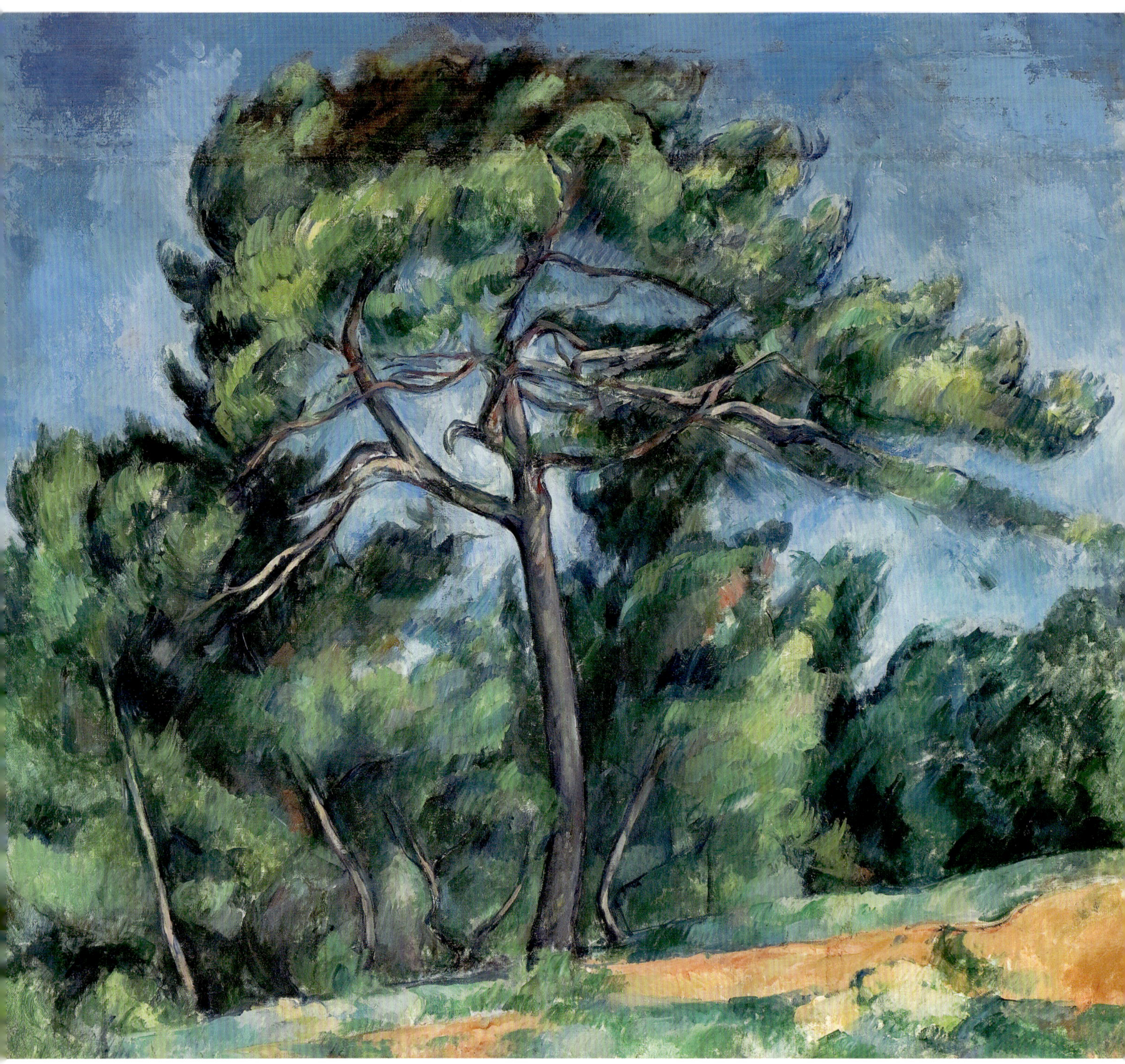

The Great Pine, 1890–96
Oil on canvas, 85.5 x 92.5 cm (33⅝ x 36⅜ in)
• São Paulo Museum of Art, São Paulo

In this picture Cézanne sees something iconic in an ordinary umbrella pine, its stubborn resistance to the elements conveyed in the direction of the painter's brushstrokes for the pine and the surrounding scrub, as if shaped by the wind.

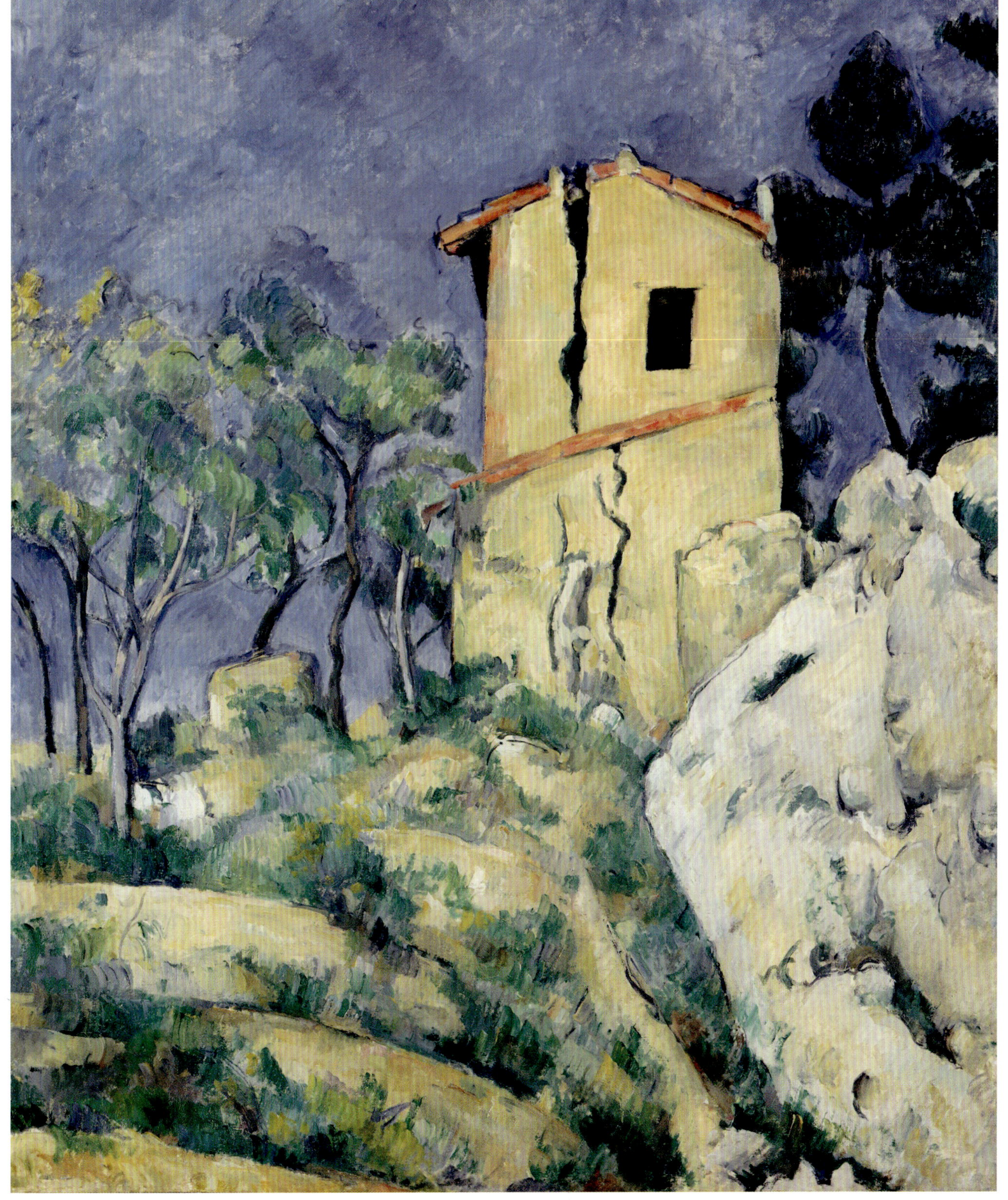

The House with the Cracked Walls, 1892–94
Oil on canvas, 80 x 64.1 cm (31½ x 25¼ in)
• Metropolitan Museum of Art, New York

Cézanne spent long hours over many decades exploring the landscape around Aix for painting motifs. It is no surprise he chose this one, depicting it frontally to make the most of the unique feature that makes it such a compelling subject.

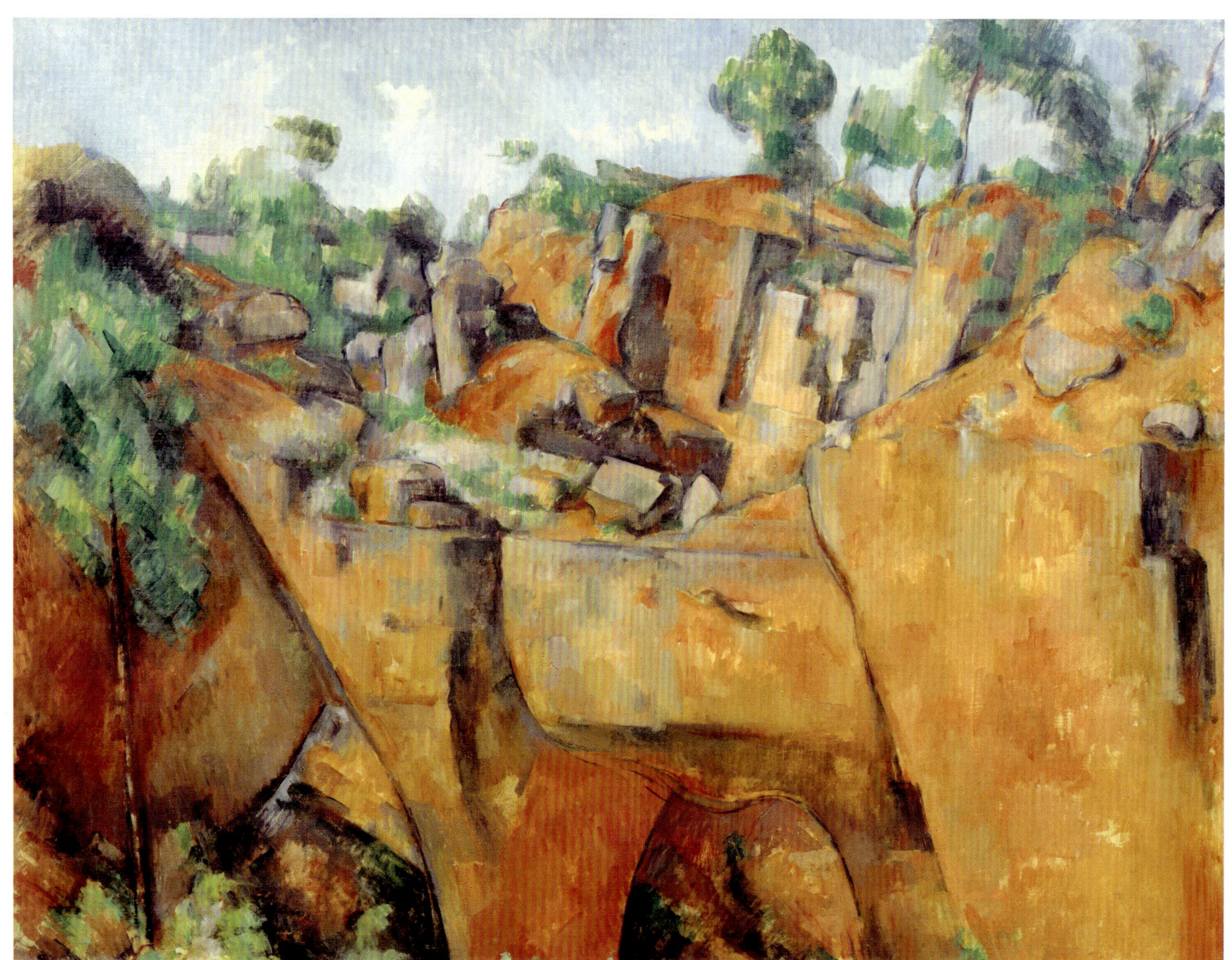

The Quarry at Bibémus, 1895
Oil on canvas, 65 x 81 cm (25⅝ x 31⅞ in) • Museum Folkwang, Essen

The old Bibémus stone quarry provided an endless variety of motifs for Cézanne. The cut rocks fascinated him for the complexity of planes they offered up, as well as the rich ochre colour unique to the geology of the region.

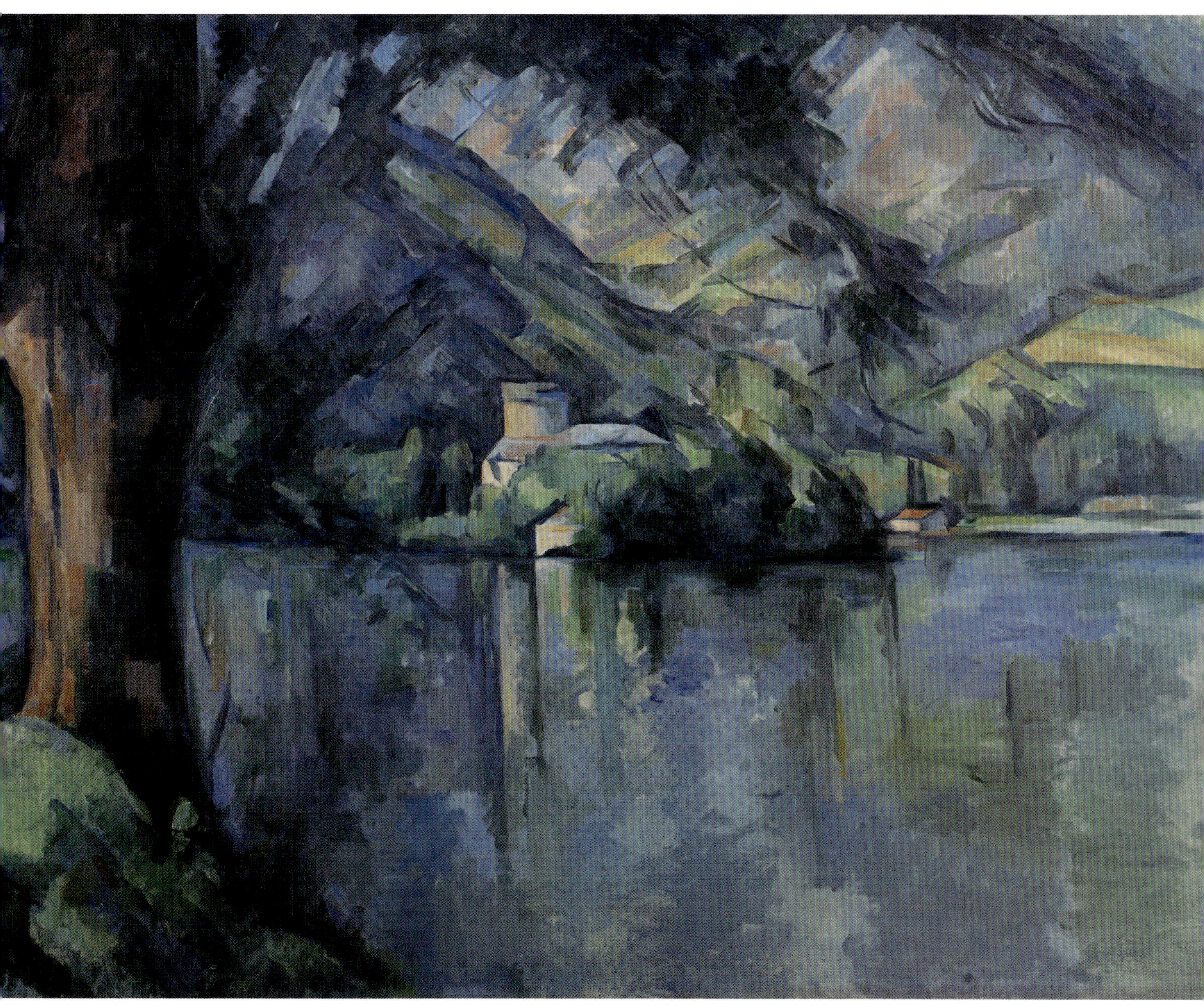

Lac d'Annecy, 1896
Oil on canvas, 65 x 81 cm (25⅝ x 31⅞ in)
• Courtauld Institute of Art, London

One of his most intimate landscapes, this painting of Lac d'Annecy, close to the Swiss border with France, is also the only canvas to have emerged from the two extended holidays Cézanne took with his wife and son in the 1890s.

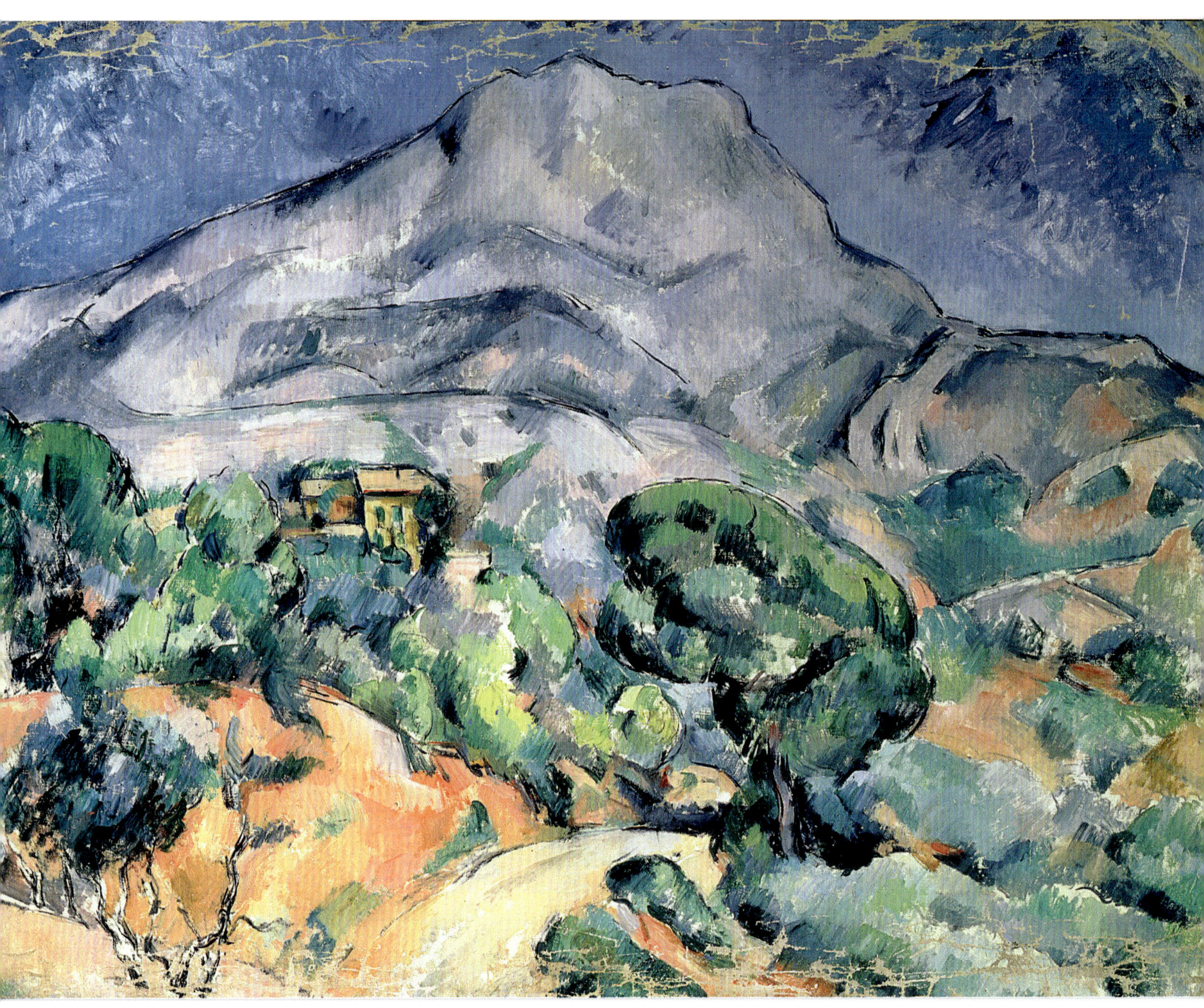

Mont Sainte-Victoire, *c.* 1896–98
Oil on canvas, 78 x 99 cm (30¾ x 39 in)
• The State Hermitage Museum, St Petersburg

Cézanne's growing obsession with Mont Sainte-Victoire is reflected in the composition of the images he now made of it. Increasingly, the other motifs present in previous paintings were eliminated, as he focused his mind on the mountain.

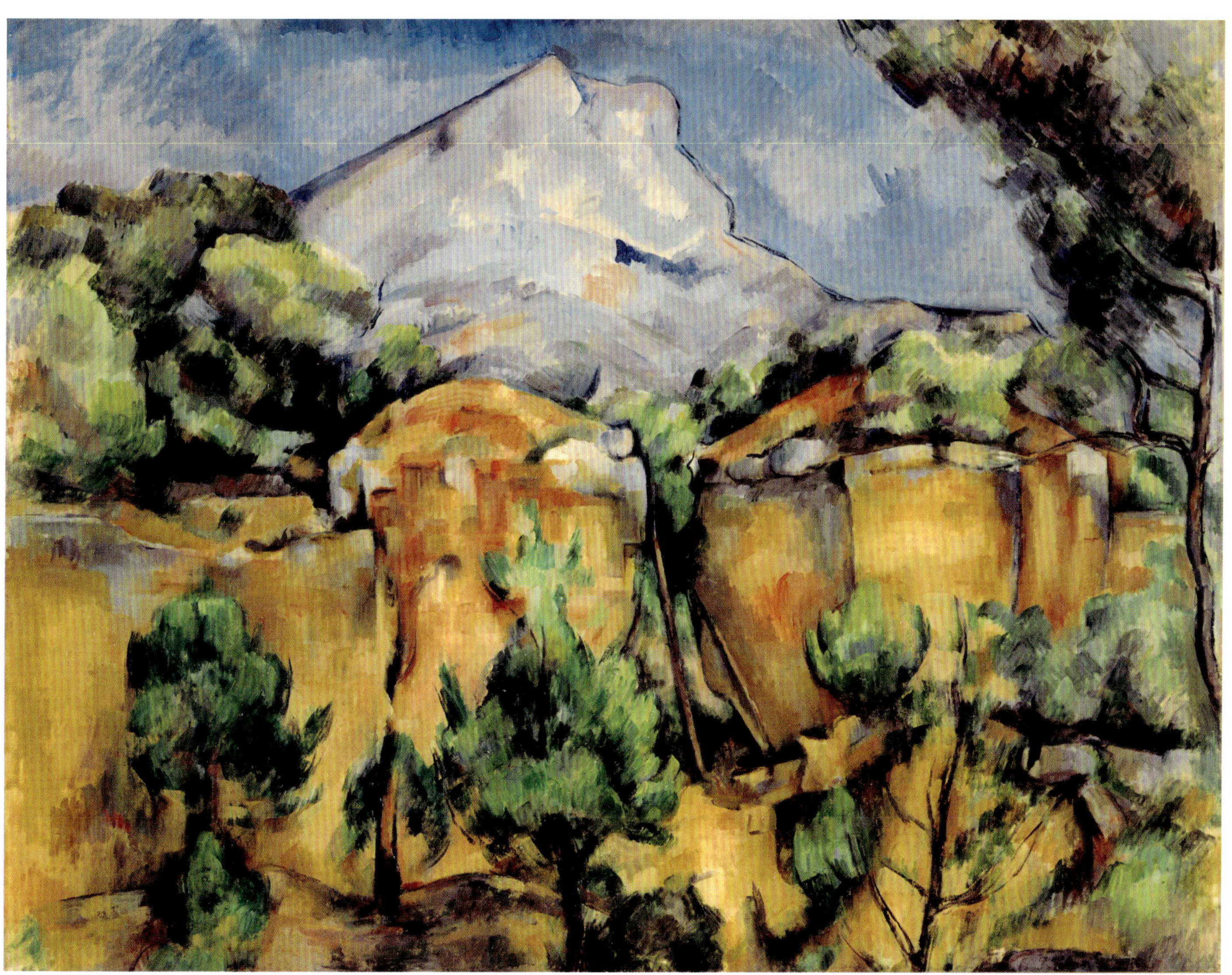

Mont Sainte-Victoire Seen from the Bibémus Quarry, *c.* 1897
Oil on canvas, 65.1 x 81.3 cm (25⅝ x 32 in)
• Baltimore Museum of Art, Baltimore

In this image, Mont Sainte-Victoire looms over the Bibémus quarry where Cézanne rented an old cottage. He would live there while painting the man-made bluffs of ochre rocks, whose colour contrasts so strongly with the distant mountain.

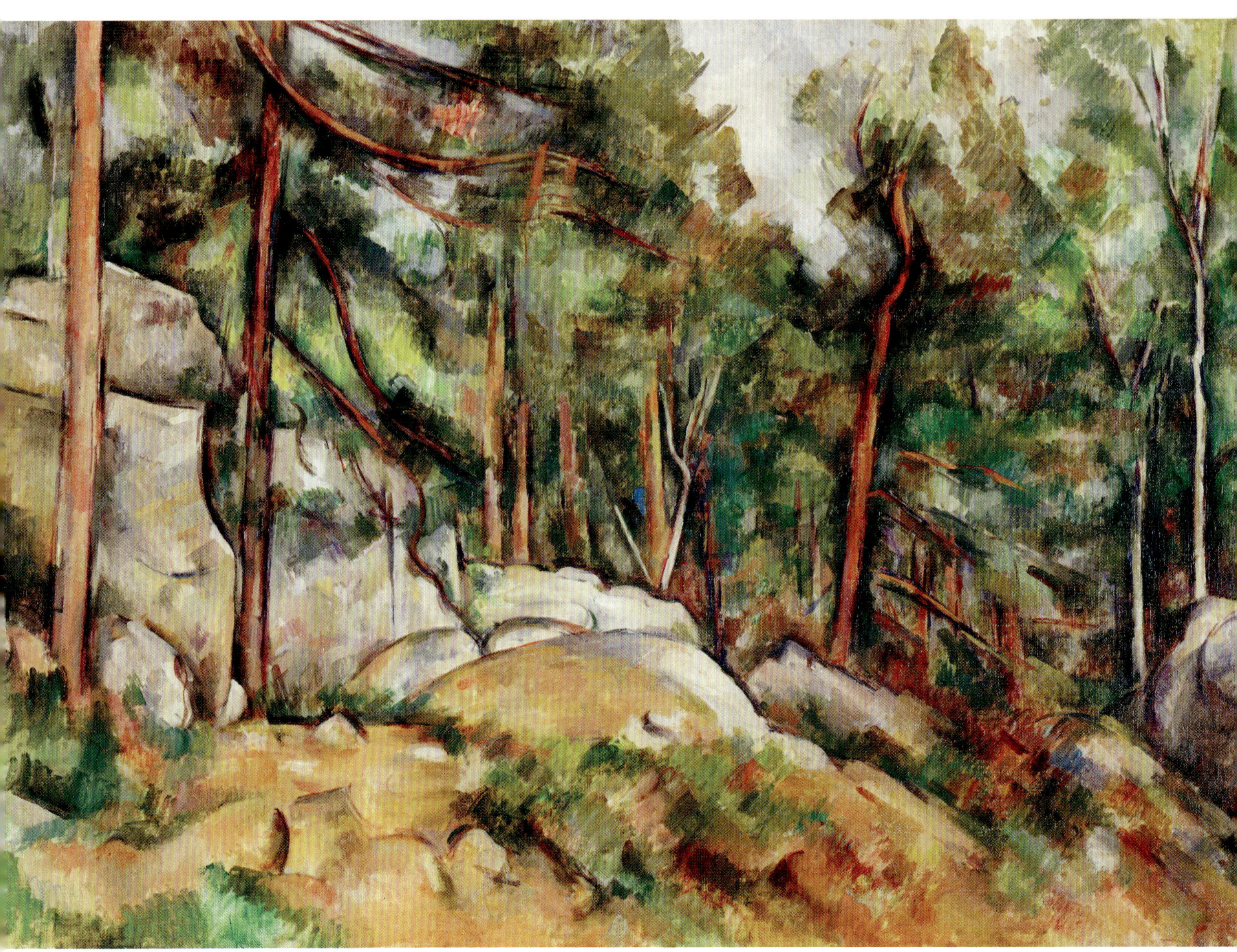

Forest Interior, 1898–99
Oil on canvas, 61 x 81.3 cm (24 x 32 in) • De Young Museum, Fine Arts
Museums of San Francisco

This image was painted in the vicinity of the Château Noir, a half-finished Neo-Gothic mansion close to the Bibémus quarries, west of Aix. By this point, the ageing Cézanne was taking a carriage on excursions to his favourite painting spots.

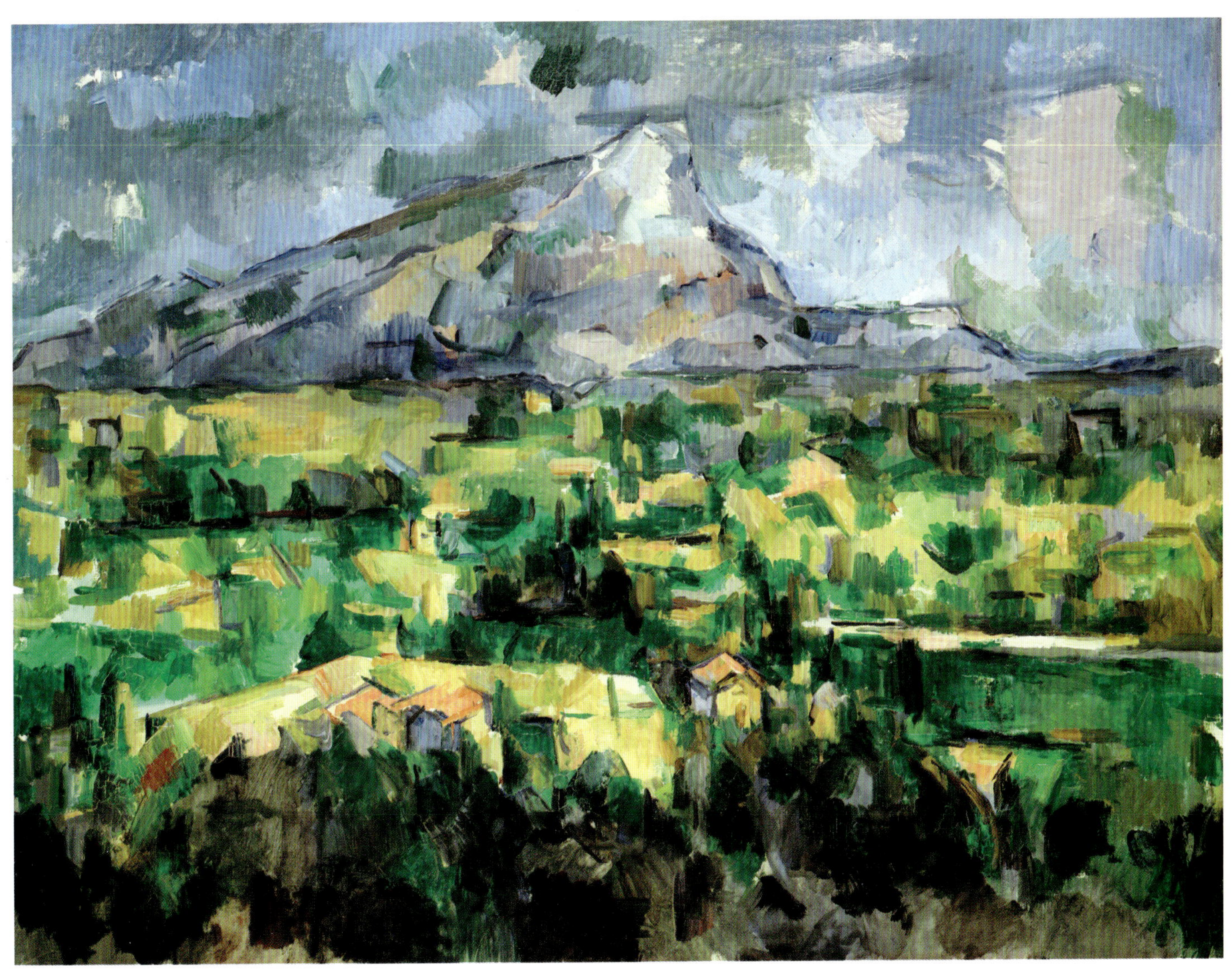

Mont Sainte-Victoire, 1902–04
Oil on canvas, 73 × 91.9 cm (28¾ × 36¼ in)
• Philadelphia Museum of Art, Philadelphia

In the early 1900s, Cézanne painted 11 oils and 17 watercolours of the mountain from his vantage point up the hill from his studio. In many of these, the scenery, though still discernible, dissolves in a spectacle of pure colour.

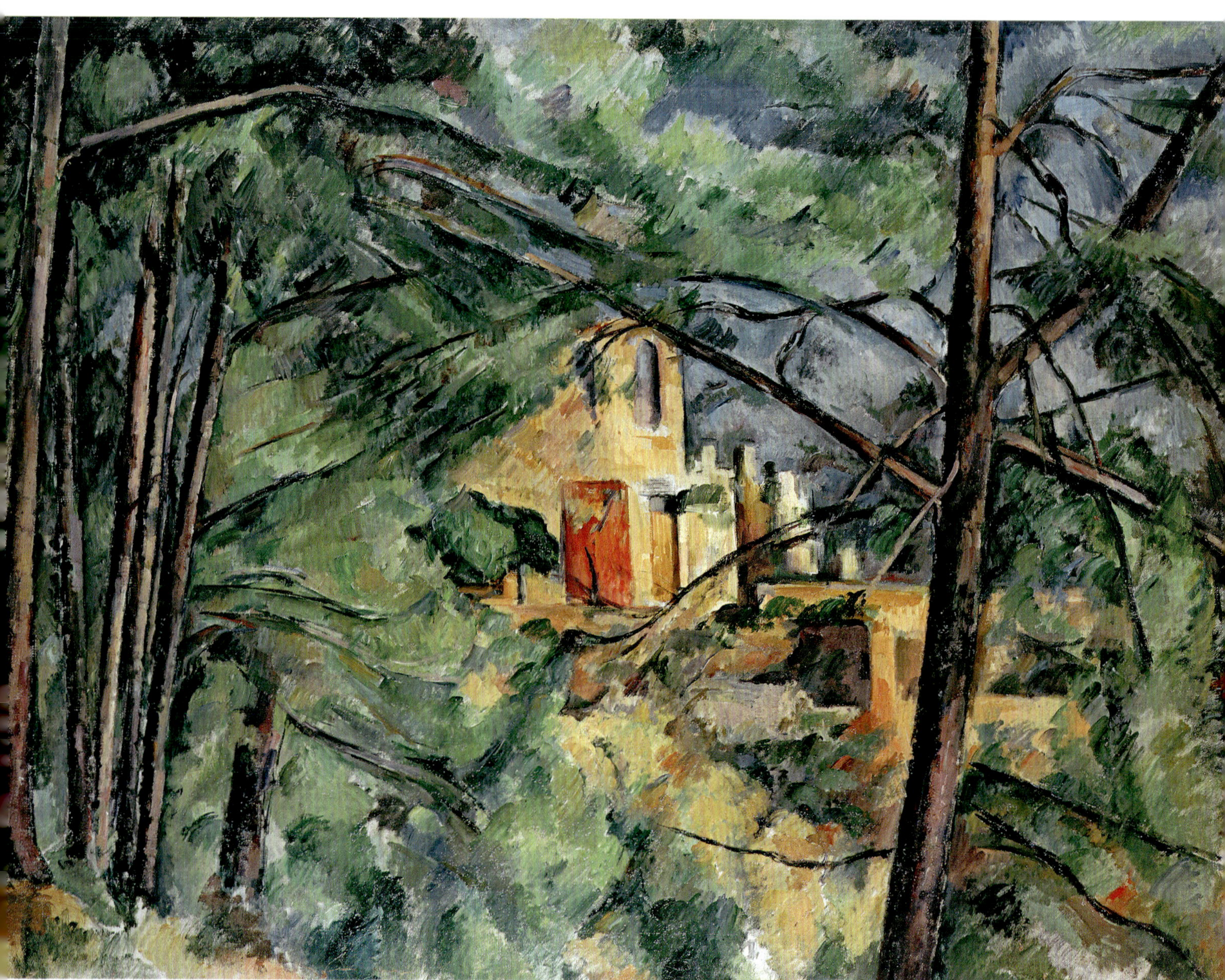

Château Noir, *c.* 1904
Oil on canvas, 73 x 92 cm (28¾ x 36¼ in) • Private Collection

The terrace of the Château Noir, here seen through trees, was where Cézanne sometimes set himself up to paint the mountain. Having tried, unsuccessfully, to persuade the owner to sell the unfinished mansion, he ended up renting a room there.

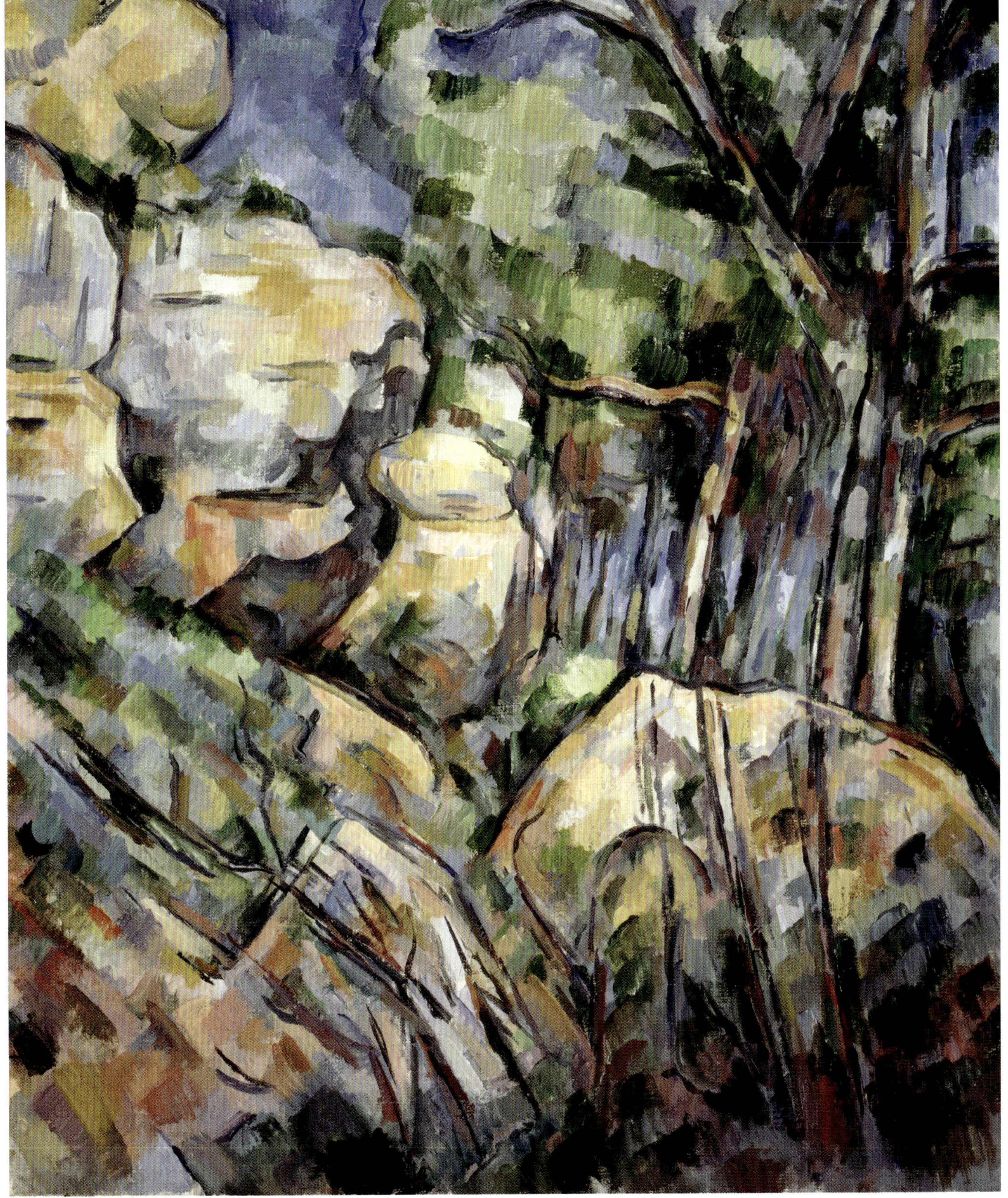

Boulders Near the Caves Above Château Noir, _c._ 1904
Oil on canvas, 65.5 x 54.5 cm (25¾ x 21½ in) • Musée d'Orsay, Paris

The remarkable distribution of colour in this canvas is almost Impressionist in approach. But only almost: the evanescent vision depicted here is not the fleeting perceptual impression of the eye, but the hazy sensation of the conceptual mind.

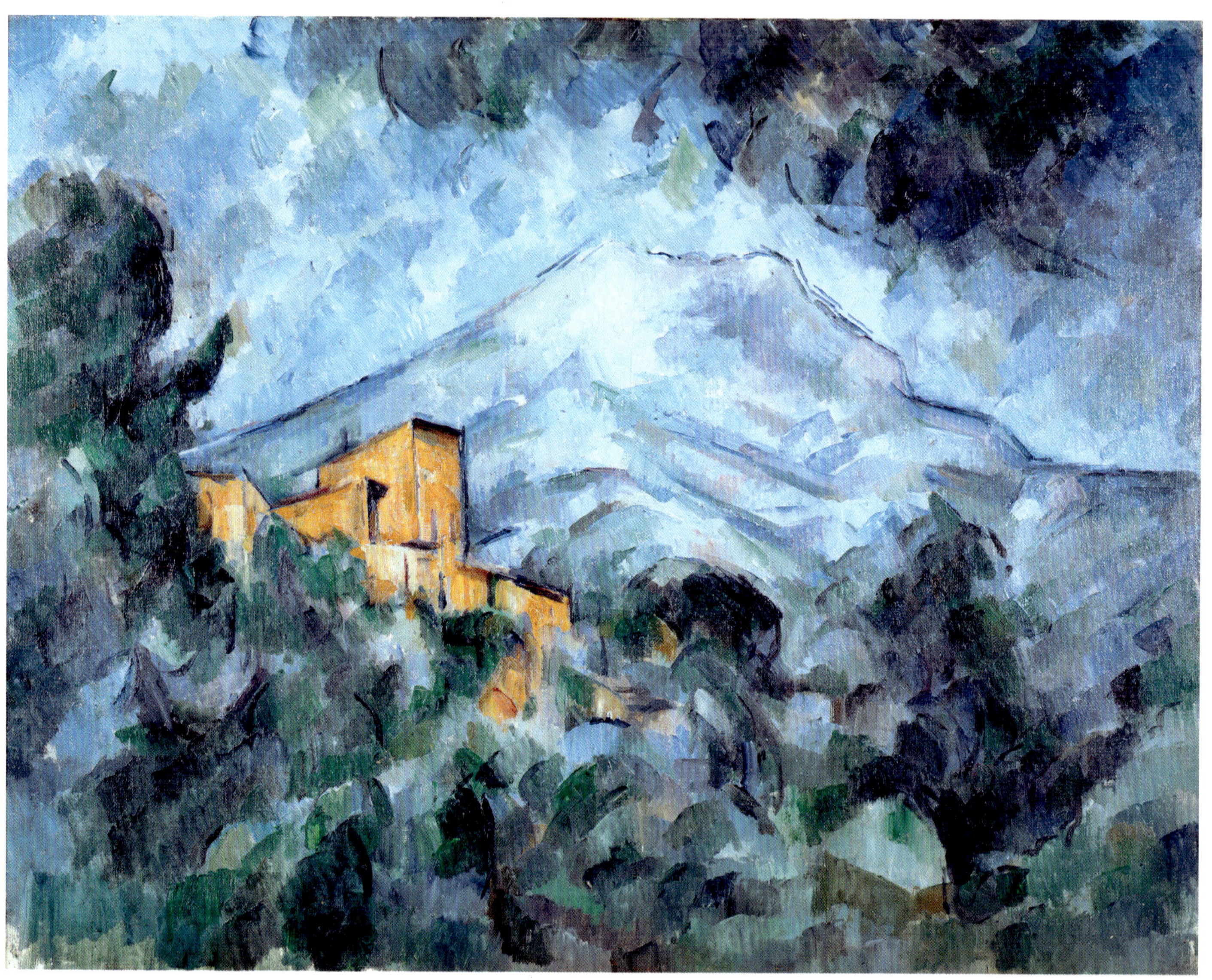

Mont Sainte-Victoire and Château Noir, *c.* 1904–06
Oil on canvas, 65.6 x 81 cm (25⅞ x 31⅞ in) • Artizon Museum, Tokyo

In this image, both mountain and sky are depicted with the same range of colours, only distinguishable from each other by the outline of the mountain. In this context, the Château Noir's stark contrast in colour and geometry is a revelation.

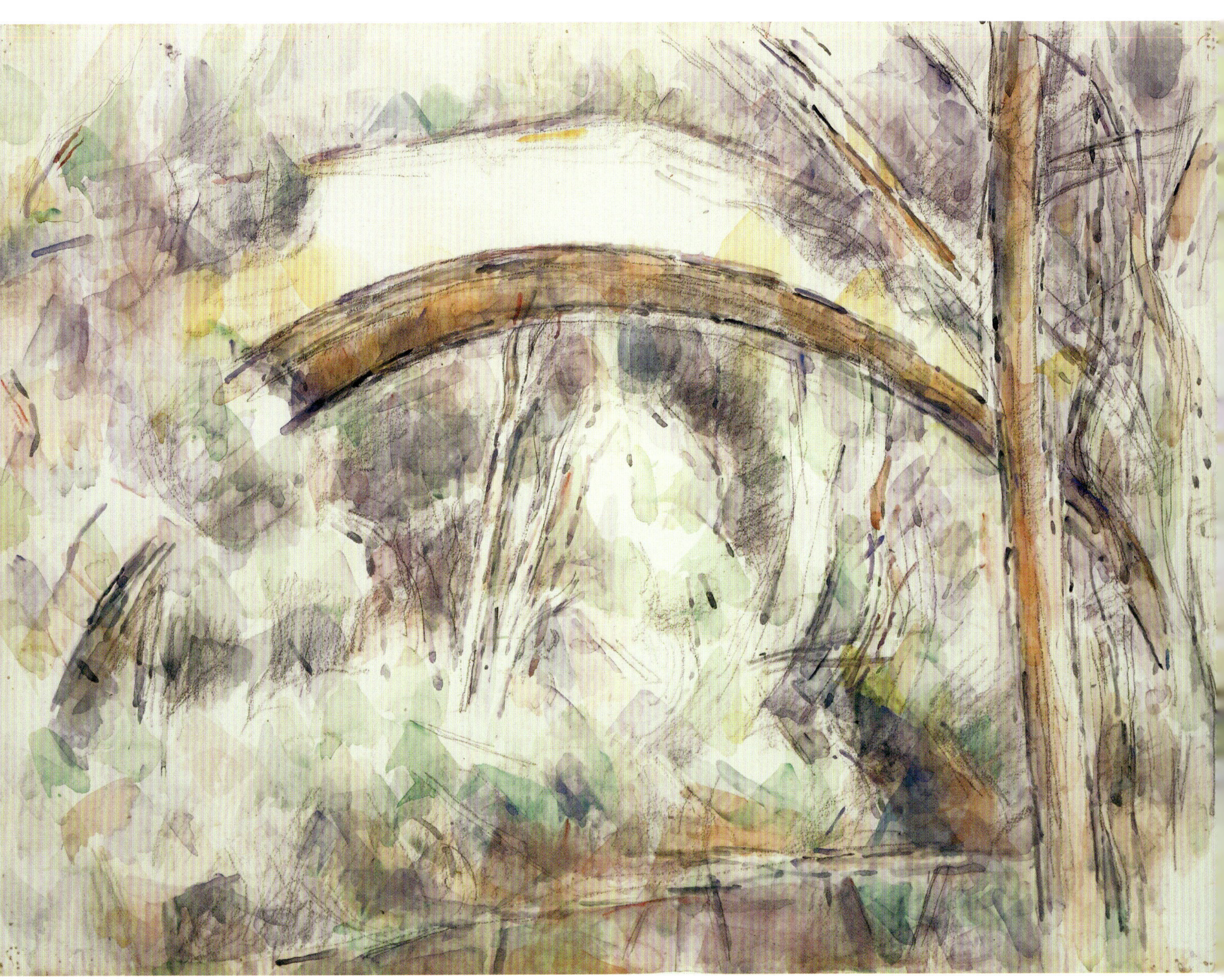

The Bridge of Trois-Sautets, _c._ 1906
Watercolour and pencil on paper, 40.8 x 54.3 cm (16 x 21⅜ in)
• Cincinnati Art Museum, Ohio

Comparing this exquisite late watercolour, of an ancient bridge in a village just south of Aix, with the canvases Cézanne painted during his final years shows just how much his approach to one medium now informed his treatment of the other.

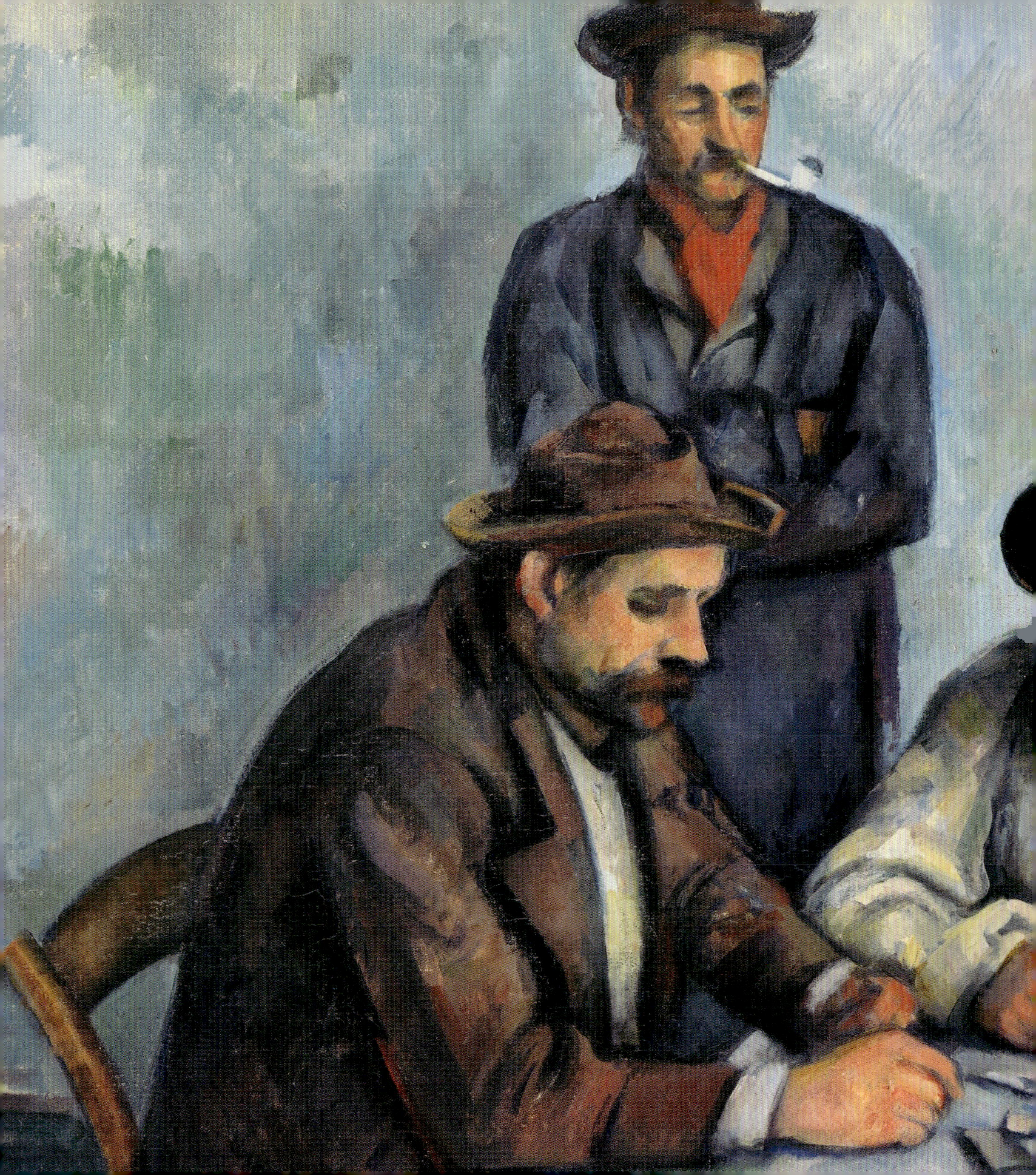

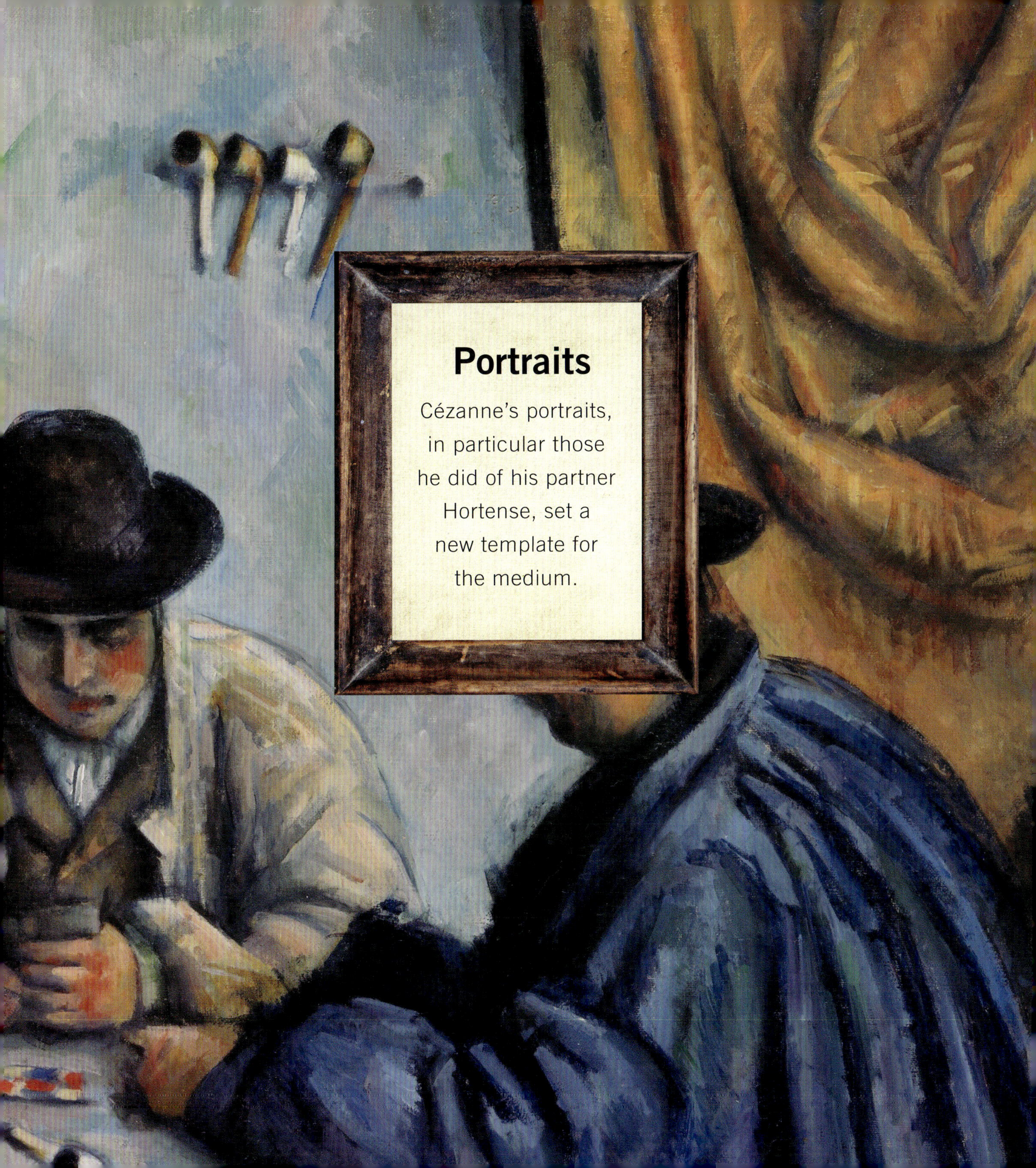

Portraits

Cézanne's portraits, in particular those he did of his partner Hortense, set a new template for the medium.

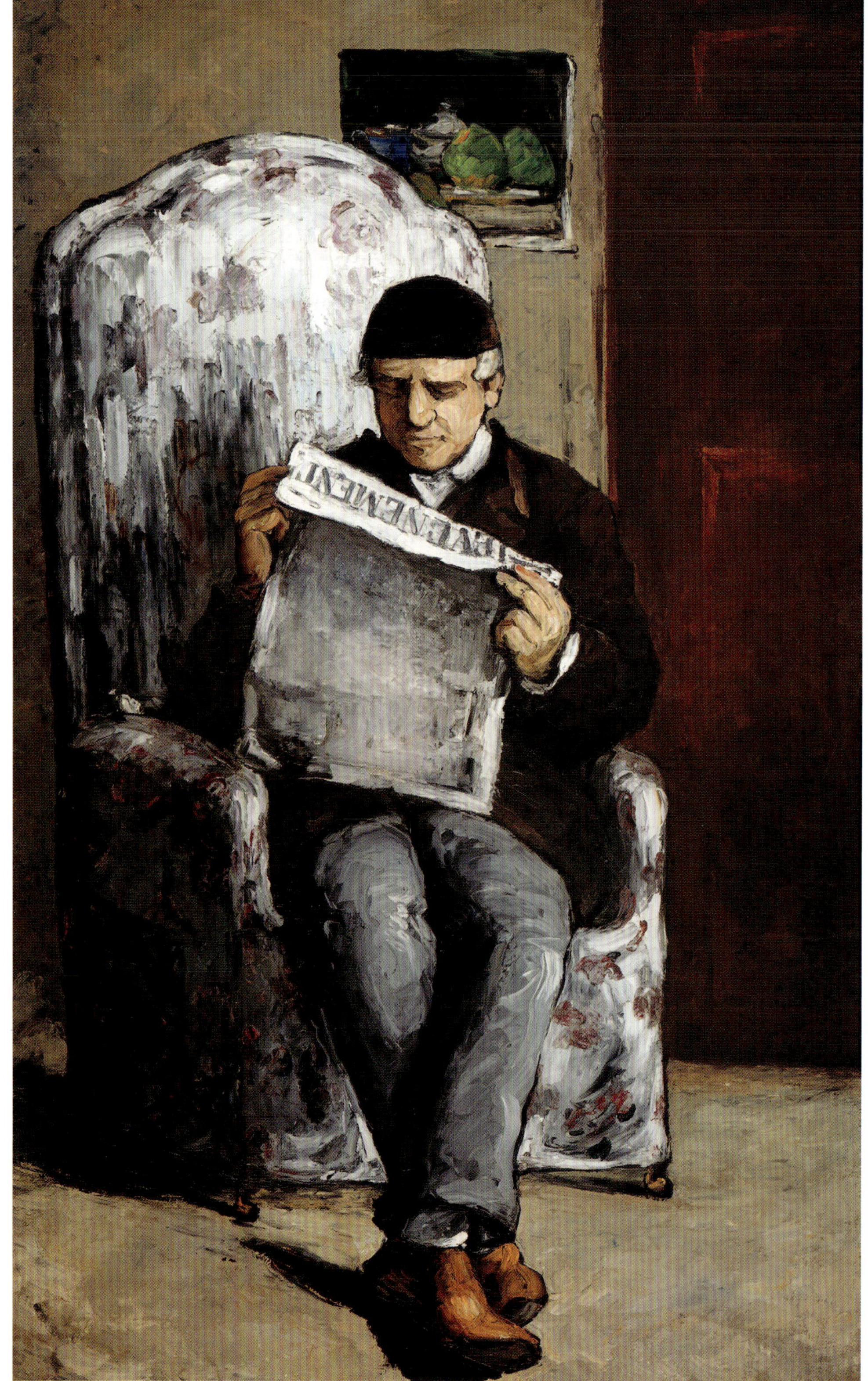

The Artist's Father, Reading _L'Événement_, 1866
Oil on canvas, 198.5 x 119.3 cm (78⅛ x 47 in)
• National Gallery of Art, Washington, D.C.

Cézanne painted his father in two separate canvases of the mid-1860s. In both he is reading the newspaper and wearing an unusual piece of headgear. This one, the second of the two, is the more convincing.

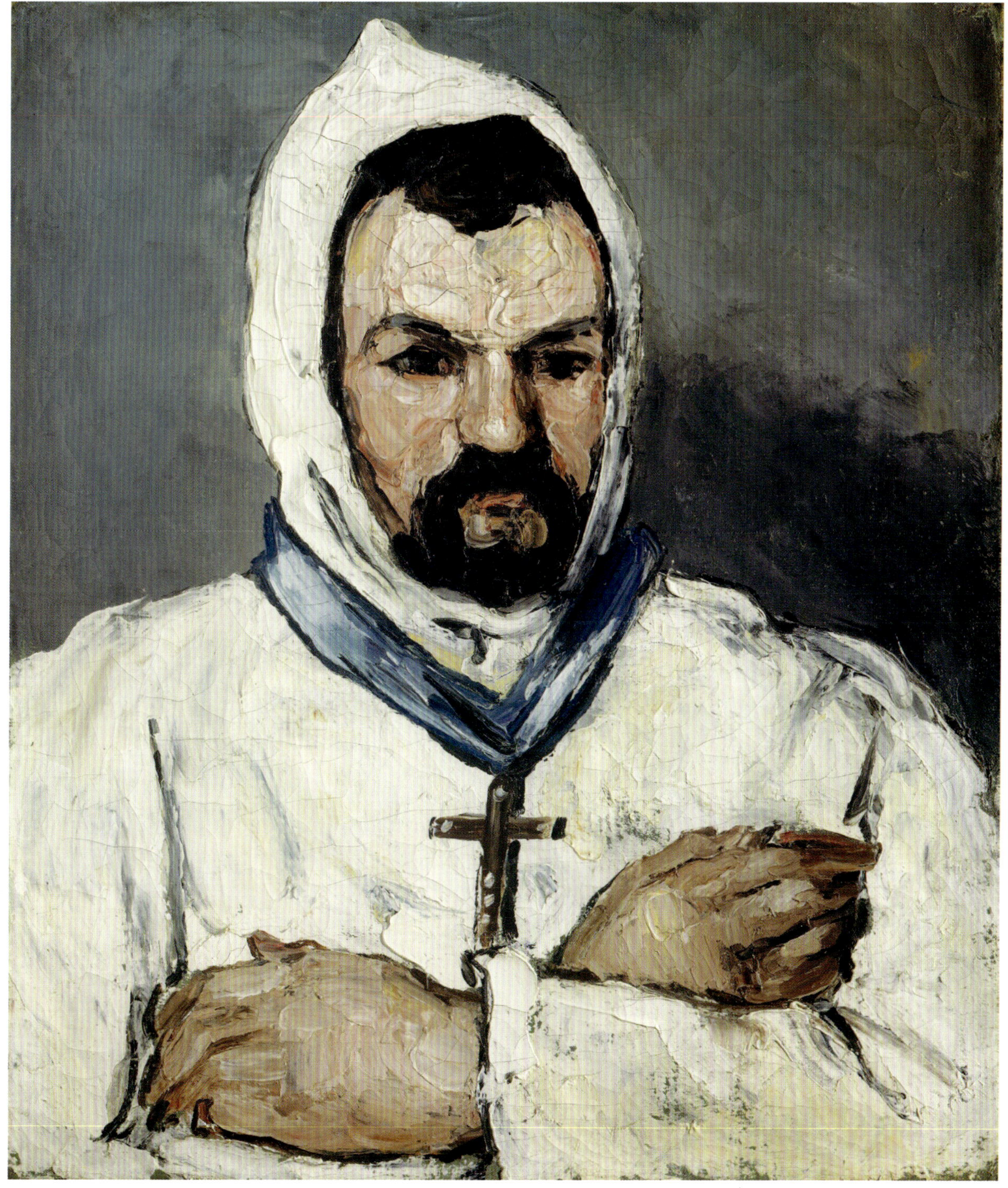

Portrait of Uncle Dominique as a Monk, 1866
Oil on canvas, 65.1 x 54.6 cm (25⅝ x 21½ in)
• Metropolitan Museum of Art, New York

Dominique Aubert (1817–?), Cézanne's mother's younger brother, seems to have been very amenable to indulging his nephew's artistic fancy, sitting for at least eight different portraits in a variety of guises in the mid-1860s.

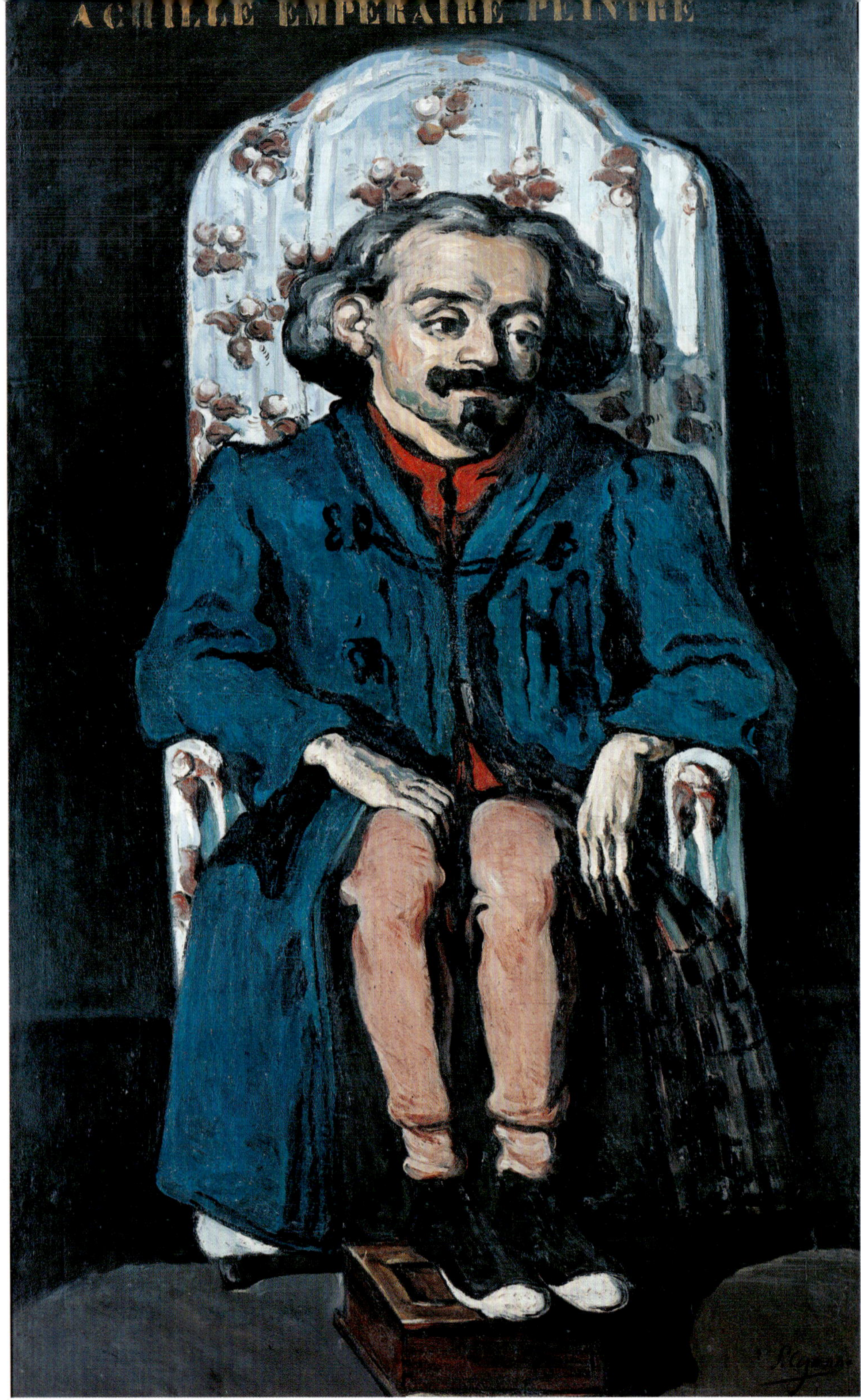

Achille Emperaire, 1867–68

Oil on canvas, 200 x 120 cm (78¾ x 47¼ in) • Musée d'Orsay, Paris

Achille Empéraire was among a group of friends Cézanne met while attending the drawing school in Aix. He later came to Paris to study before pursuing a career as a painter. But without private means he struggled to make a living.

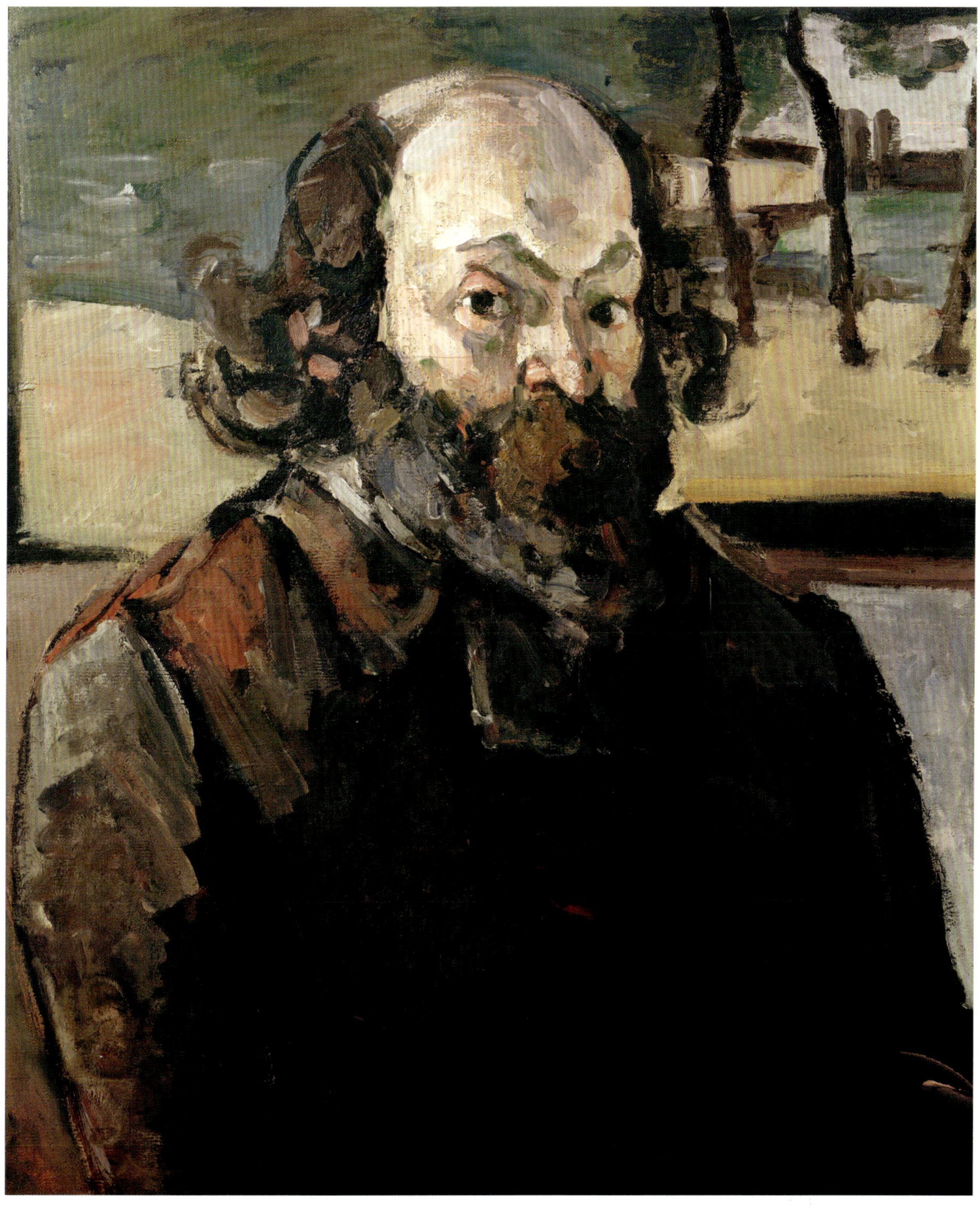

Self-Portrait, c. 1875
Oil on canvas, 65 x 54 cm (25½ x 21¼ in) • Musée d'Orsay, Paris

The full beard Cézanne is wearing in this self-portrait gives him the reticent, even truculent air for which he became known. But the animated eyes tell a different story, as reflected in the testimonies of many who knew him to be a lively companion.

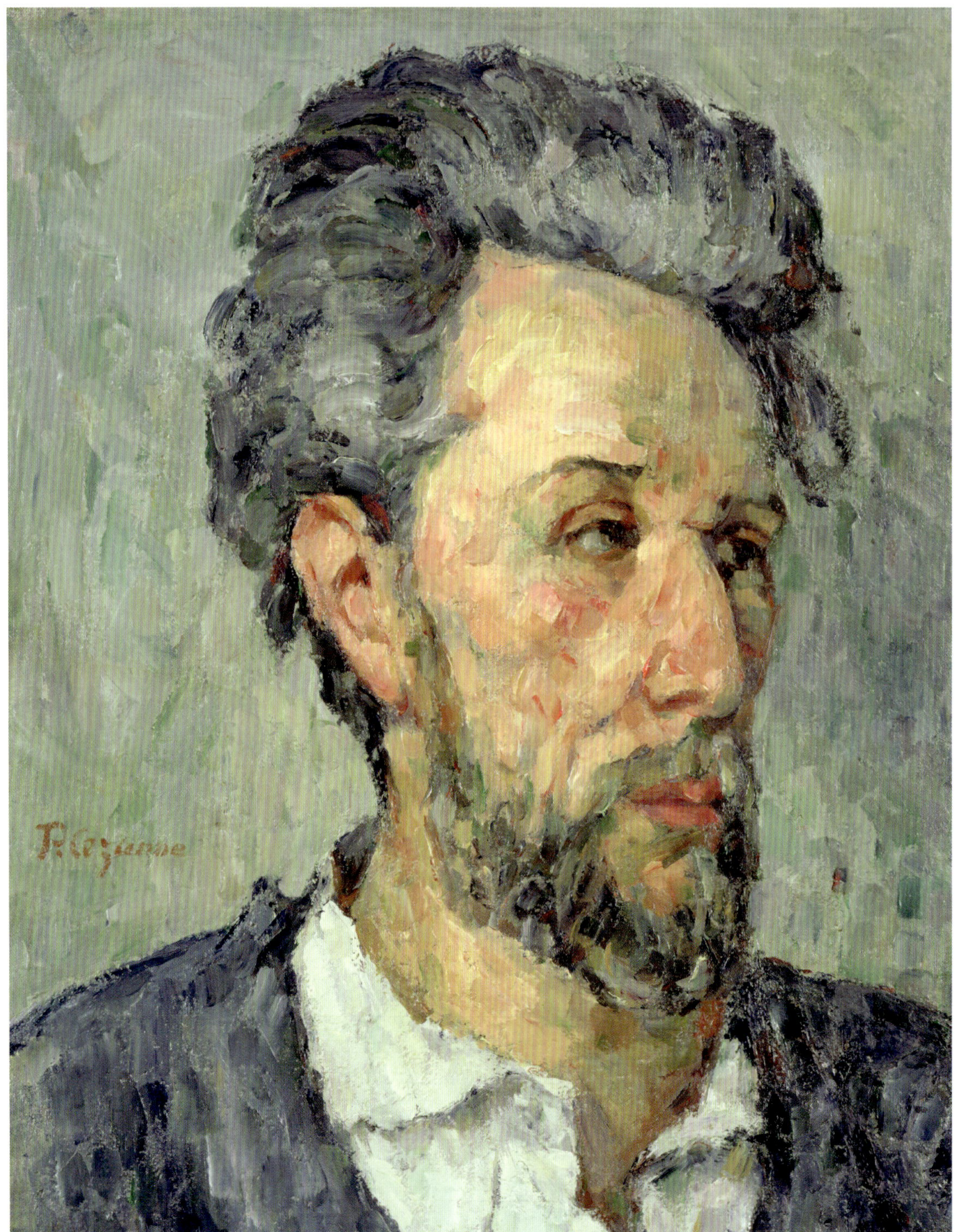

Portrait of Victor Chocquet, 1876–77
Oil on canvas, 45.7 x 36.8 cm (18 x 14½ in) • Private Collection

Chocquet must have been a special human being, because the same qualities of gentleness and openness that Cézanne conveys in this charming portrait are also present in Renoir's portraits of Chocquet from the same period.

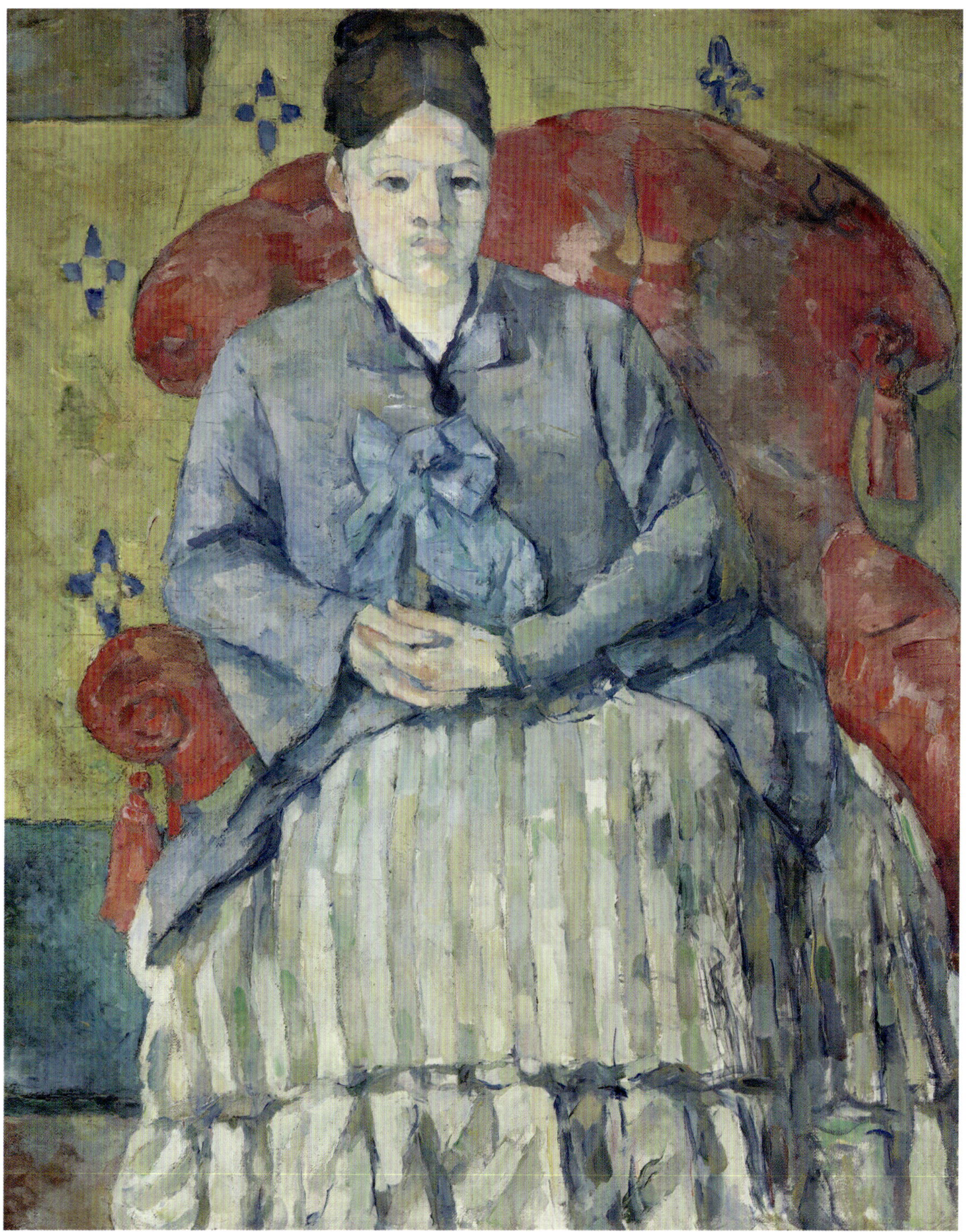

Madame Cézanne in a Red Armchair, *c.* 1877
Oil on Canvas, 72.4 x 55.9 cm (28½ x 22 in) • Museum of Fine Arts, Boston

In this portrait of his future wife, then still Hortense Fiquet, Cézanne uses the primary colours, simply but effectively, to determine the various planes of the picture. By the time it was painted, the couple had a five-year-old son.

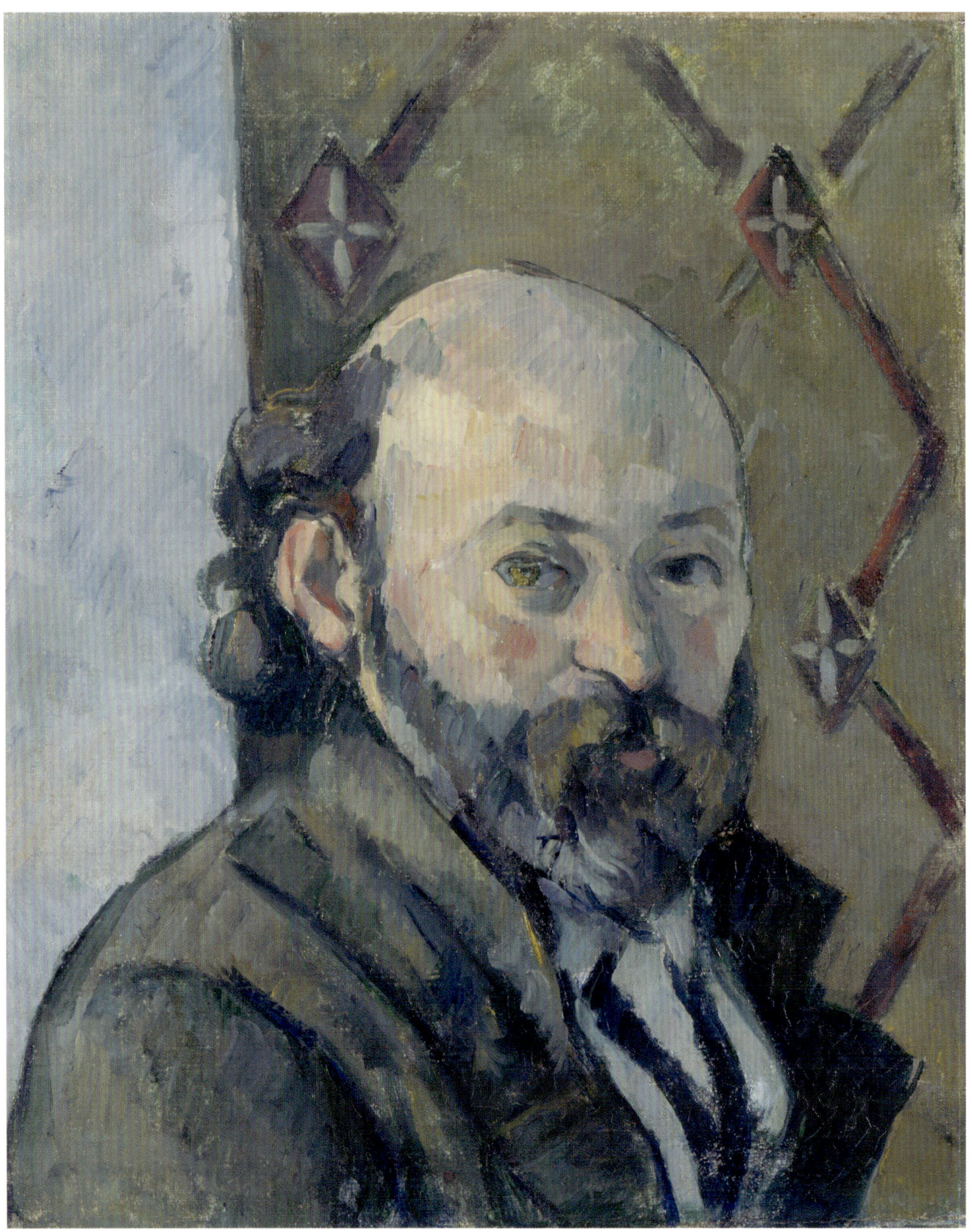

Self-Portrait, *c.* 1880–81
Oil on canvas, 34.7 x 27 cm (13⅝ x 10⅝ in) • National Gallery, London

Cézanne painted some 26 self-portraits across his career, but they don't give much away. To his young confidants later in his life, he made reference to this lack of self-disclosure, describing himself in one letter as 'that non-existent man'.

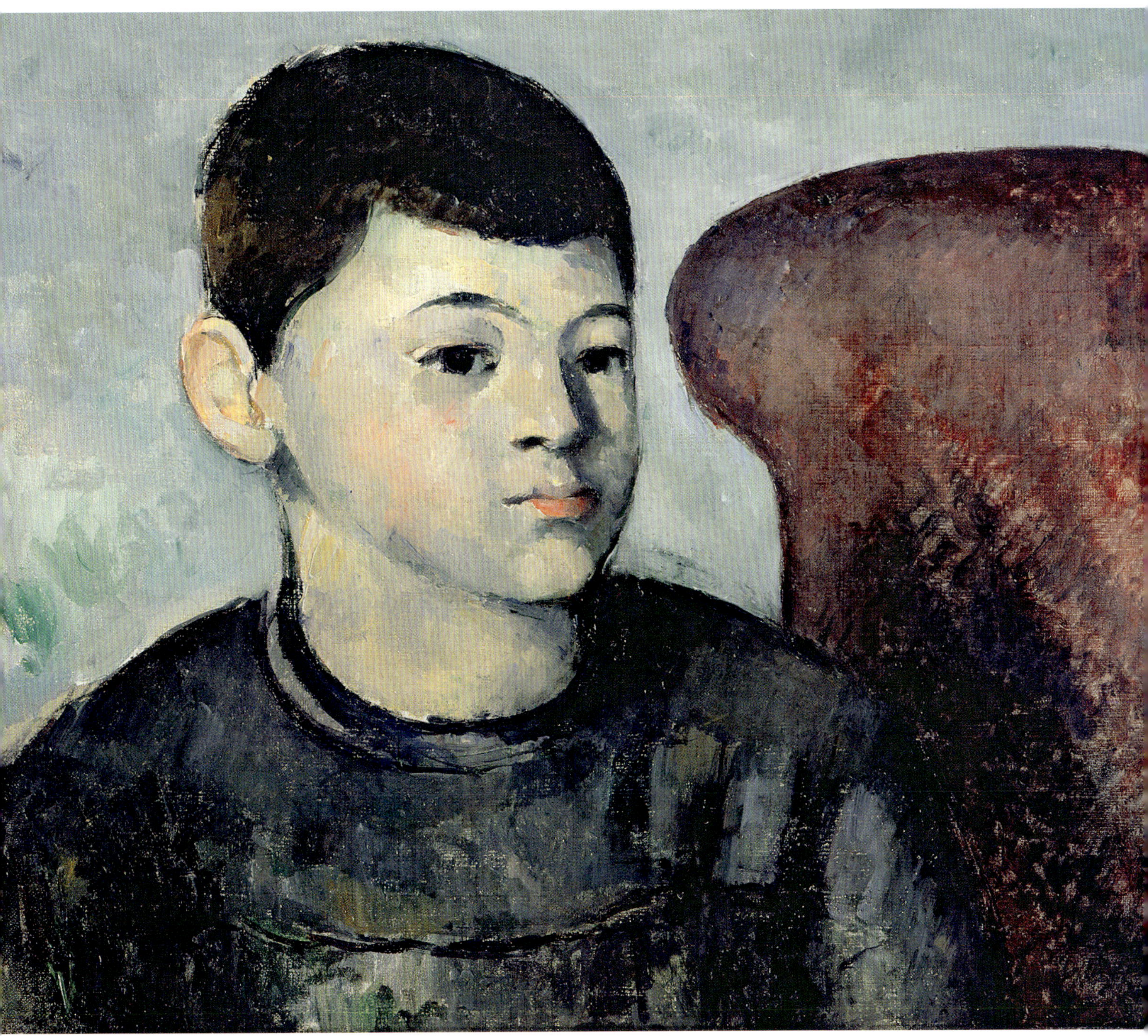

Portrait of the Artist's Son, 1881–82
Oil on canvas, 35 x 38 cm (13¾ x 15 in) • Musée de l'Orangerie, Paris

This portrait is the most charming of the several Cézanne did of his son Paul as a boy or young man. Cézanne seems to have been a classic absent father, absorbed in his painting and often not even living with his family.

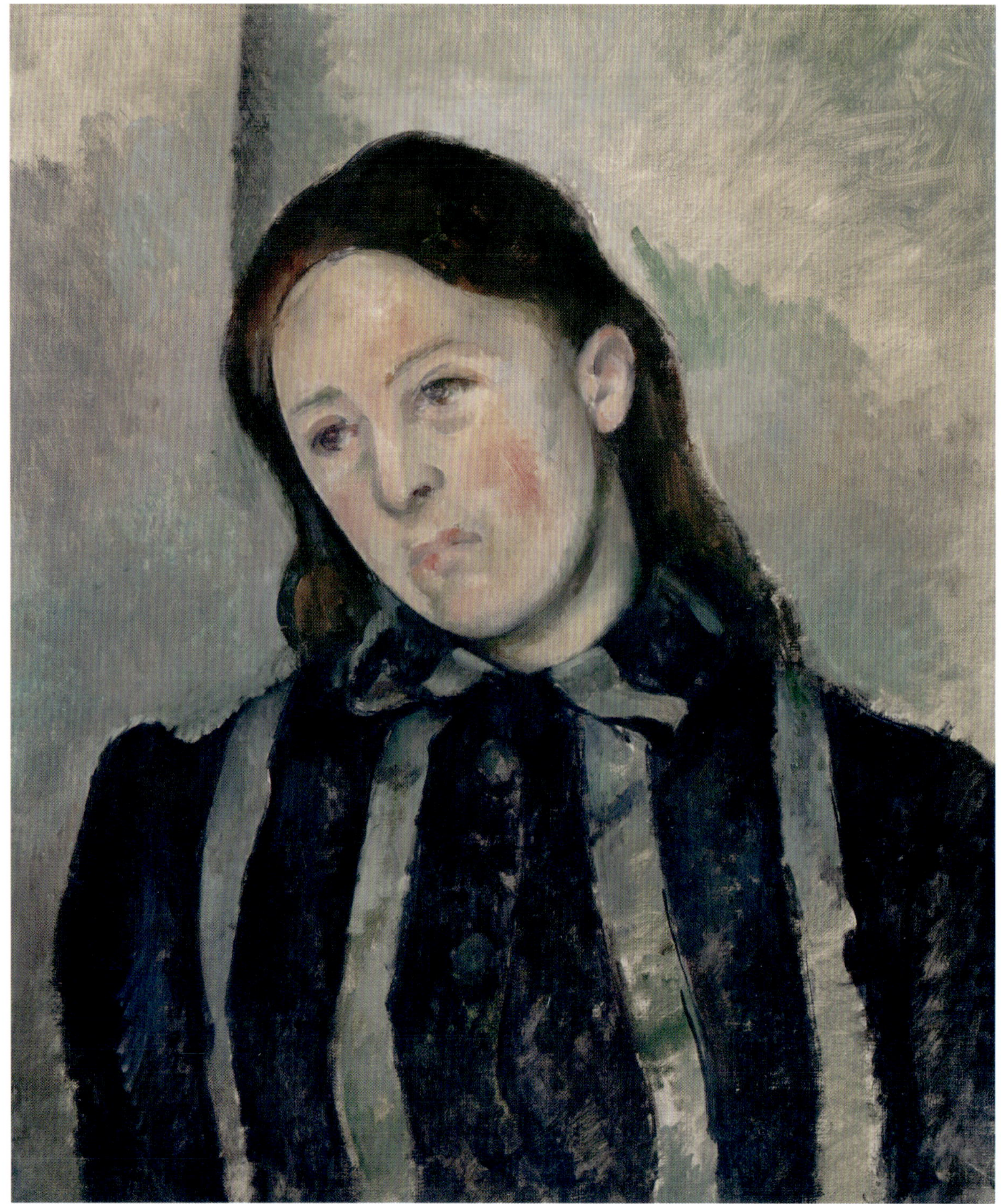

Portrait of Madame Cézanne, 1885–86
Oil on canvas, 61.9 × 51.1 cm (24⅜ × 20⅛ in)
• Philadelphia Museum of Art, Philadelphia

Few spouses have been so often and so sensitively depicted. An odd couple, the Cézannes lived as much apart as together, but Hortense still sat with admirable patience for the many, sometimes hundreds of, sittings it took her husband to finish each picture.

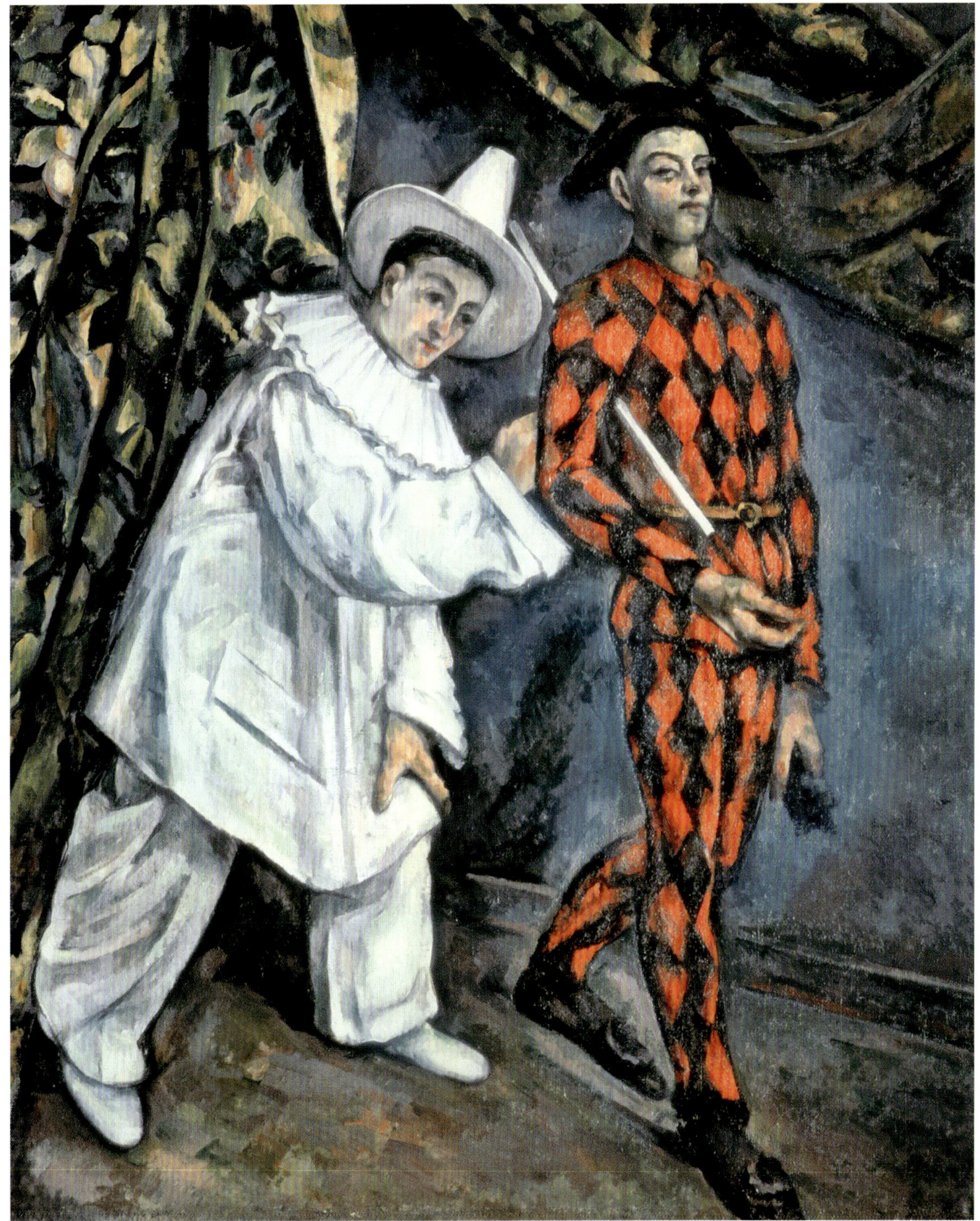

Pierrot and Harlequin, c. 1888
Oil on canvas, 102 x 81 cm (40 x 32 in) • Pushkin Museum, Moscow

The commedia dell'arte figure of Harlequin that a young Picasso depicted in several early works was inspired by the attenuated figures in this painting by Cézanne, in which his son Paul poses as Harlequin with his friend Louis Guillaume as Pierrot behind.

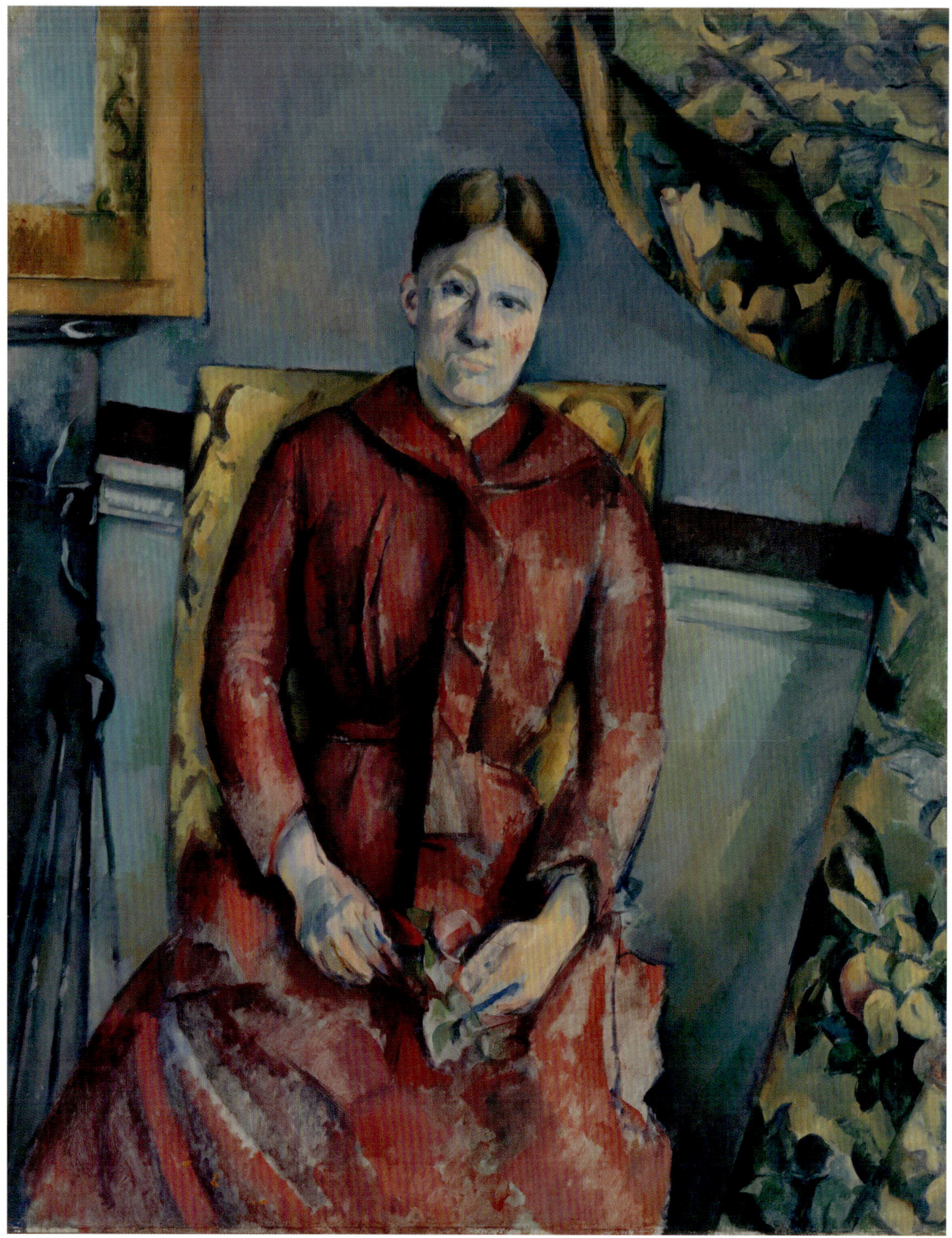

Madame Cézanne in a Red Dress, 1888–90
Oil on canvas, 116.5 x 89.5 cm (45⅞ x 35¼ in)
• Metropolitan Museum of Art, New York

This painting seems to defy gravity, with the verticals of a fireplace and a mirror to the left at odds with the slope of the wall moulding, itself bisected by the yellow chair on which Hortense is so uncertainly perched.

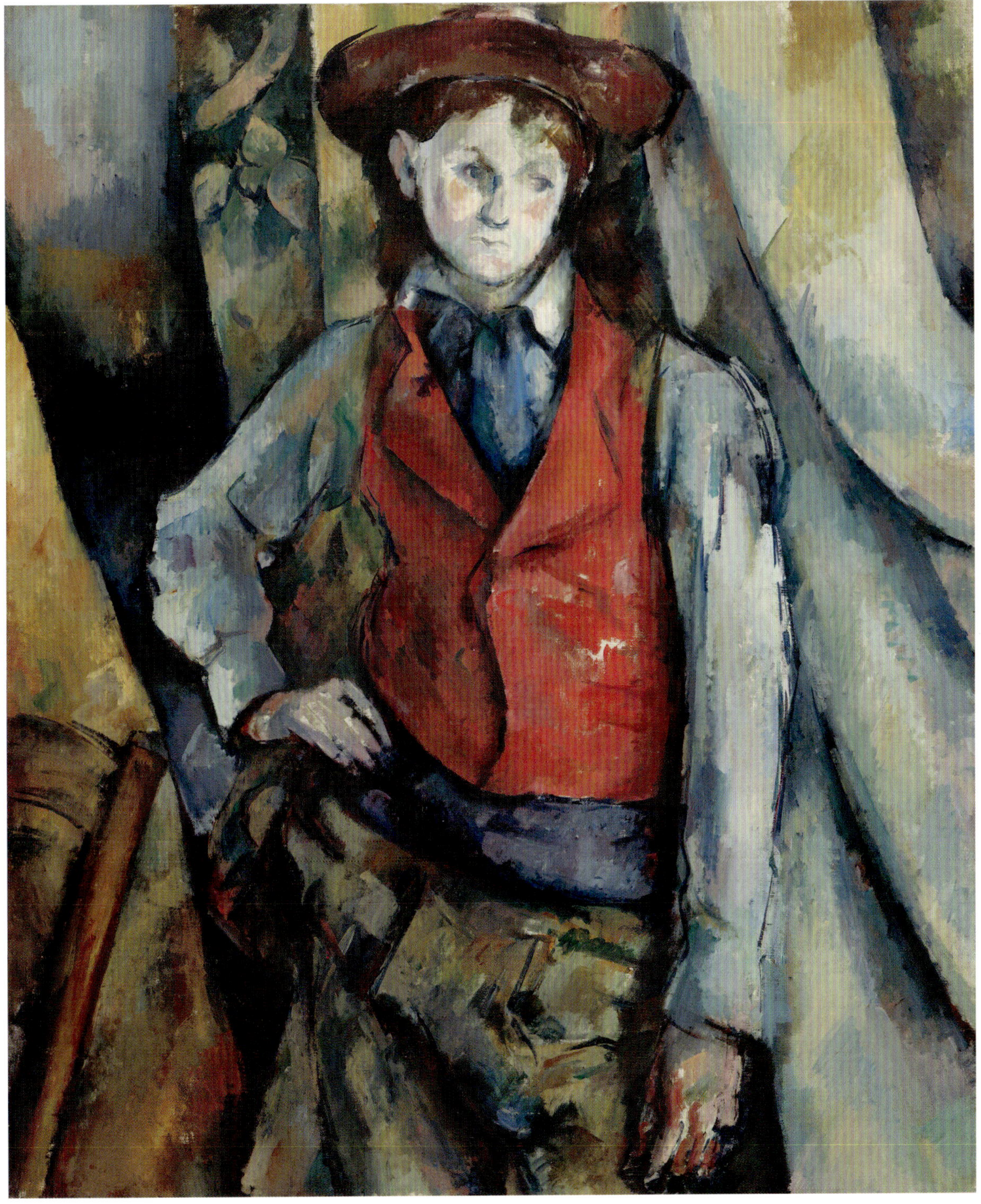

Boy in a Red Waistcoat, 1888–90
Oil on canvas, 89.5 x 72.4 cm (35¼ x 28½ in)
• National Gallery of Art, Washington, D.C.

The boy in this painting was called Michelangelo de Rosa. This is one of three similar pictures featuring de Rosa in the same garb in different poses, evoking the Florentine Mannerist art of Pontormo (1494–1556/7) and Bronzino (1503–72).

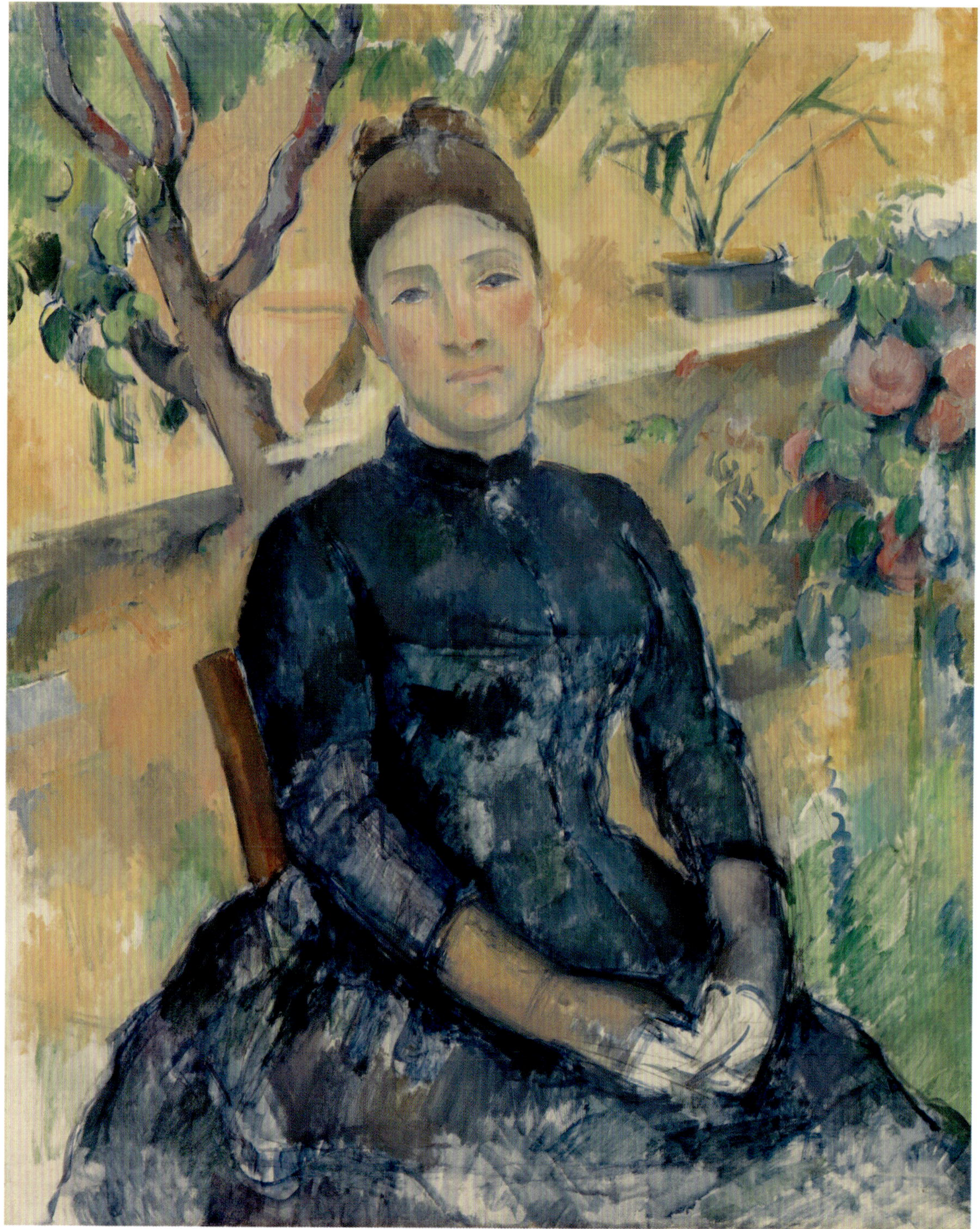

Madame Cézanne in the Conservatory, 1891
Oil on canvas, 92.1 x 73 cm (36¼ x 28¾ in)
• Metropolitan Museum of Art, New York

The perfect oval of Hortense's face, further emphasized by her hairline, lends this portrait an artificial air that is further enhanced by the mask-like appearance of her features. It is one of the most impersonal of Cézanne's many images of his wife.

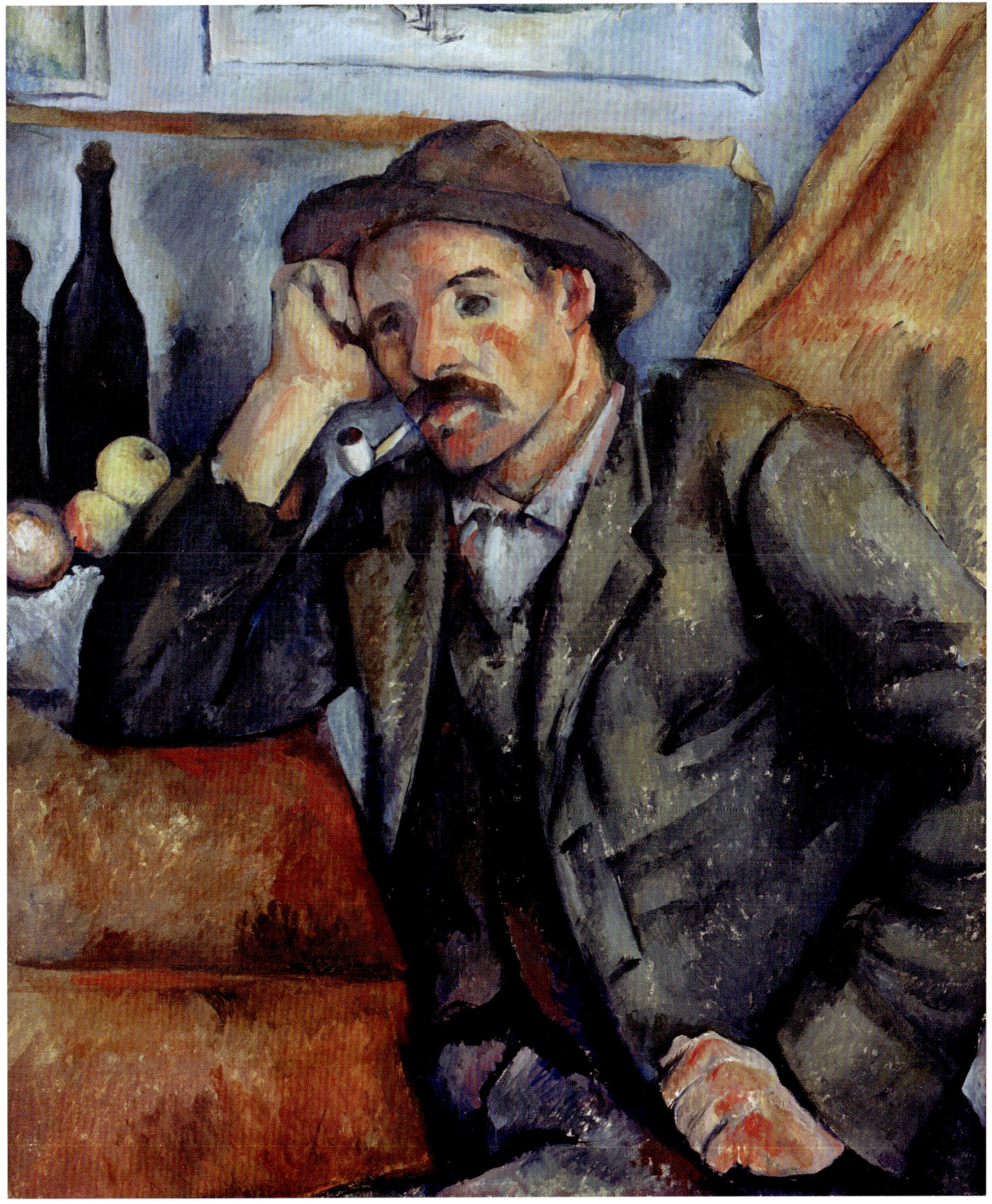

Man with a Pipe, 1890
Oil on canvas, 91 x 72 cm (35¾ x 28⅜ in)
• The State Hermitage Museum, St Petersburg

After the death of his father, Cézanne went back to live permanently at the Jas de Bouffan. He found endless motifs not only in the grounds but also among the peasants and day labourers who worked there, who were pressed into posing for him.

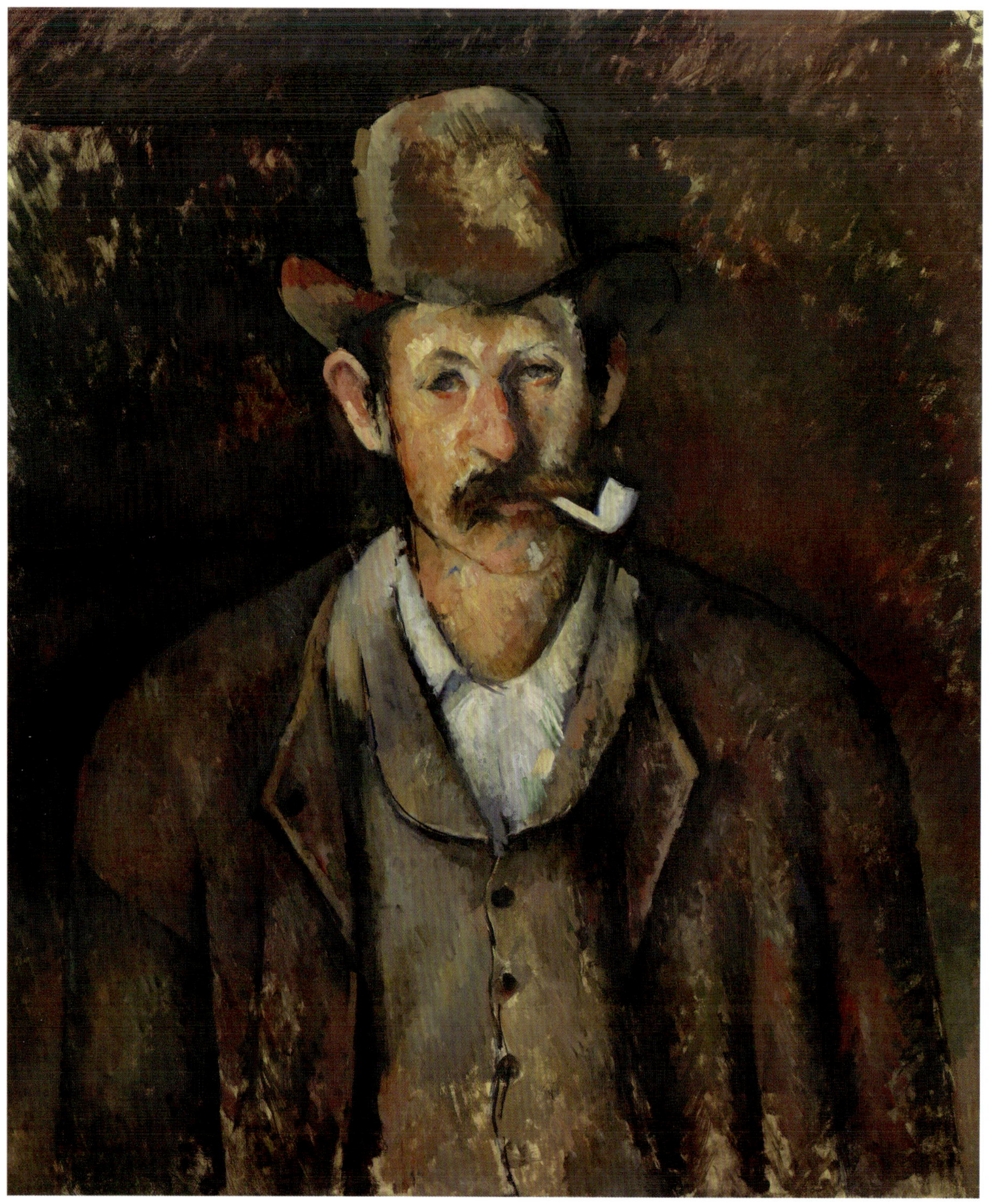

Man with a Pipe, 1892

Oil on canvas, 73 x 60 cm (28¾ x 23⅝ in)

• Courtauld Institute of Art, London

This is one of several different images of men smoking pipes that Cézanne painted in the early 1890s.
Though clearly a portrait, it hardly matters that the sitter is not named; nor is he a type, but simply a man.

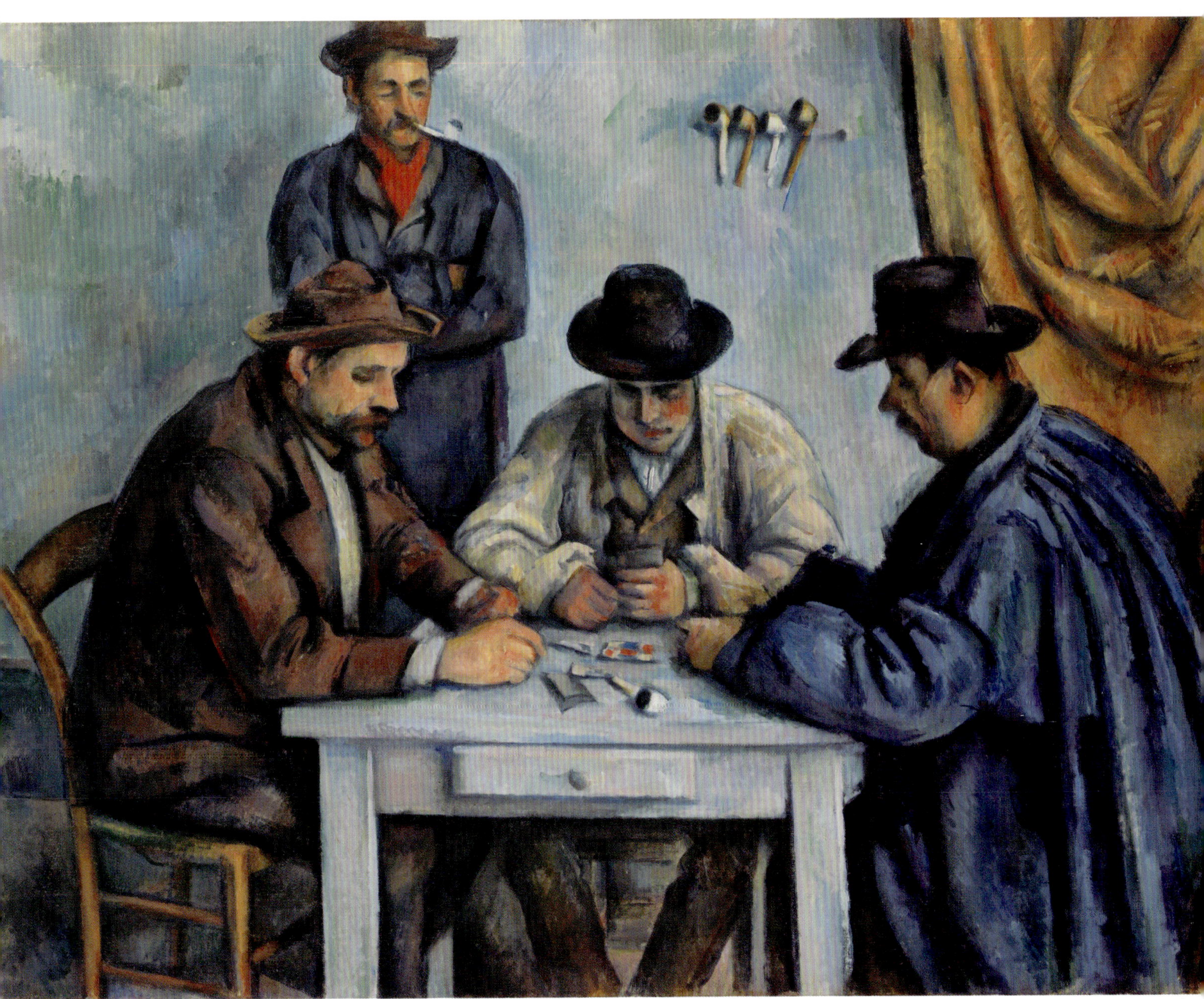

The Card Players, 1890–92
Oil on canvas, 65.4 x 81.9 cm (25¾ x 32¼ in)
• Metropolitan Museum of Art, New York

The models for this great genre painting were all workers on the Cézanne family estate. This is one of five images he painted with the same theme, of which one other was a group composition similar to this.

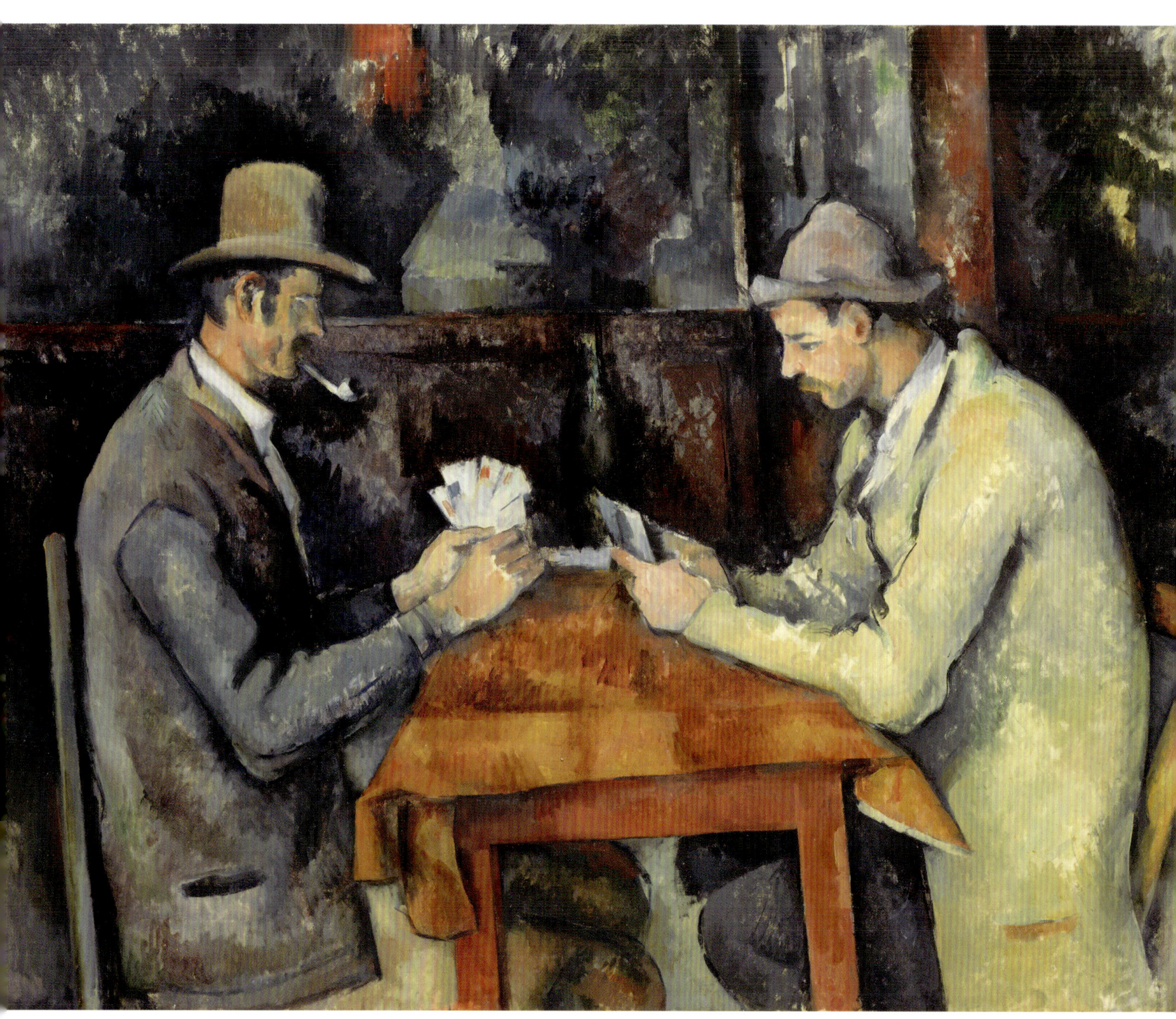

The Card Players, 1892–96
Oil on canvas, 60 x 73 cm (23⅝ x 28¾ in)
• Courtauld Institute of Art, London

One of two paintings of pairs in the *Card Players* series, the painter's own absorption in the game the men are playing is betrayed by the angle of view tilting away from vertical, as if he were too caught up in the hand to notice.

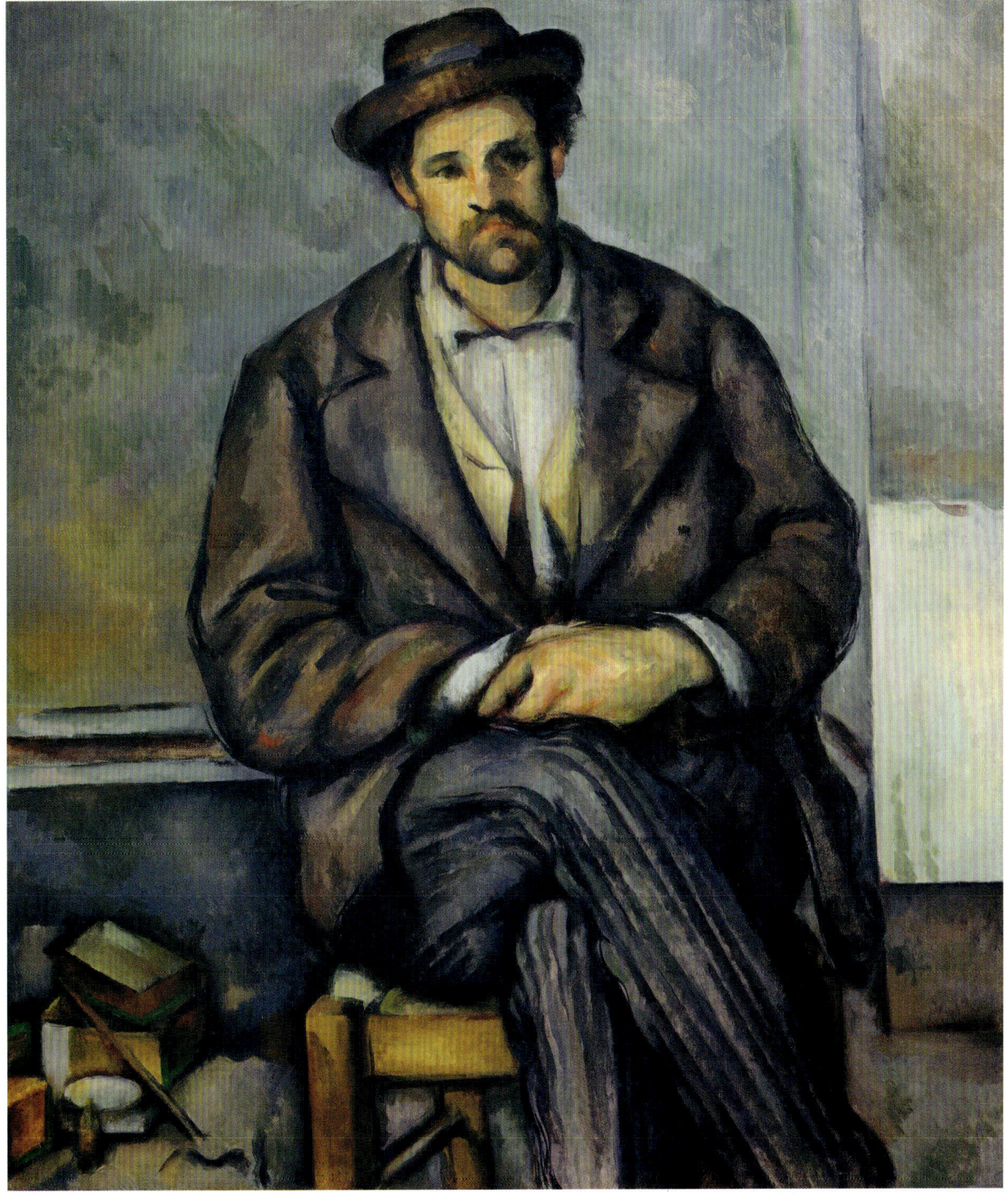

Seated Peasant, c. 1892–96
Oil on canvas, 54.6 x 45.1 cm (21½ x 17¾ in)
• Metropolitan Museum of Art, New York

Peasants had been the subject of paintings by earlier French painters like the seventeenth-century Le Nain brothers and more recently Jean-François Millet. But the peasant in this image is a more sophisticated figure, painted in what was an era of rapid social change.

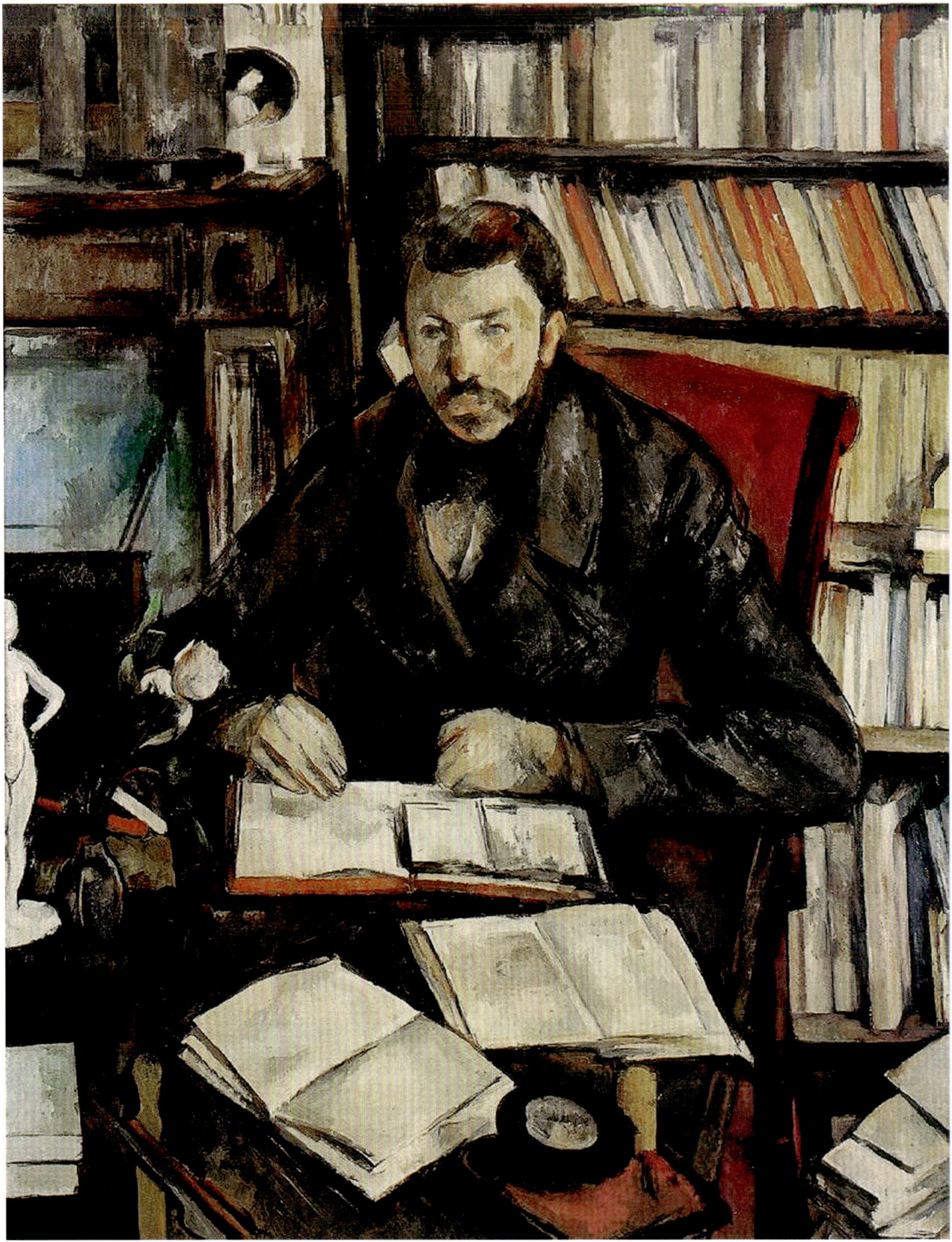

Portrait of Gustave Geffroy, 1895–96
Oil on canvas, 117 x 89.5 cm (46 x 35¼ in) • Musée d'Orsay, Paris

The writer and critic Gustave Geffroy became one of the most supportive advocates of Cézanne's work in print. Cézanne worked on this portrait almost every day for some three months before declaring it a failure and giving up.

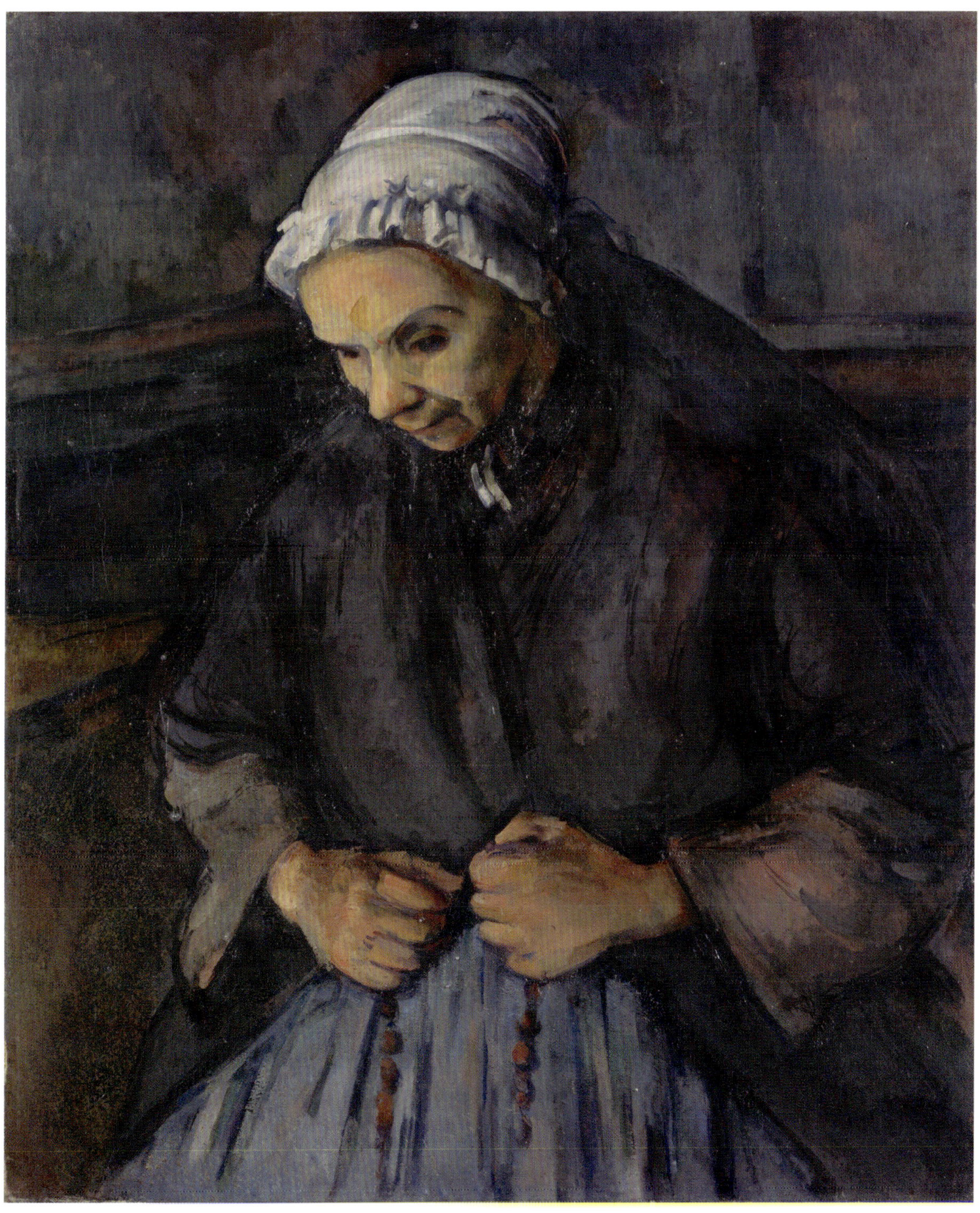

An Old Woman with a Rosary, _c._ 1895–96
Oil on canvas, 80.6 x 65.5 cm (31¾ x 25¾ in) • National Gallery, London

Another painting Cézanne regarded as unfinished is this absorbing image of an old woman clutching a rosary. The model seems to be praying but in reality she was a nun who had lost her faith, left her convent and whom Cézanne had taken in.

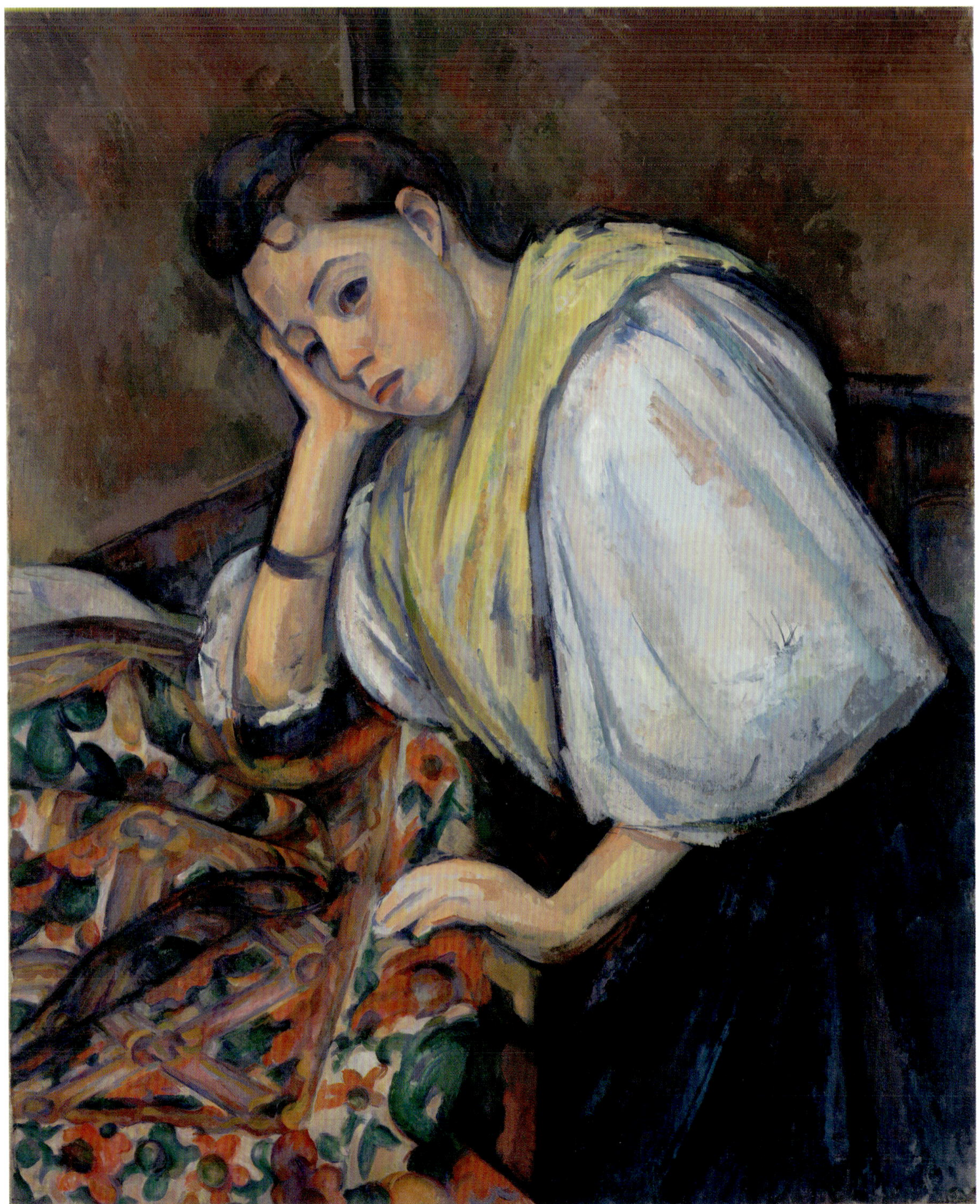

Young Italian Woman at a Table, *c.* 1895–1900
Oil on canvas, 92.1 × 73.5 cm (36¼ × 29 in) • J. Paul Getty Museum,
The Getty Center, Los Angeles

The model for this painting was probably a worker at the Jas de Bouffan. Her studied pose is traditionally associated with melancholy, but the mask-like face resists such a reading. It was unusual for Cézanne to paint women other than his wife.

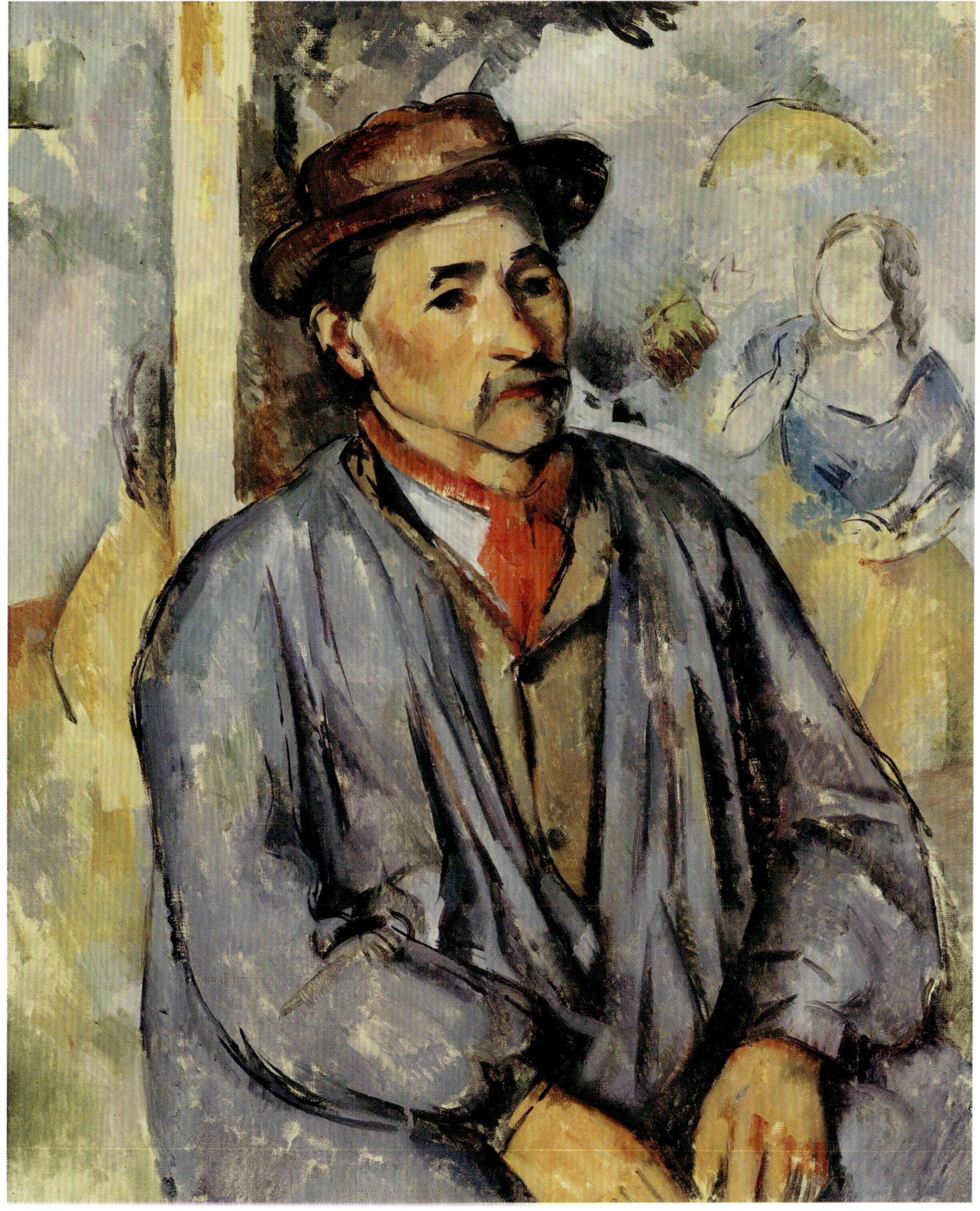

Man in a Blue Smock, *c.* **1896–97**
Oil on canvas, 81.5 x 64.8 cm (32 x 25½ in)
• Kimbell Art Museum, Fort Worth, Texas

While earlier painters had depicted peasants in genre paintings, Cézanne conferred on them the dignity of the portrait. Though they were never named, his serious interest in them reflected the solidarity he felt with the ordinary people of his region.

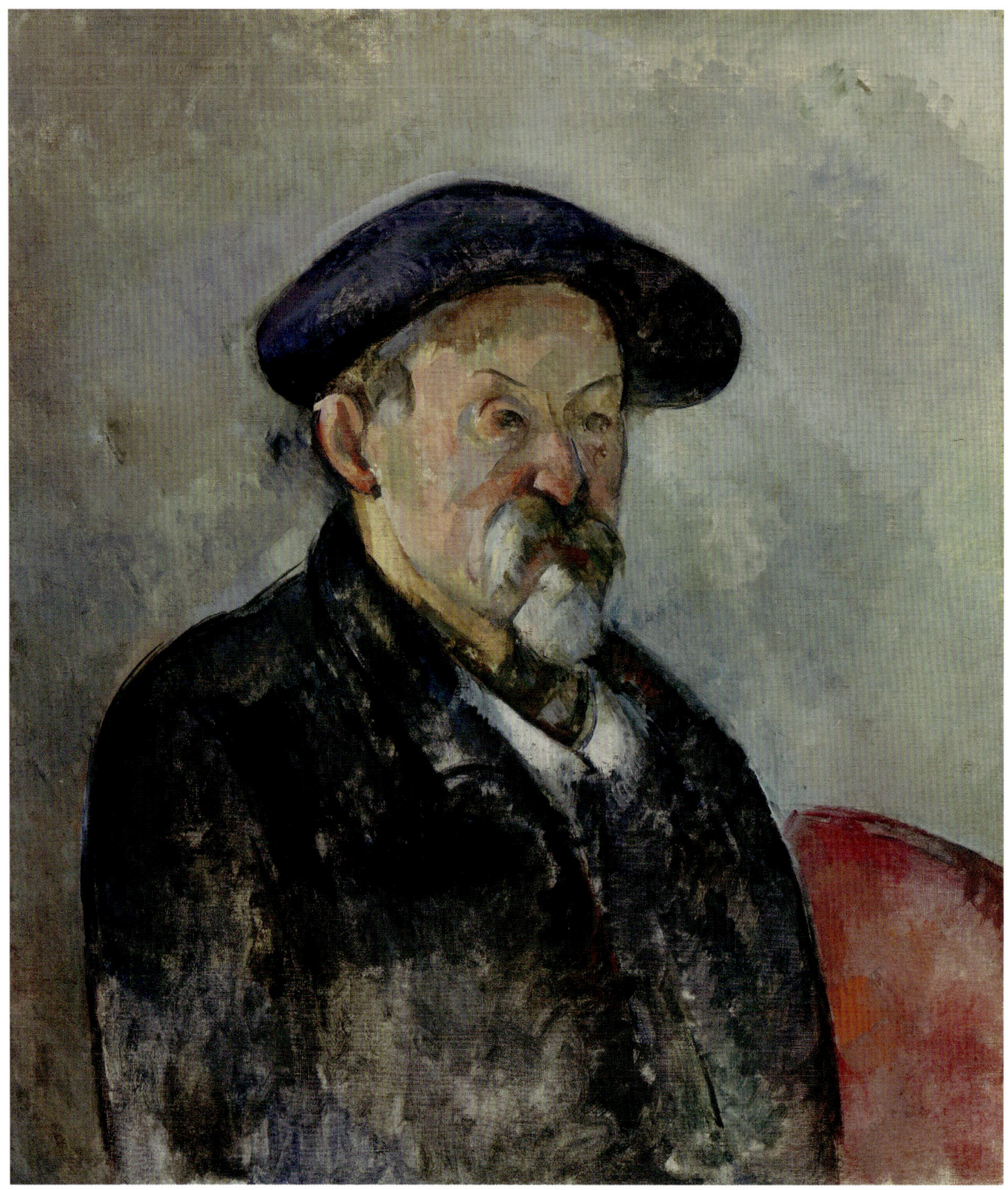

Self-Portrait with Beret, 1898–1900
Oil on canvas, 64 x 51 cm (25¼ x 20⅛ in) • Museum of Fine Arts, Boston

Like Rembrandt (1606–69) before him, in his understated way Cézanne was rather fond of dressing up. Among his many self-portraits, there are a number that show him wearing various kinds of headgear, though the facial expression is always the same.

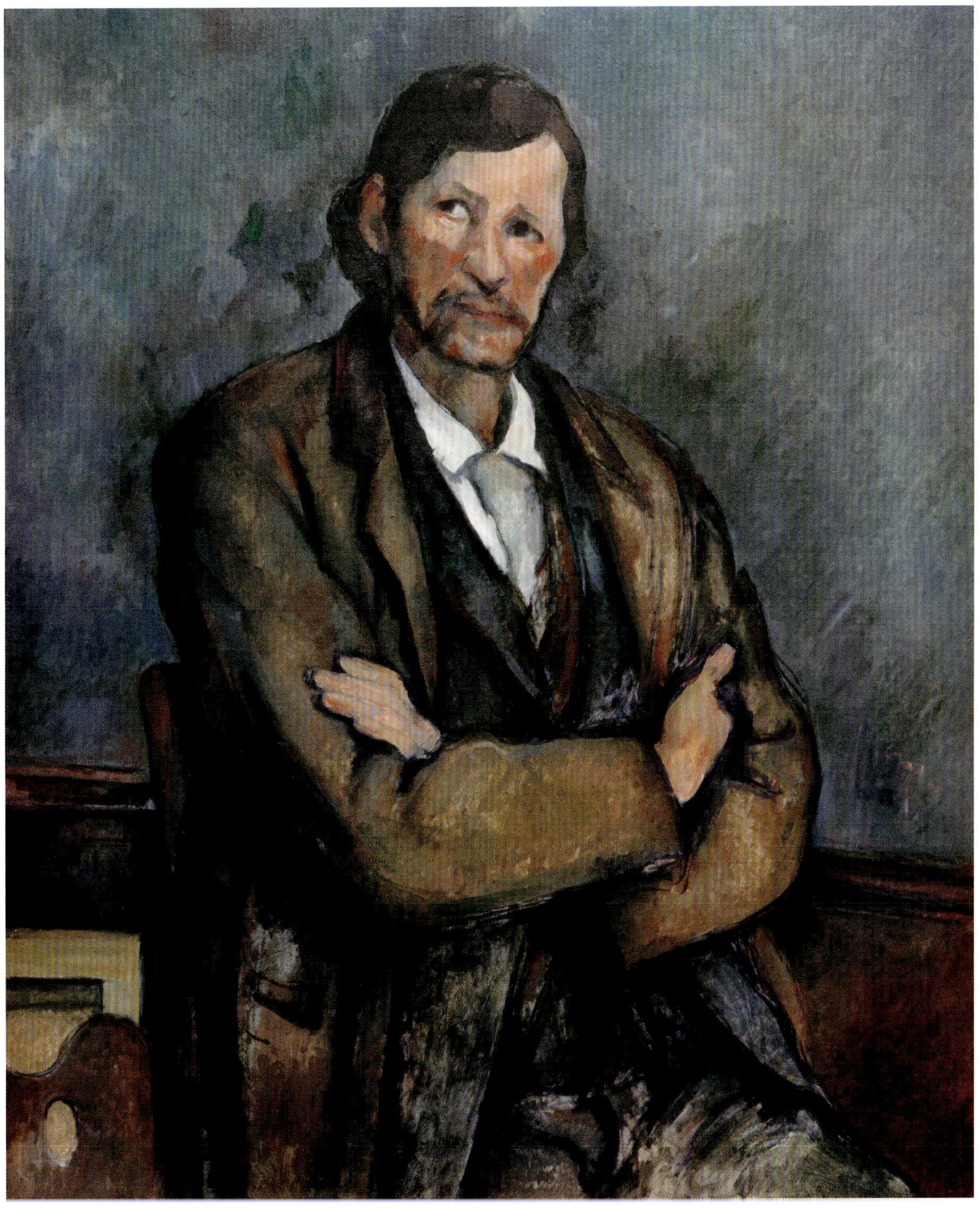

Man with Crossed Arms, *c.* 1897
Oil on canvas, 92 x 72.7 cm (36¼ x 28⅝ in)
• Solomon R. Guggenheim Museum, New York

This portrait is most striking for the distracted expression on the sitter's face, reinforced by crossed arms, suggesting an attitude of truculence or even boredom with the process of posing he is having to endure.

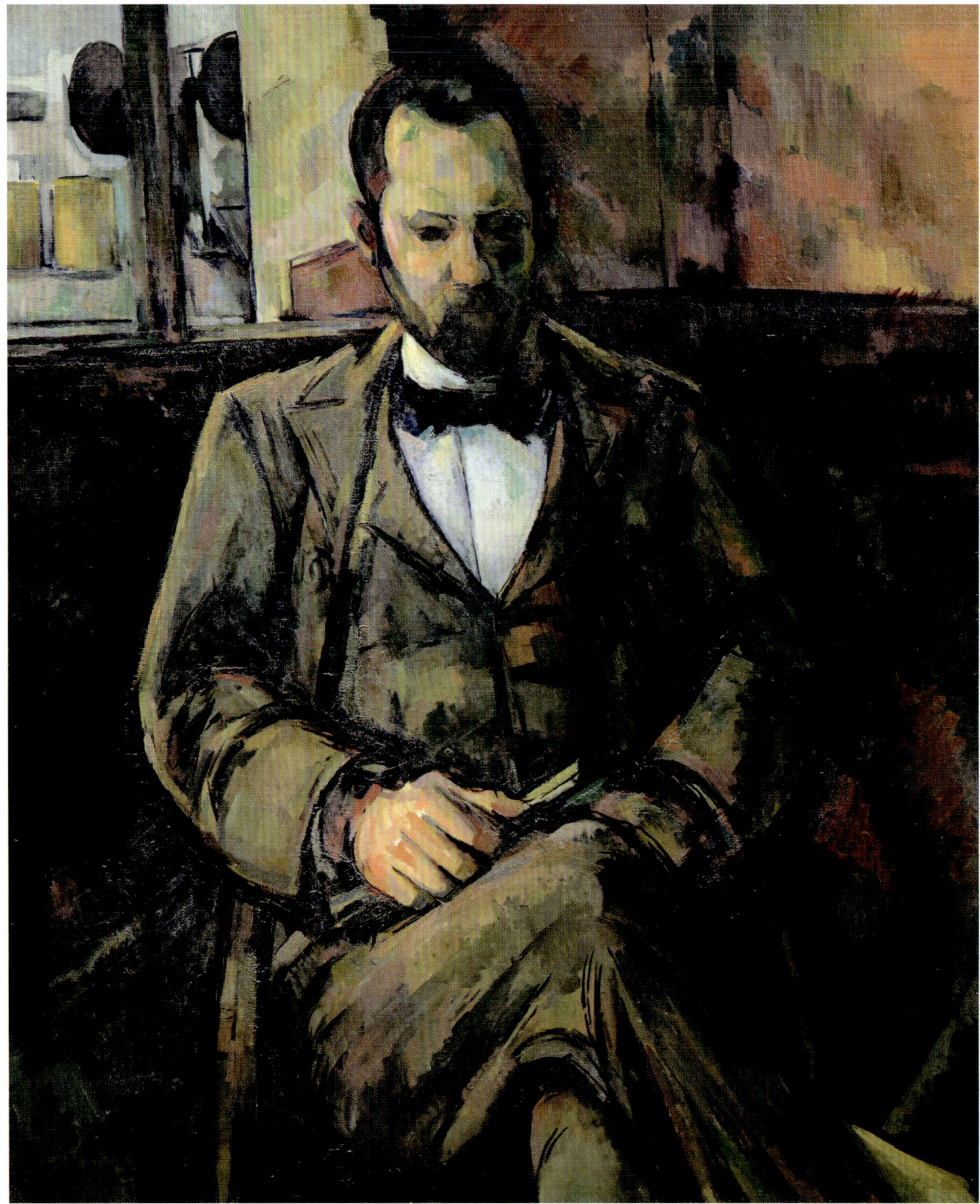

Portrait of Ambroise Vollard, 1899
Oil on canvas, 100 x 81 cm (39⅜ x 31⅞ in) • Musée du Petit Palais, Paris

This depiction of Cézanne's dealer remained unfinished in the painter's estimation, though Vollard had sat for more than 100 sessions at Cézanne's Paris studio by the time he abandoned it. This was not uncommon among Cézanne's later portraits.

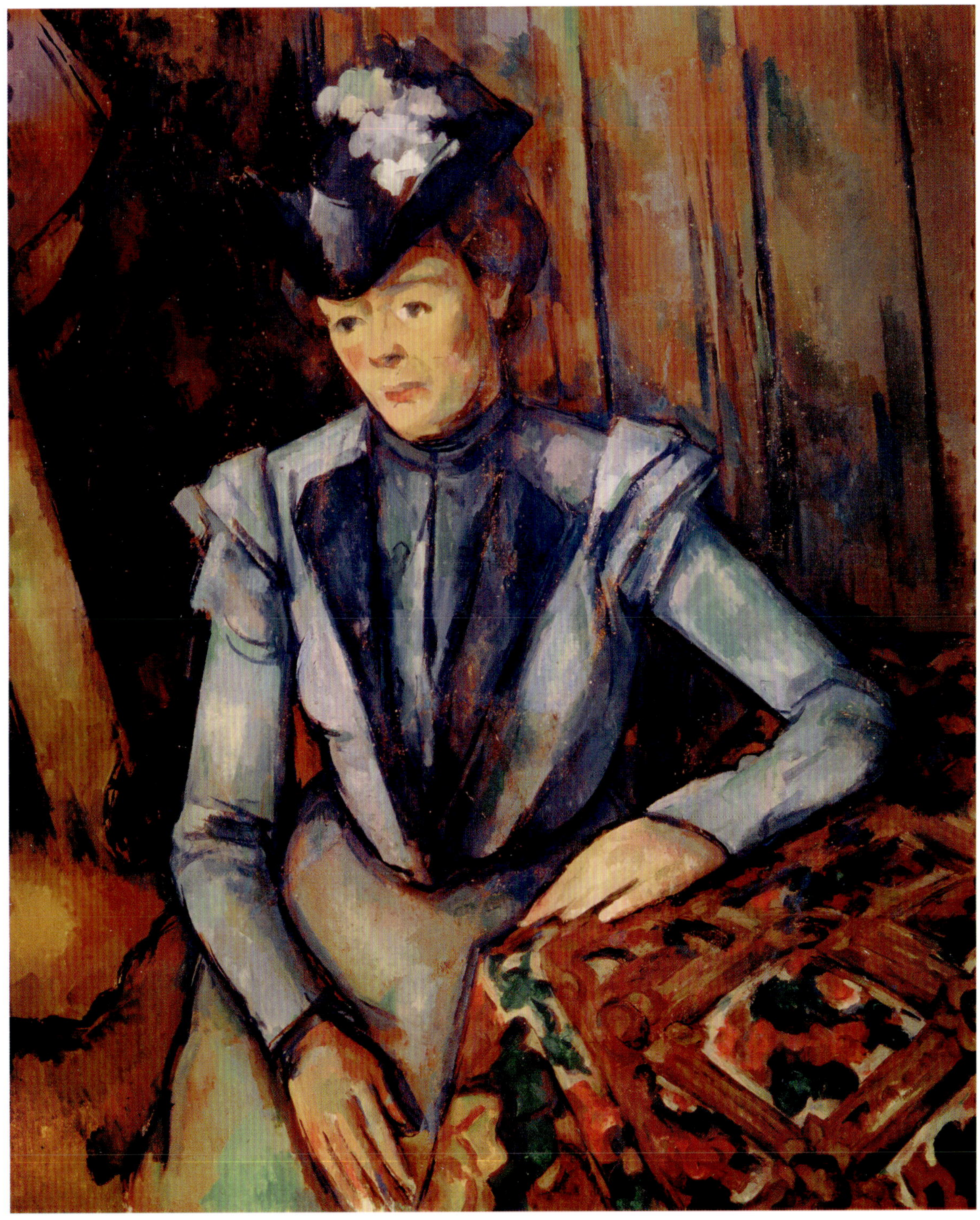

Lady in Blue, c. 1900
Oil on canvas, 90 x 73.5 cm (35⅜ x 29 in)
• The State Hermitage Museum, St Petersburg

This is thought to be Cézanne's last portrait of Hortense. Though they seem to have lived largely separate lives for most of their marriage, neither one seems to have tired of the roles – of artist and model – in which they had first met.

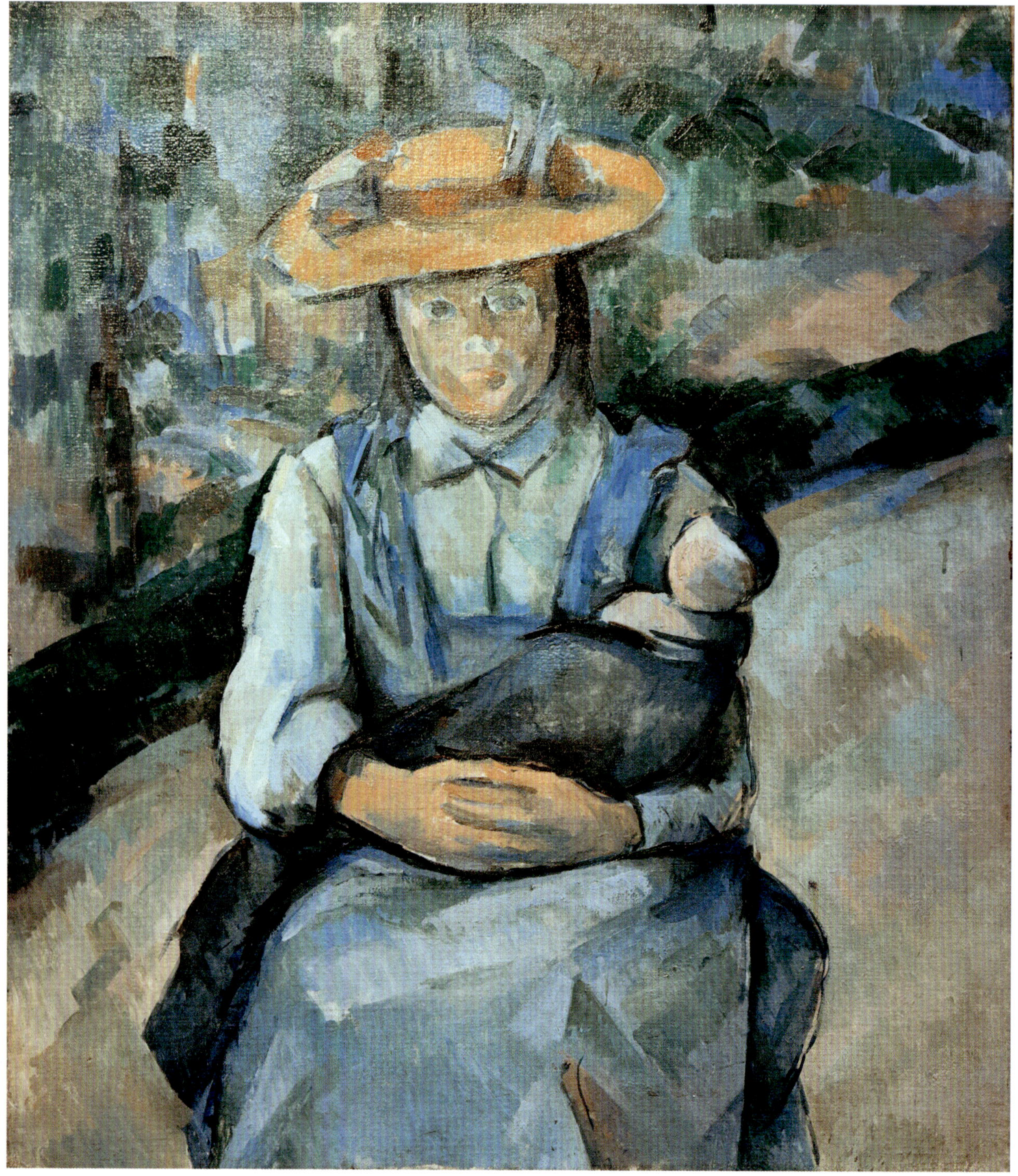

Little Girl with a Doll, 1902–04
Oil on canvas, 73 x 60 cm (28¾ x 23⅜ in) • Private Collection

The girl in this painting is hardly less doll-like than the figure she is cradling. The abstraction of vision in Cézanne's late portraits subordinates notions of personality and human separateness to the overall pattern of the image.

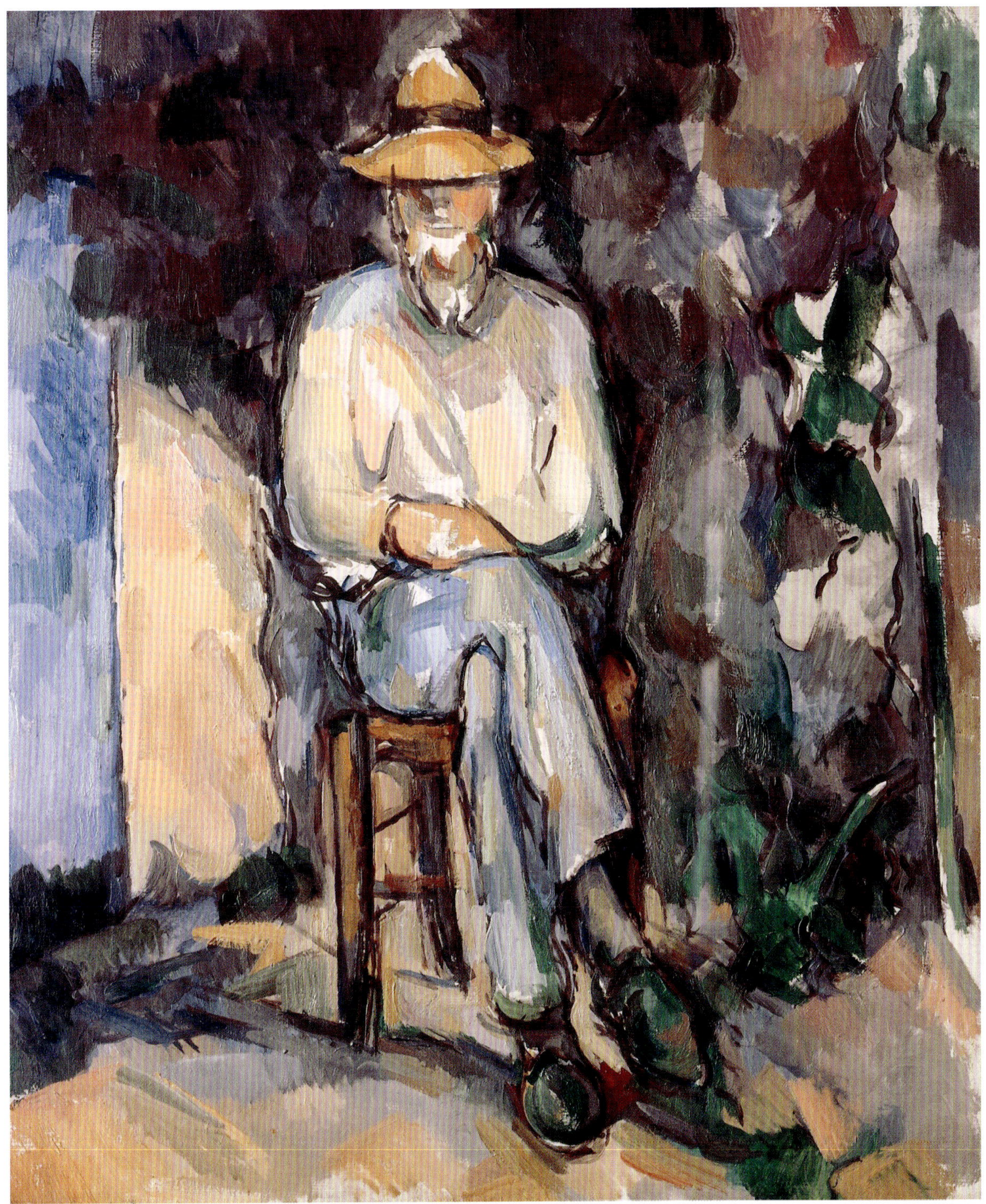

The Gardener Vallier, *c.* 1906
Oil on canvas, 65.4 x 54.9 cm (25¾ x 21⅝ in) • Tate Modern, London

As well as being the gardener and odd-job man, Vallier was also Cezanne's final model, though here a more radical idea of man's unity with his environment has replaced the quiet integrity of the peasant portraits of the previous decade.

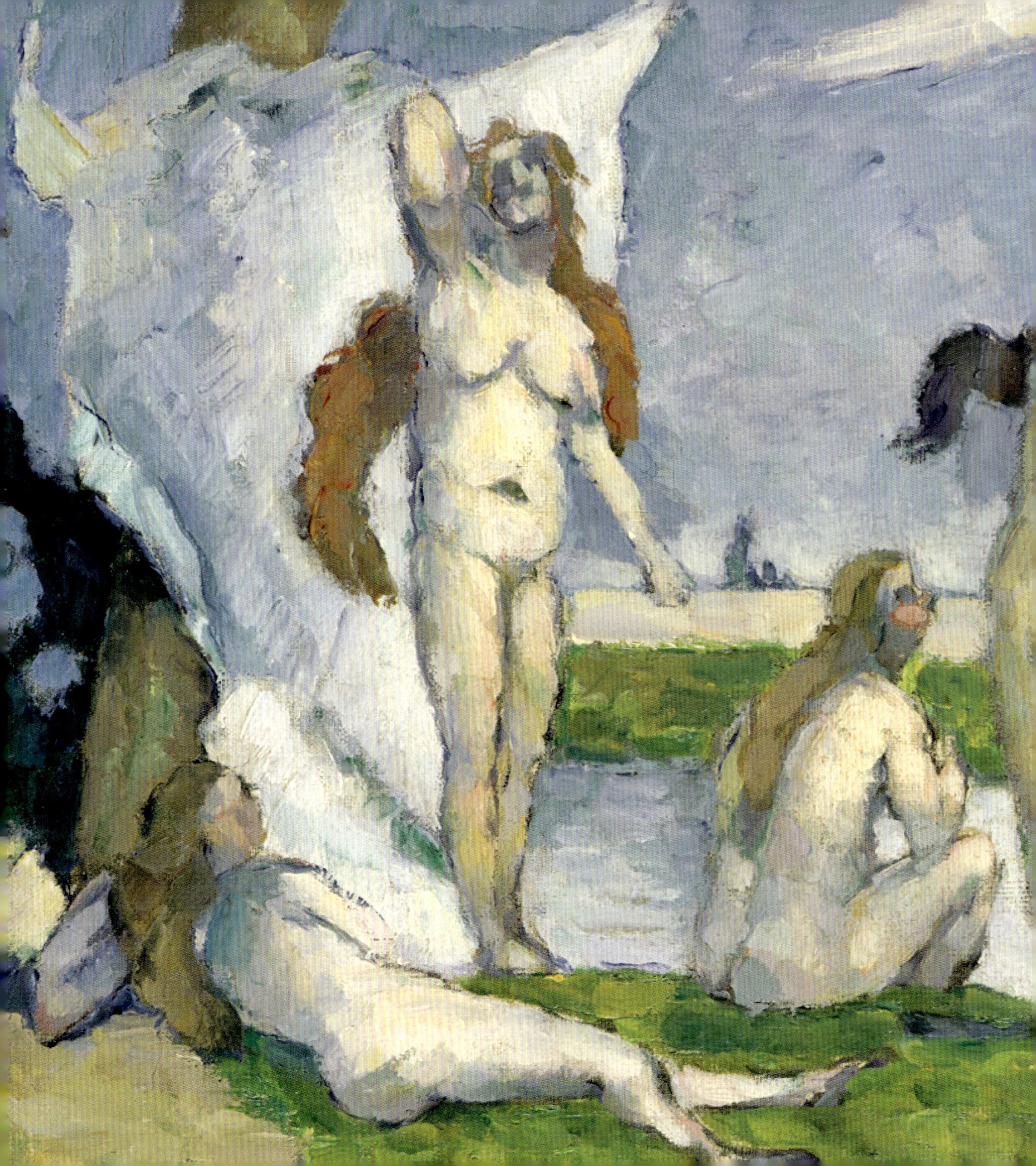

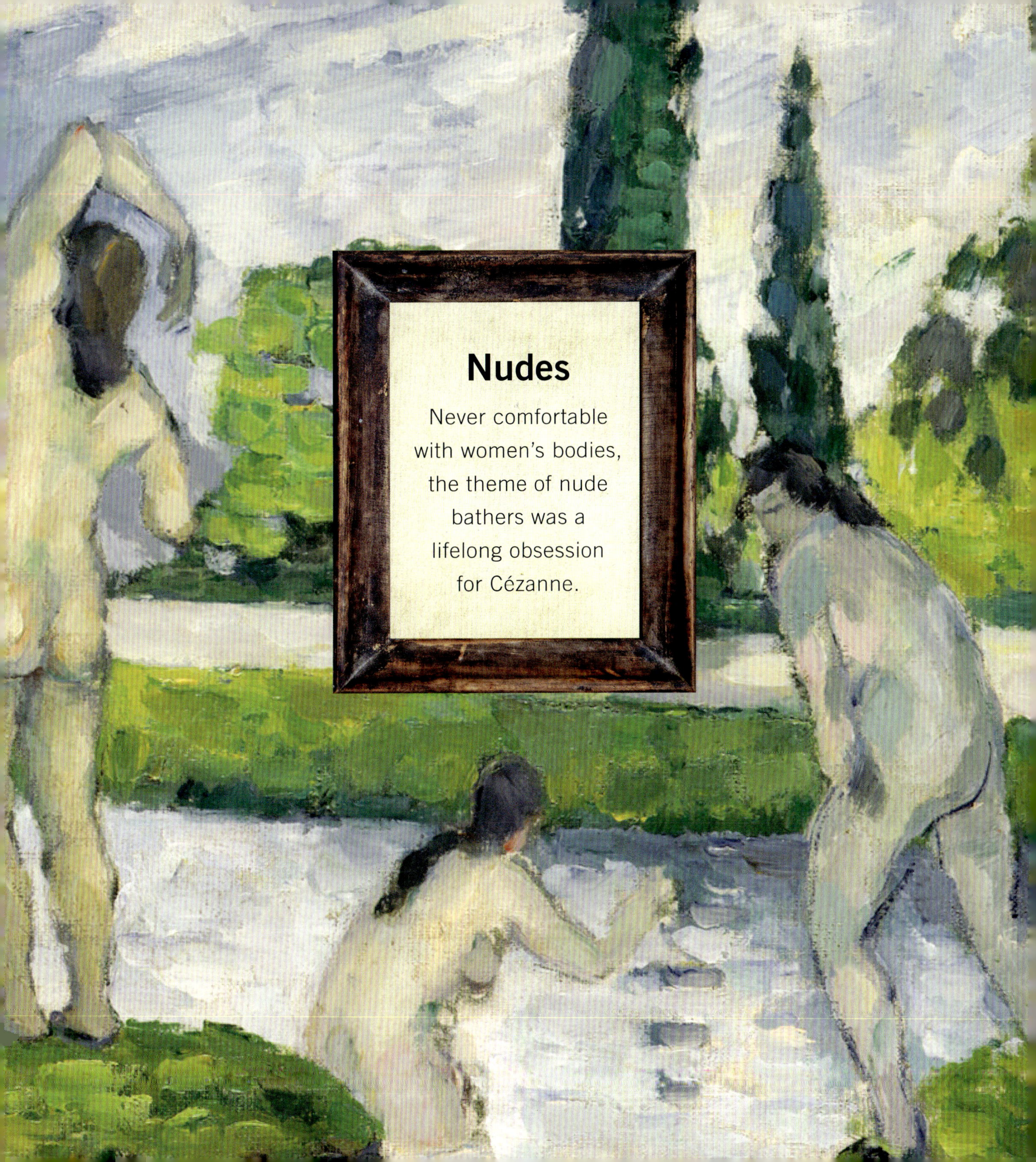

Nudes

Never comfortable
with women's bodies,
the theme of nude
bathers was a
lifelong obsession
for Cézanne.

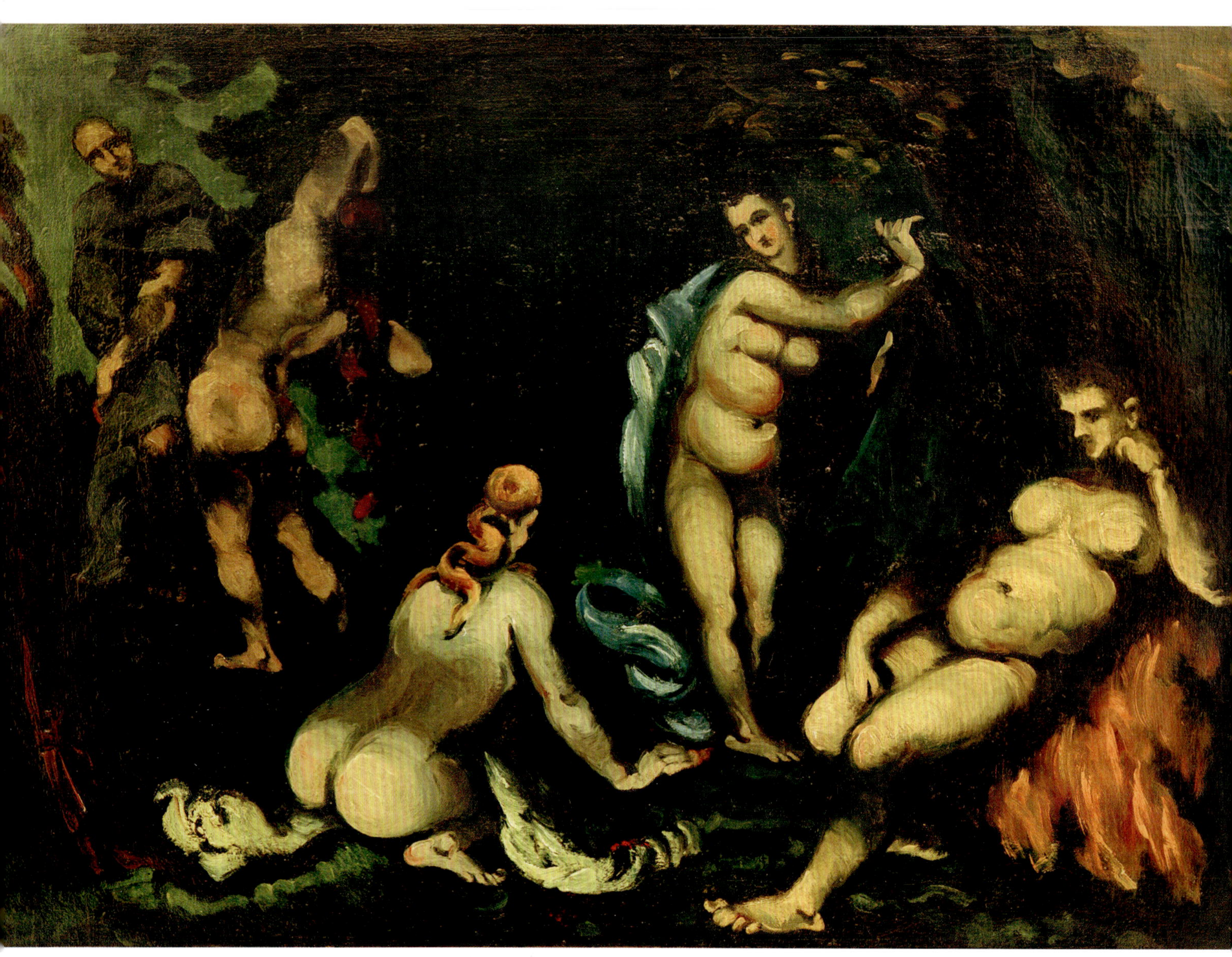

The Temptation of St Anthony, *c.* 1870
Oil on canvas, 57 x 76 cm (22½ x 29⅞ in)
• Emil Bührle Collection, Zurich

This dark, brooding image from the end of Cézanne's Romantic period is concerned solely with the figures. Later embracing the need to work directly from nature, he would go on to confront the challenge of integrating the human body with its environment.

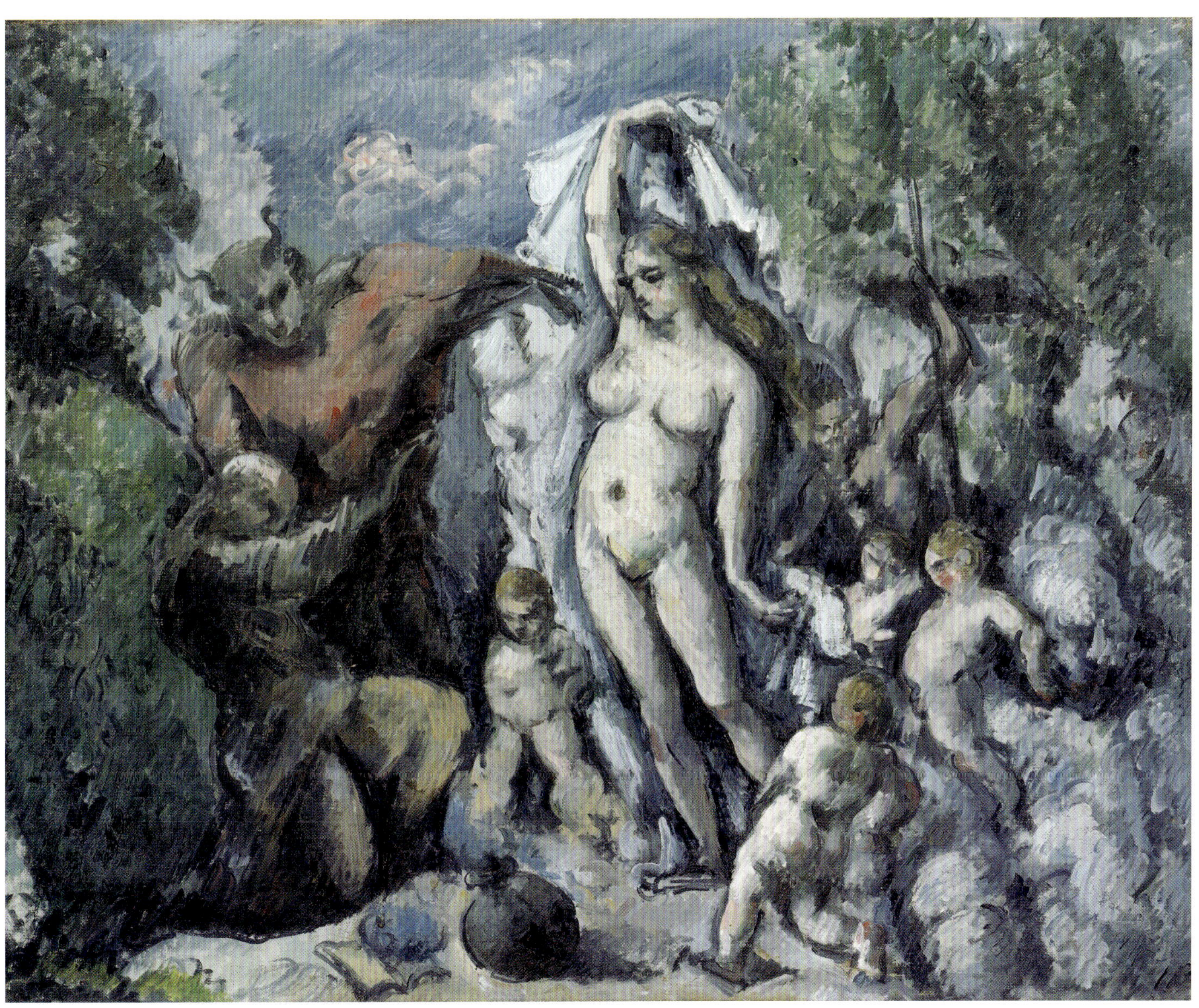

The Temptation of St Anthony, c.1877
Oil on canvas, 47.2 x 56 cm (18⅝ x 22 in) • Musée d'Orsay, Paris

Seven years later than the previous painting on this theme, this canvas shows how much Cézanne's outlook had changed. The dark colouring and ambivalent sensuality of the first picture has been replaced by a bright palette and a purposeful, confident nude.

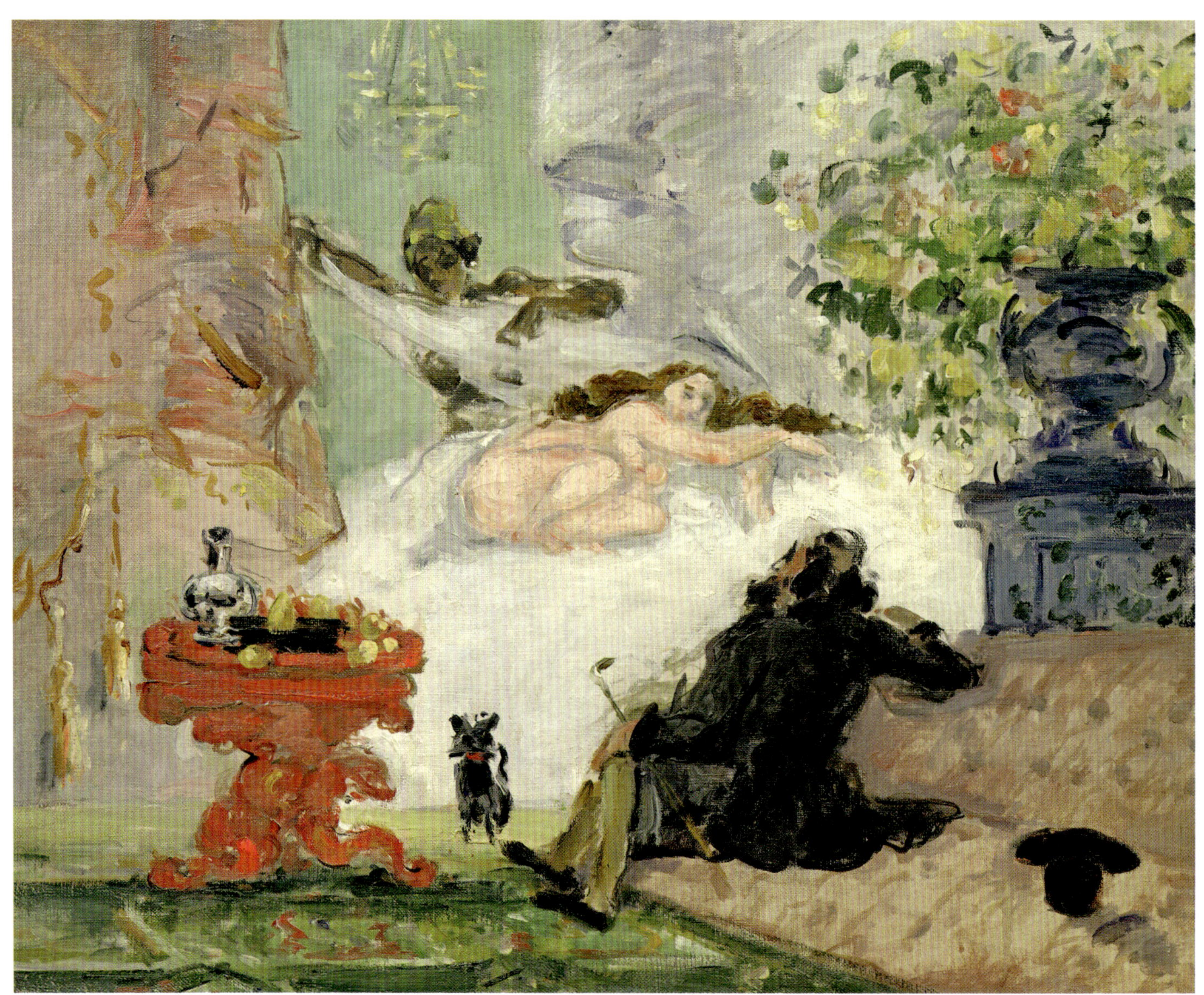

A Modern Olympia, 1873–74

Oil on canvas, 46.2 x 55.5 cm (18¼ x 21⅞ in) • Musée d'Orsay, Paris

A knowing homage to Manet's *Olympia*, Cézanne's honest depiction of artistic voyeurism is rendered with Impressionist brushwork of such obvious agitation that one critic who saw it called him 'a sort of madman who paints in delirium tremens'.

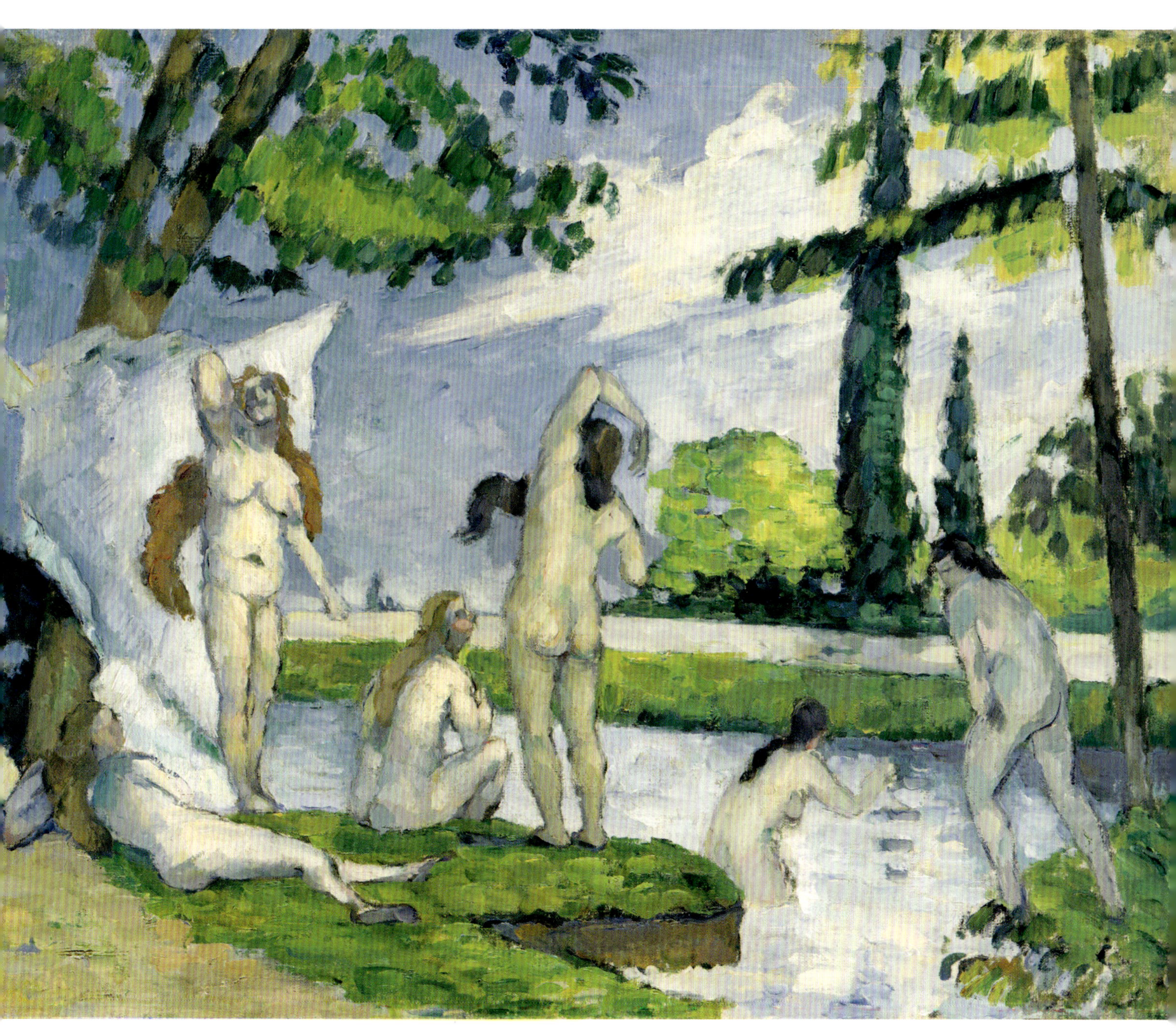

Bathers, 1874–75
Oil on canvas, 38.1 x 46 cm (15 x 18⅛ in)
• Metropolitan Museum of Art, New York

This small painting, an early example of a theme Cézanne would pursue until the end of his life, is notable for its use of a bright but limited palette of mainly blues, greens and yellows, giving the picture an innocent and charming sensuality.

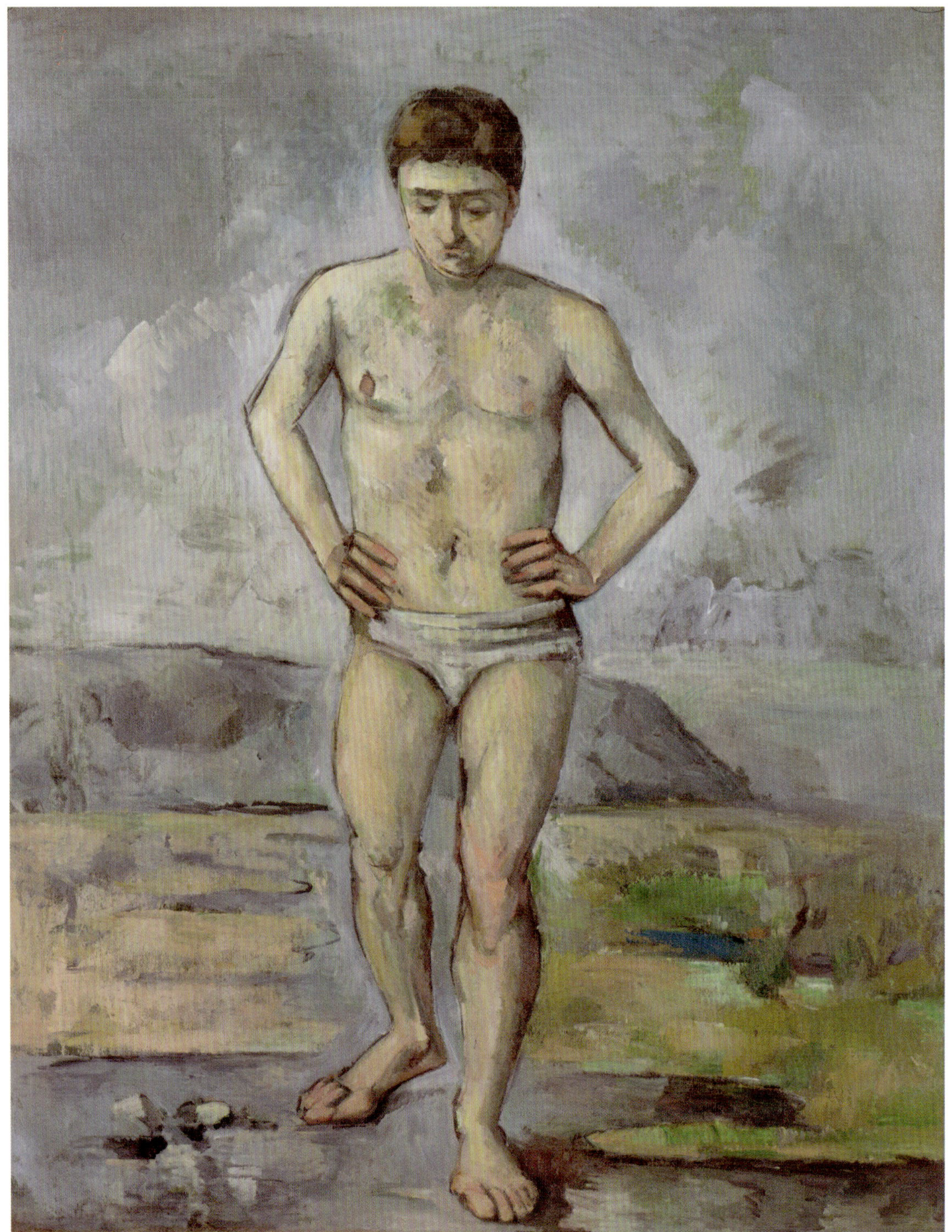

The Bather, *c.* 1885
Oil on canvas, 127 x 96.8 cm (50 x 38⅛ in)
• Museum of Modern Art, New York

The same semi-naked figure appears centrally in a painting and various related studies of a group of male bathers Cézanne painted in the 1870s. This one is by far the most successful, both anatomically and in the figure's integration with his surroundings.

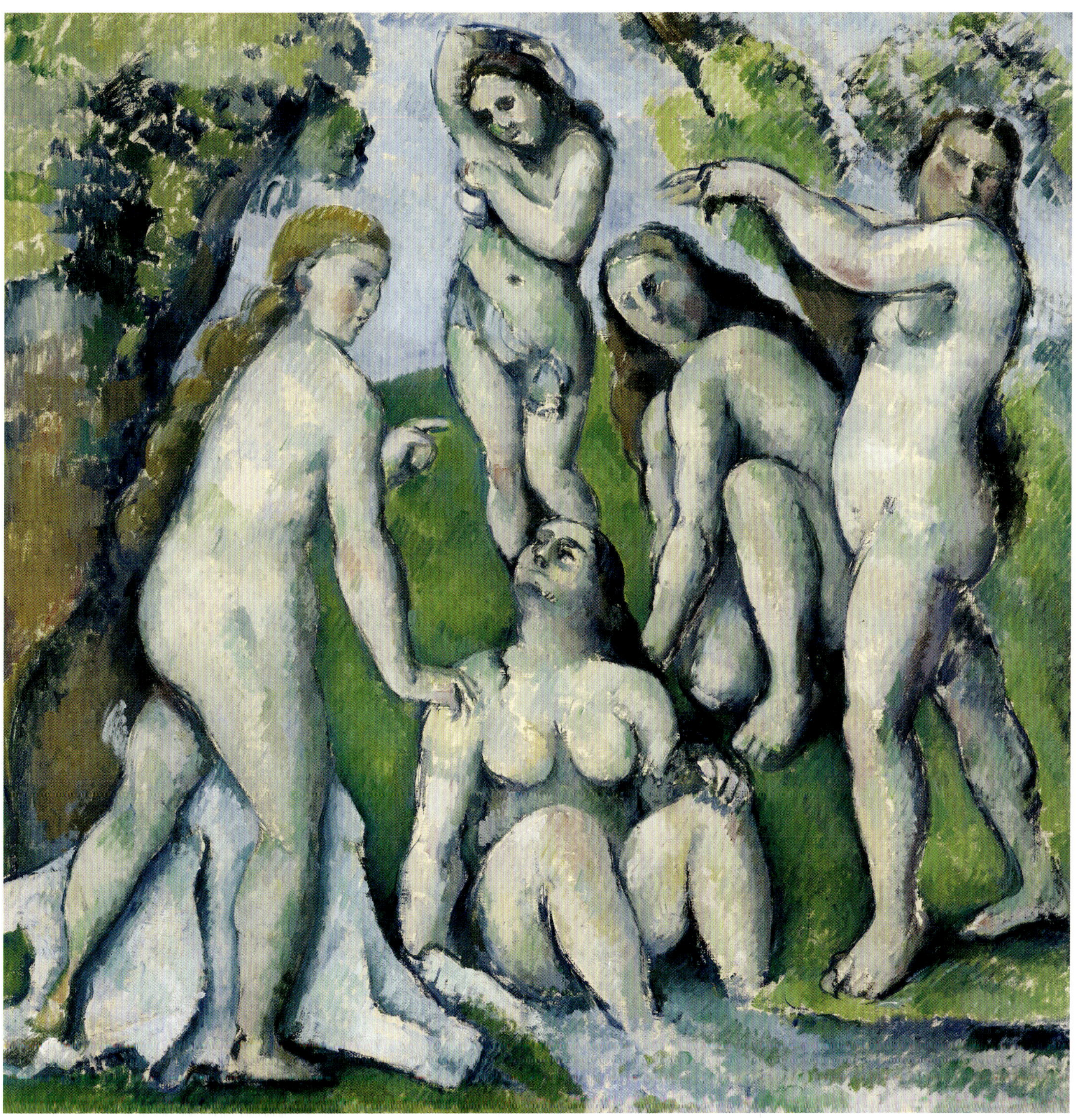

Five Bathers, 1885–87
Oil on canvas, 65.3 x 65.3 cm (25¾ x 25¾ in) • Kunstmuseum, Basel

In this painting, in the framing foliage that apparently meets at an unseen apex, Cézanne has begun to explore the pyramidal structure that would come to define the monumental canvases, known as *The Large Bathers*, which he began in the 1890s.

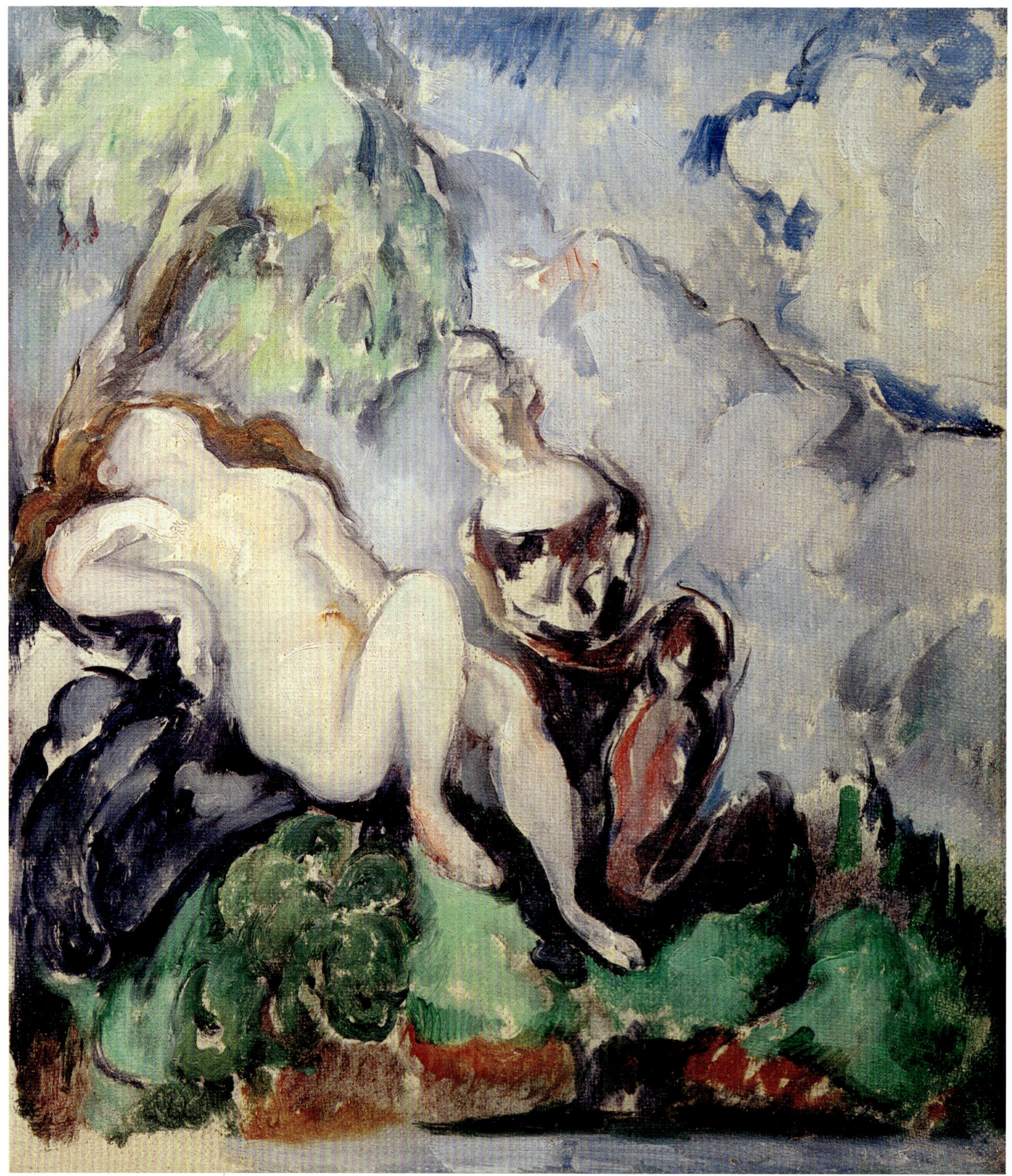

Bathsheba, 1885–90
Oil on canvas, 29 x 25 cm (11⅜ x 9⅞ in)
• Musée Granet, Aix-en-Provence

The erotic Biblical story of David and Bathsheba has long been a favourite for painters. Given his ambition to paint a large picture of bathers, here Cézanne is trying to integrate a sexually charged subject with the surrounding environment.

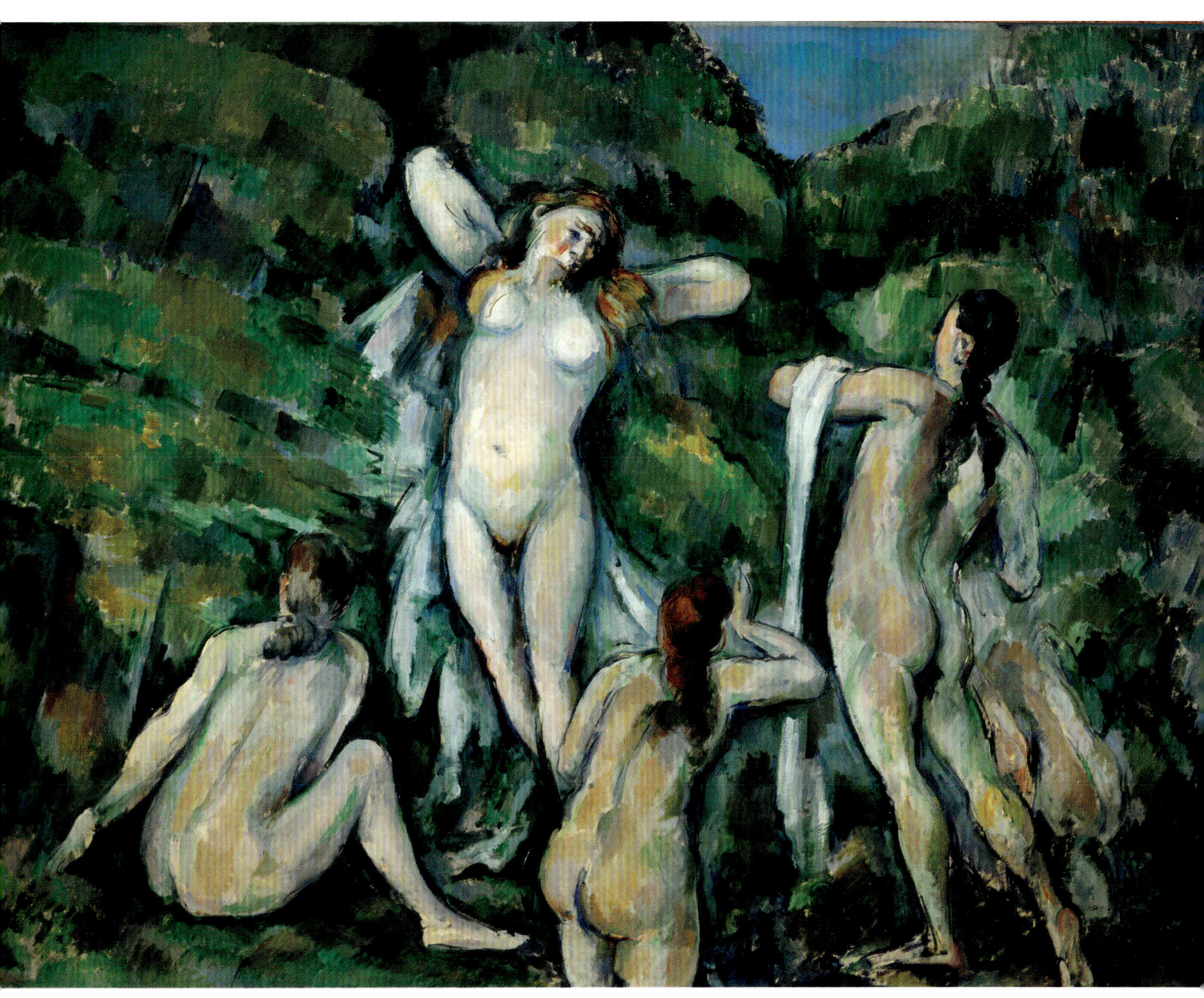

Women Bathing, 1888–90
Oil on canvas, 73 x 92 cm (28¾ x 36¼ in)
• Ny Carlsberg Glyptotek, Copenhagen

In this image of bathers, the female nudes have begun to assume the languidness we find in *The Large Bathers*, while the skin tones of the bodies are subtly harmonized with the colours of the surrounding foliage.

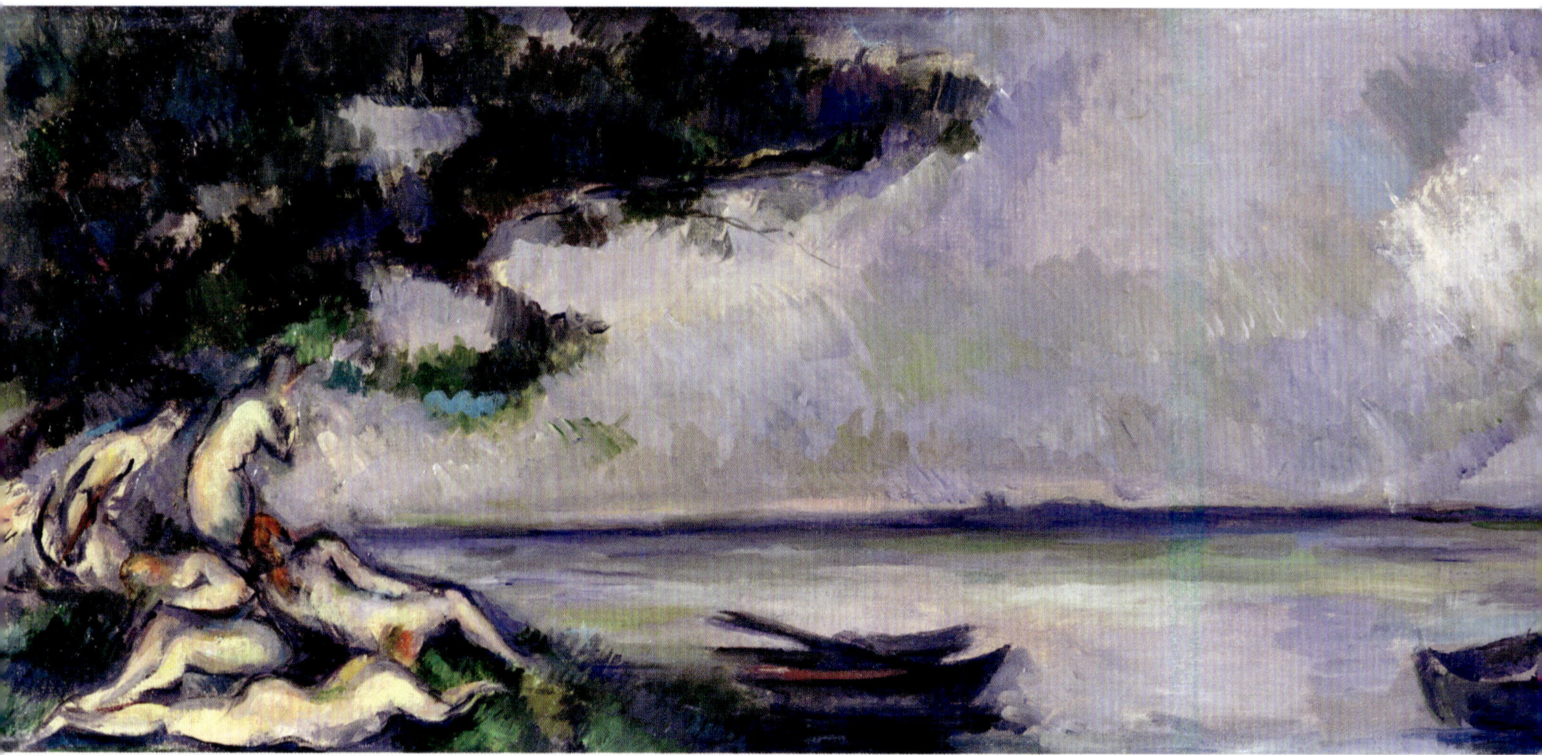

Boat and Bathers, 1890
Oil on canvas, 30 x 125 cm (11¾ x 49¼ in) • Musée de l'Orangerie, Paris

This unusual image of two groups of bathers remained unfinished when Victor Chocquet, the man who commissioned it as a decorative panel for his Paris apartment, died in 1891. Later cut up into three sections, it was only reassembled in 1973.

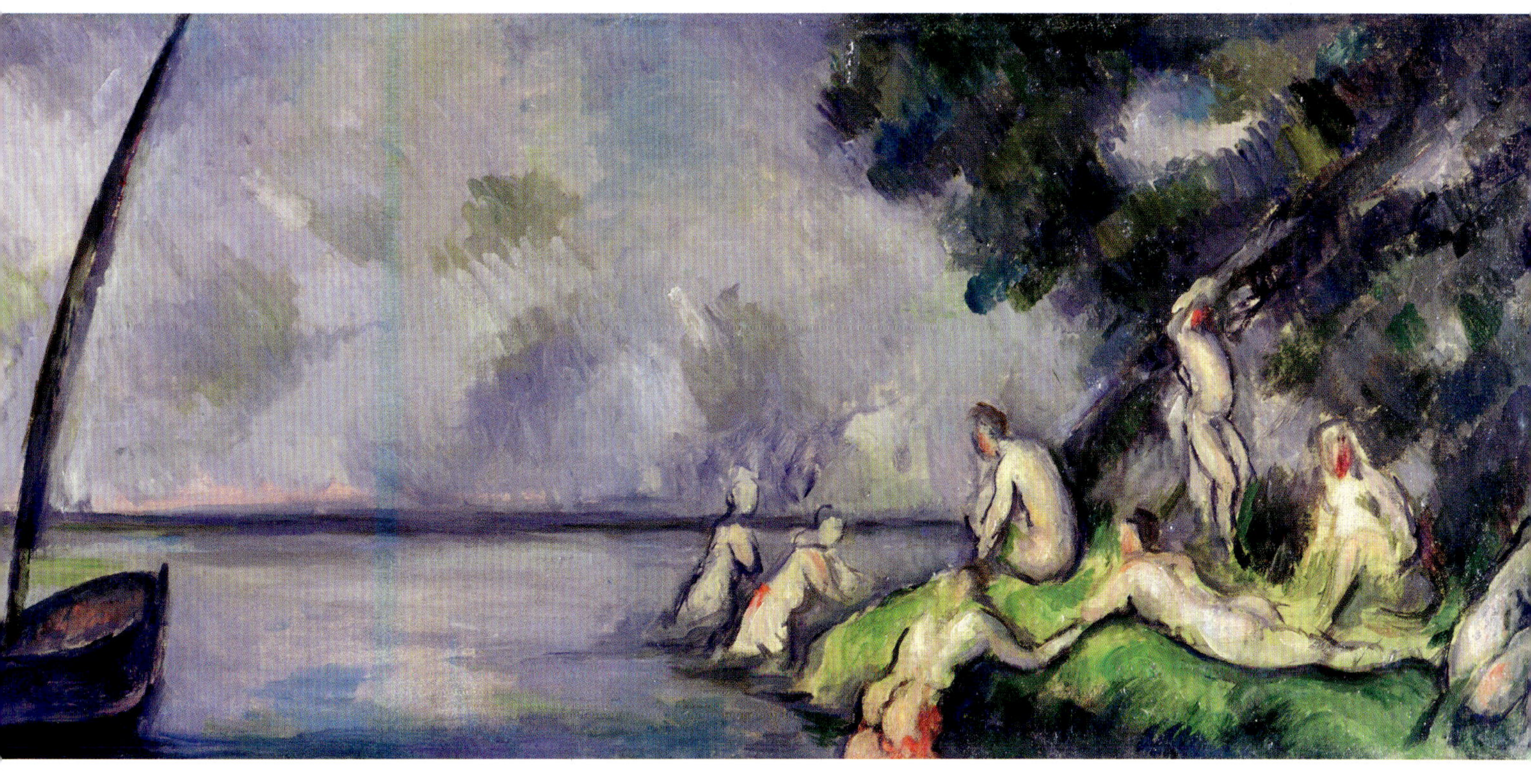

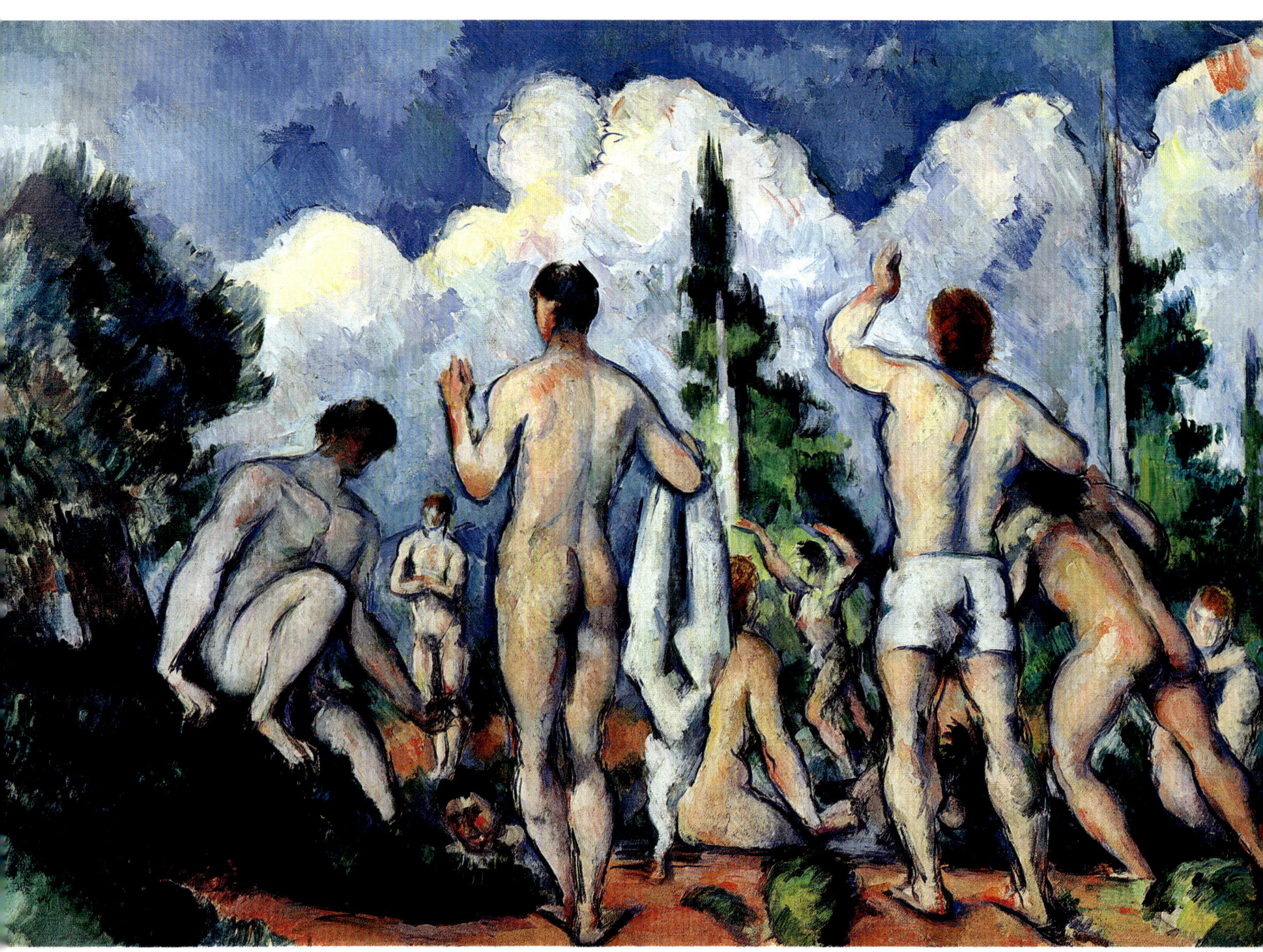

Bathers, *c.* 1890
Oil on canvas, 60.5 x 82.5 cm (23¾ x 32½ in)
• Musée d'Orsay, Paris

Cézanne painted several versions of this picture around the same period, building on similar groups of male bathers depicted in earlier images going back to the 1870s. This one exhibits the greatest colour contrast among the set.

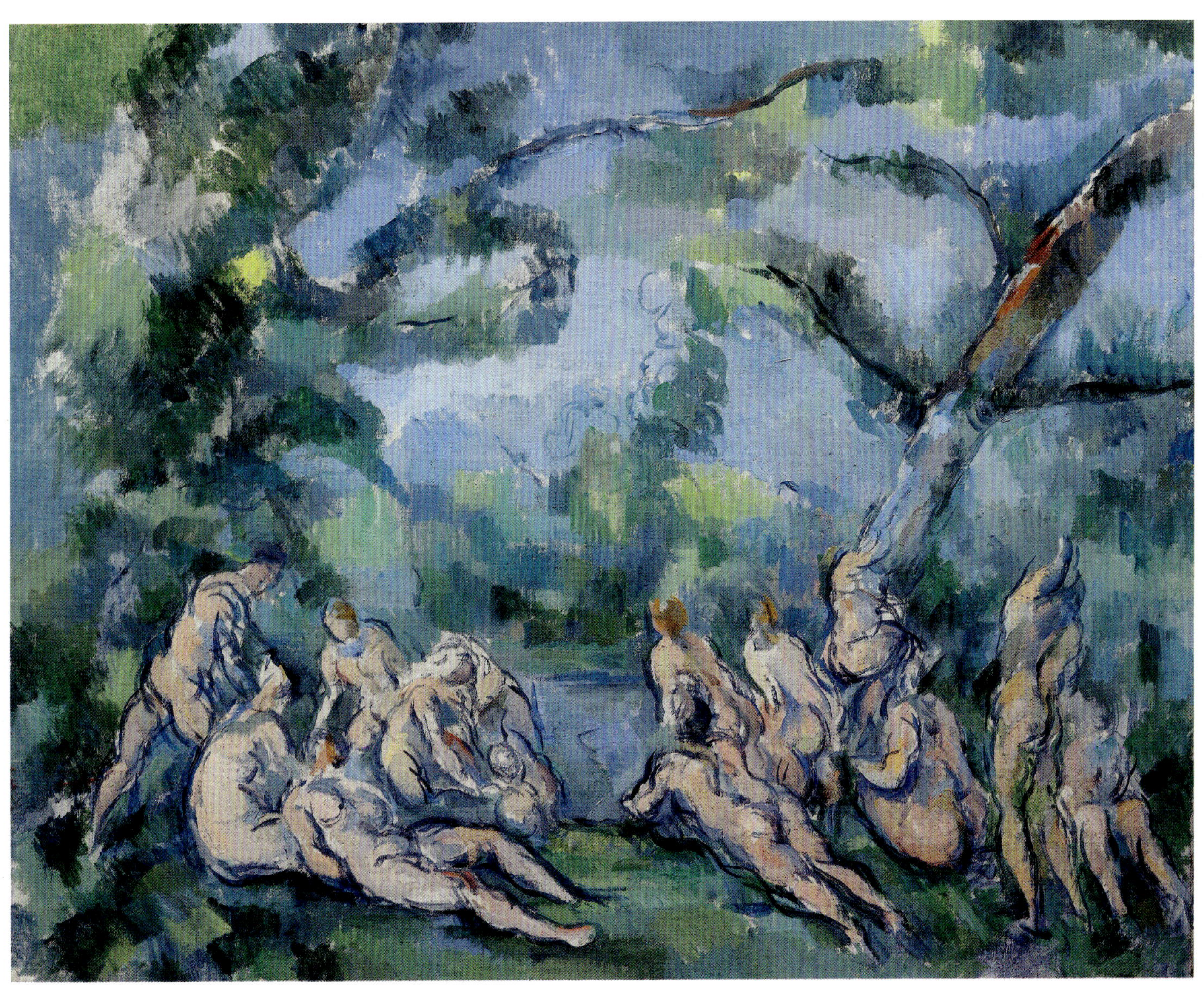

Bathers, 1899–1904
Oil on canvas, 51.3 × 61.7 cm (20⅓ × 24¼ in)
• Art Institute of Chicago, Chicago

Cézanne made many studies for the paintings we now know as *The Large Bathers*. Though his religious sister Marie ordered the many discovered after his death to be burned on grounds of obscenity, some 60 escaped the flames.

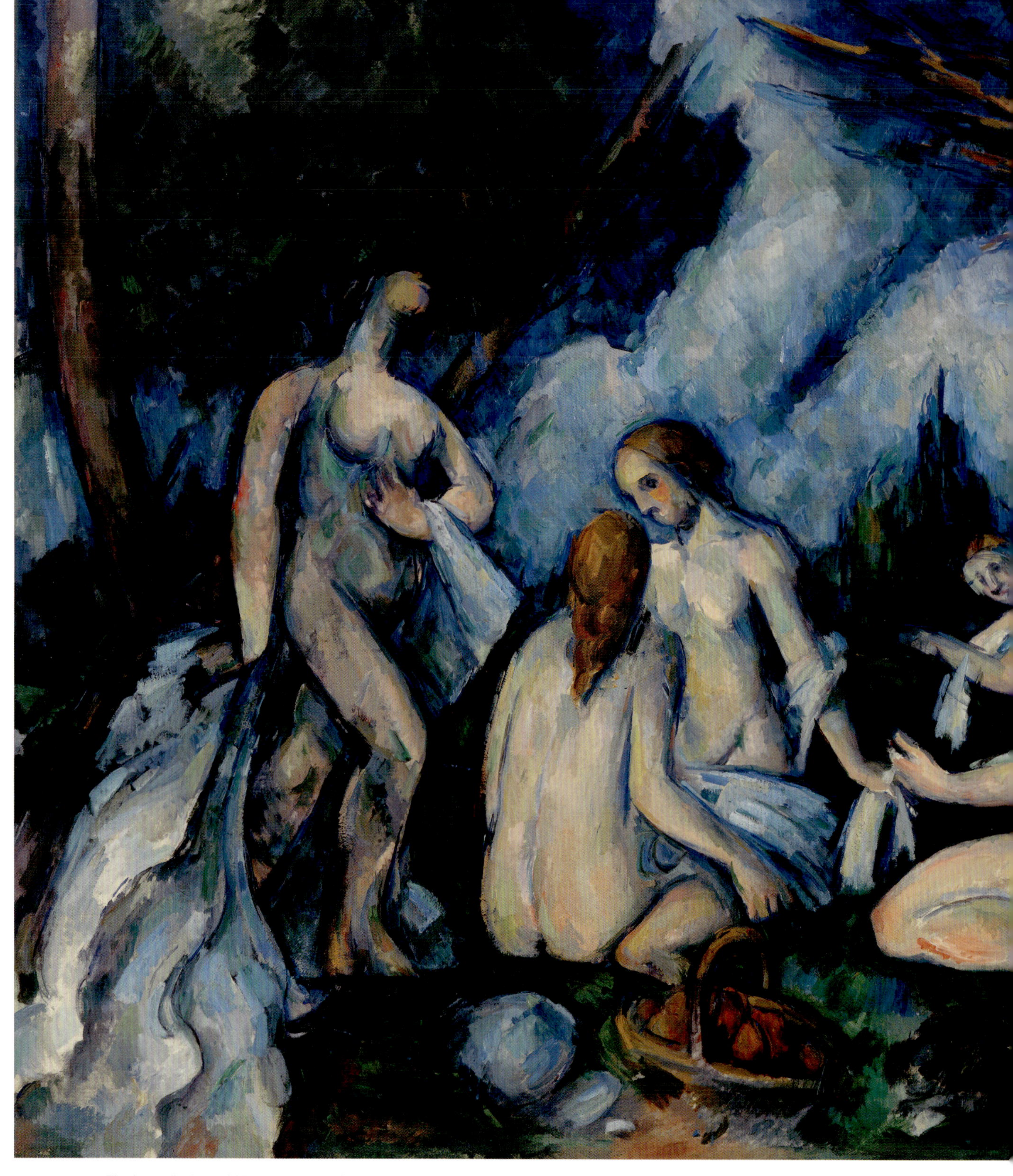

The Large Bathers, 1895–1906
Oil on canvas, 132.4 x 219.1 cm (52⅛ x 86¼ in)
• Barnes Foundation, Merion, Pennsylvania

Cézanne worked on the three huge paintings we call *The Large Bathers* throughout the last decade of his life, using a purpose-built easel that could be taken outside to paint the background landscapes that feature in these pictures.

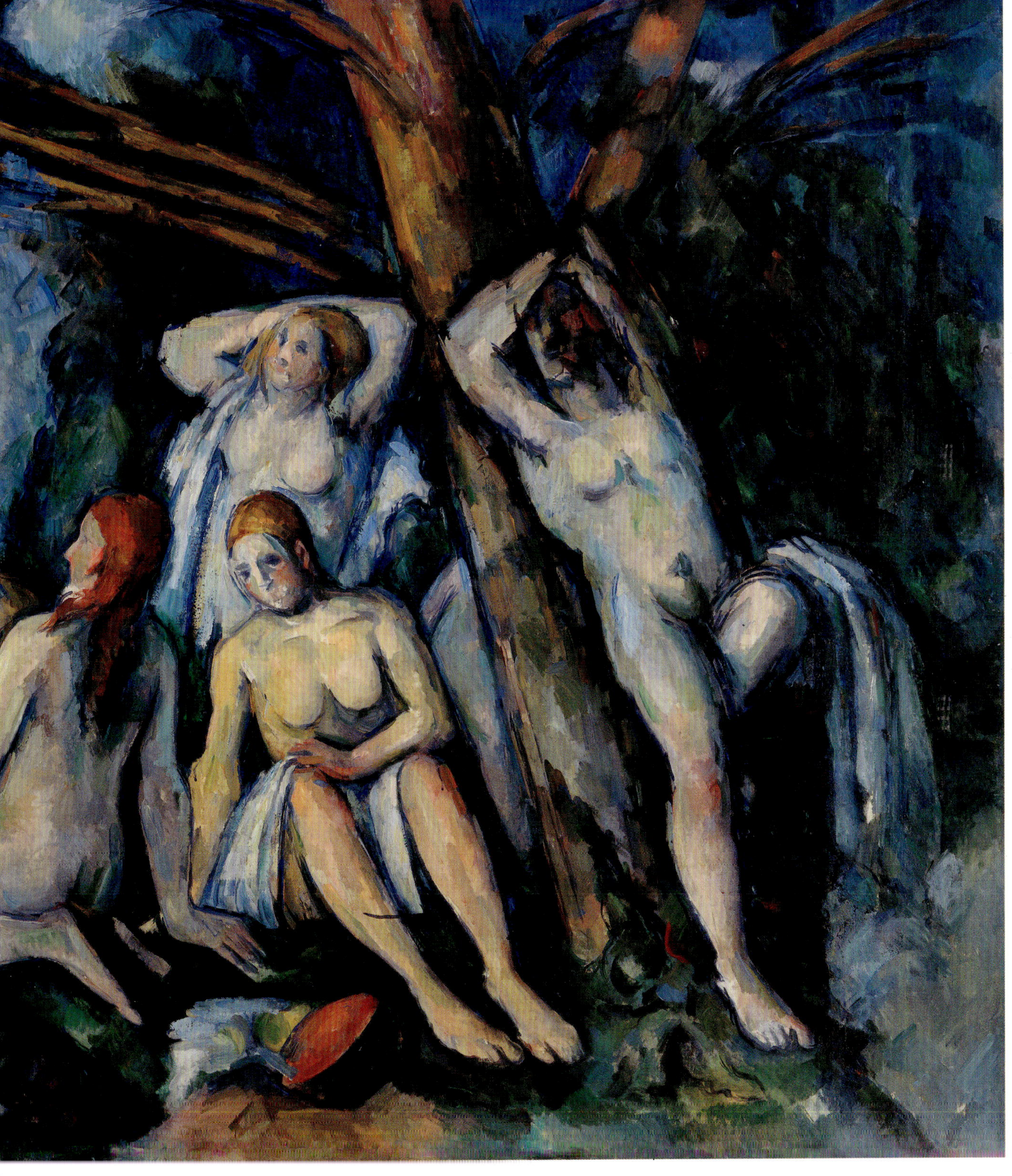

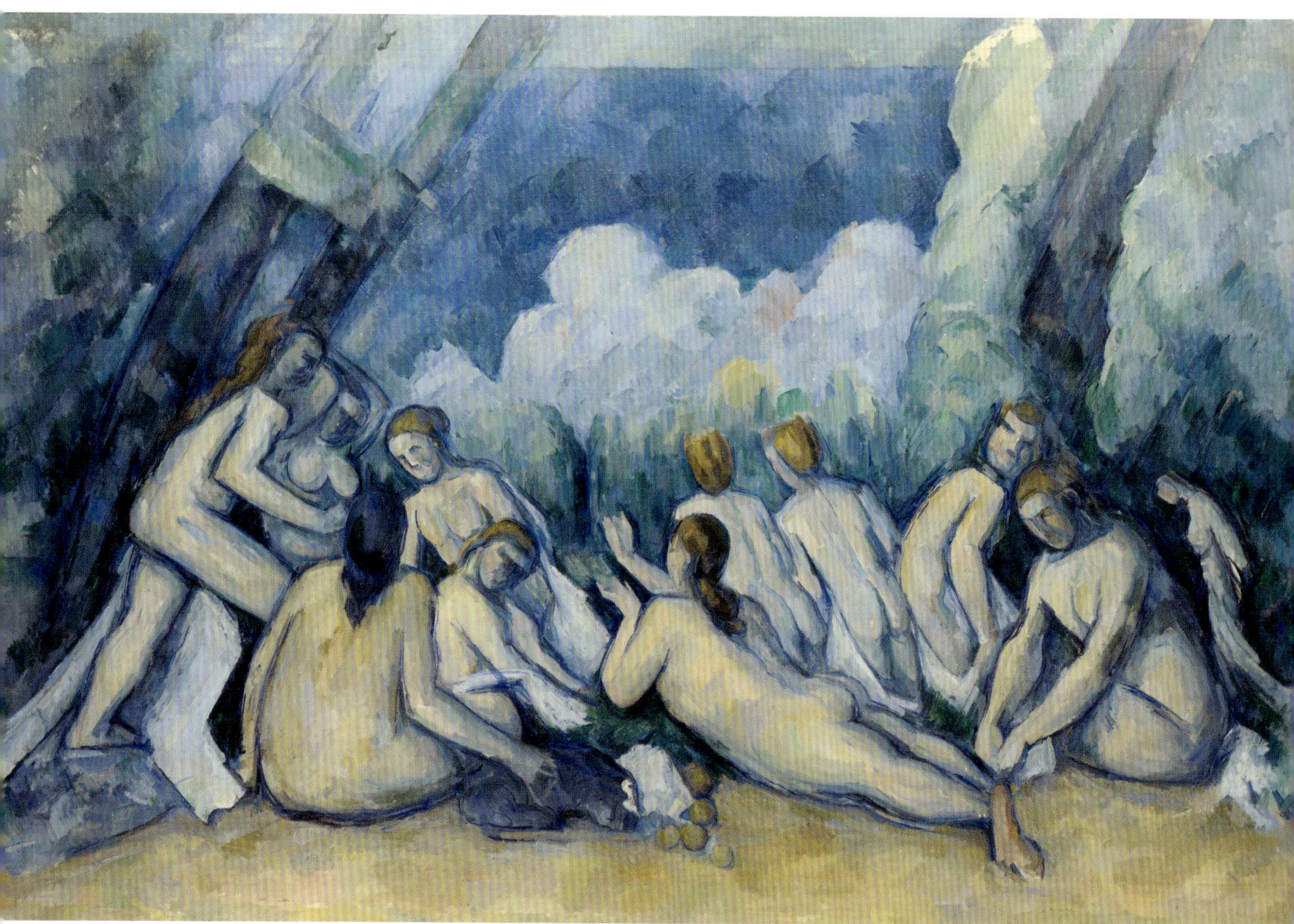

The Large Bathers, *c.* 1894–1905
Oil on canvas, 127.2 x 196.1 cm (4 ft 2⅛ x 6 ft 5¼ in)
• National Gallery, London

Close study of *The Large Bathers* in London's National Gallery reveals the women's faces to be hideous masks, with strange eyes and no mouths to speak of. They are not so much real women as spirits emerging from the landscape they inhabit.

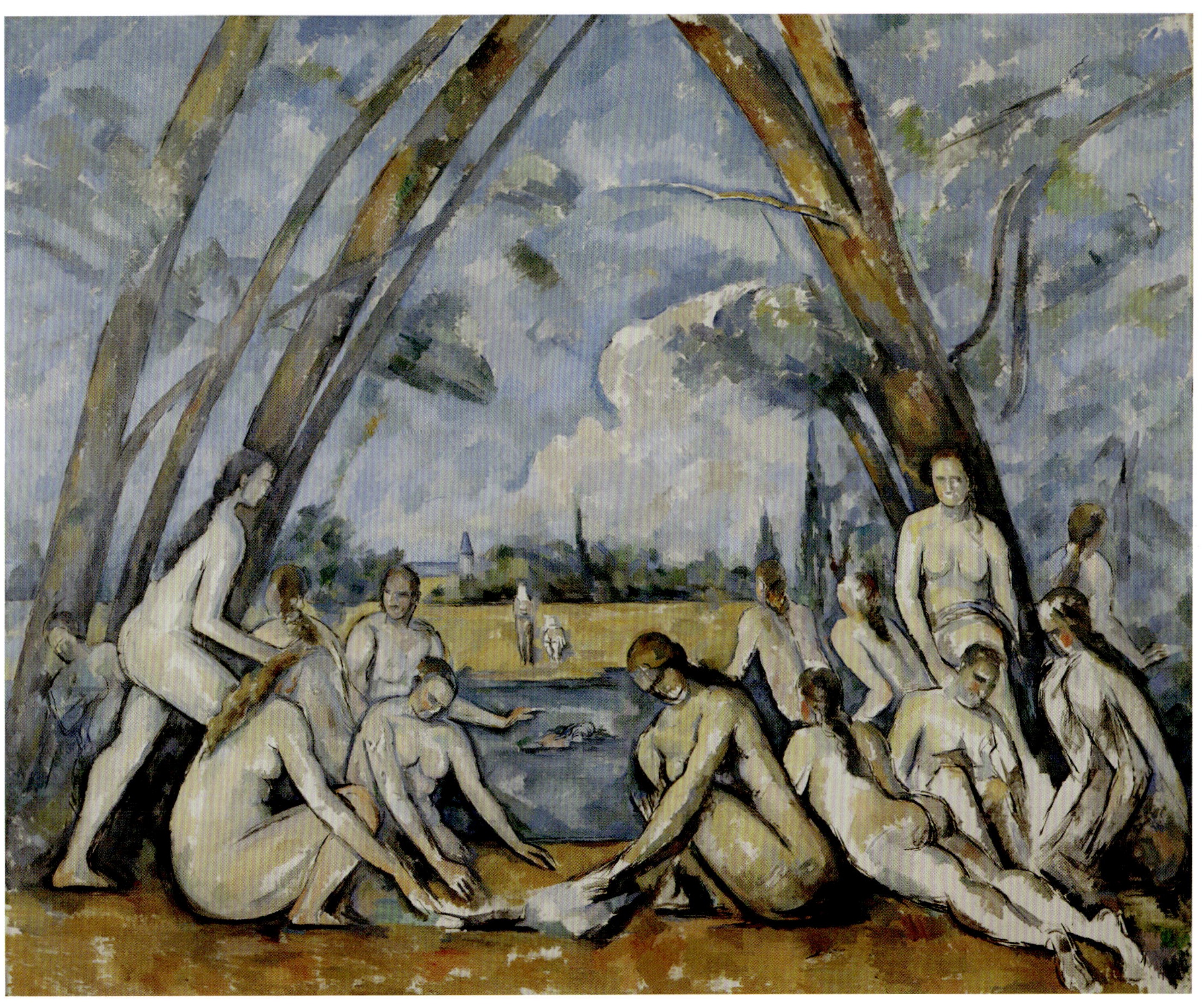

The Large Bathers, 1900–06
Oil on canvas, 210.5 × 250.8 cm (6 ft 10⅞ x 8 ft 2¾ in)
• Philadelphia Museum of Art, Philadelphia

Though Cézanne was influenced in his images of bathers by the classical paintings of Poussin, they also depict a landscape he knew well: the red earth of Provence and the silvery thread of the River Arc running close to the city of Aix.

Indexes

Index of Works

Page numbers in *italics* refer to illustrations.

A

Achille Empéraire (1867–68) *82*
Apples and Oranges (c. 1899) *42*
Artist's Father, Reading L'Évènement
   (1866) 7–8, *80*

B

Basket of Apples, The (c. 1893) *36*
Bather, The (c. 1885) *114*
Bathers (1874–75) 25, *113*
Bathers (1899–1904) *121*
Bathers (c. 1890) *120*
Bathsheba (1885–90) 25, *116*
Battle of Love, The (1877) 10
Bay of Marseille Seen from L'Estaque
   (c. 1885) 15, *60*
Black Marble Clock, The (c. 1870) 8
Blue Vase, The (1888–90) 18, *35*
Boat and Bathers (1890) *118*
Boulders Near the Caves Above
   Château Noir (c. 1904) *75*
Bouquet in a Small Delft Vase (1873)
   10, *30*
Boy in a Red Waistcoat (1888–90) *91*
Bridge at Maincy, The (1879) 11, *53*
Bridge of Trois-Sautets (c. 1906) *77*

C

Card Players, The (1890–92) 20, *95*
Card Players, The (1992–96) *96*
Château Noir (c. 1904) *74*
Château of Médan, The
   (c. 1879–80) *54*
Chestnut Trees at Jas de Bouffan (c.
   1885–86) *61*

D

Dovecote at Bellevue, The (1888–92)
   20, *63*

E

Eternal Feminine, The (1877) 10

F

Five Bathers (1885–87) 25, *115*
Forest Interior (1898–99) *72*

G

Gardanne (c. 1885) *58*
Gardener Vallier, The (c. 1906) *107*
Great Pine near Aix (1895–97) 22
Great Pine, The (1890–96) *66*

H

Hanged Man's House, Auvers-sur-
   Oise (1873) 9, 18, *50*
Hortense Nursing Paul (1872) 9
House and Dovecote at Bellevue, The
   (1890–92) *64*
House in Aix (Jas de Bouffan)
   (1887) 17
House of Doctor Gachet in Auvers,
   The (c. 1873) *51*
House of Pierre Lacroix (1873) 9
House with the Cracked Walls, The
   (1892–94) *67*

K

Kitchen Table (Still Life with Basket)
   (1888–90) *34*

L

L'Estaque with Red Roofs
   (1883–85) *57*
Lac d'Annecy (1896) 22, *69*
Lady in Blue (c. 1900) *105*
Large Bathers, The (1894–1905) *124*
Large Bathers, The (1895–1906)
   24, *122*
Large Bathers, The (1900–06) *125*
Little Girl with a Doll (1902–04) *106*

M

Madame Cézanne in a Red Armchair
   (c. 1877) 10–11, *85*
Madame Cézanne in a Red Dress
   (1888–90) 17–18, *90*
Madame Cézanne in Blue
   (1888–90) 18
Madame Cézanne in the Conservatory
   (1891) *92*
Man in a Blue Smock
   (c. 1896–97) *101*

Man with a Pipe (1890) *93*
Man with a Pipe (1892) *94*
Man with Crossed Arms
   (c. 1897) *103*
Melting Snow at L'Estaque (c. 1870) 8
Mill at the River (The Bridge of
   Maincy) (1904–05) 21
Modern Olympia, A (1873–74) 10, *112*
Mont Saint-Victoire and the Viaduct of
   the Arc River Valley (1882–85) *55*
Mont Sainte-Victoire (c. 1896–98) *70*
Mont Sainte-Victoire (c. 1902–04) *73*
Mont Sainte-Victoire and Château
   Noir (c. 1904–06) 23, *76*
Mont Sainte-Victoire from Les Lauves
   (1904–06) 26
Mont Sainte-Victoire Seen from the
   Bibémus Quarry (c. 1897) 21, *71*
Mont Sainte-Victoire with Large Pine
   (c. 1897) 21, *62*
Murder, The (c. 1870) 8

O

Old Woman with a Rosary, An
   (c.1895–96) *99*

P

Pierrot and Harlequin (c. 1888) *89*
Portrait of Ambroise Vollard
   (1899) *104*
Portrait of Gustave Geffroy
   (1895–96) *98*
Portrait of Joachim Gasquet
   (1896–97) 22
Portrait of Madame Cézanne
   (1885–86) *88*
Portrait of the Artist's Son
   (1881–82) *87*
Portrait of Victor Chocquet
   (1876–77) *84*
Pyramid of Skulls (1901) *46*

Q

Quarry at Bibémus, The (1895)
   21, *68*

R

Road at Pontoise, The (1875–77)
   11, *52*
Rocks in the Forest (c. 1893) 21

S

Seated Peasant (c. 1892–96) *97*
Self-Portrait (c. 1875) *83*
Self-Portrait (c. 1880–81) *86*
Self-Portrait with Beret (1898–1900)
   102
Still Life with Apples and Biscuits (c.
   1877) *32*
Still Life with Apples and Peaches (c.
   1908) *47*
Still Life with Apples on a Sideboard
   (1900–06) *45*
Still Life with Milk Jug and Fruit
   (c. 1900) *43*
Still Life with Onions (1896–98)
   18, *41*
Still Life with Open Drawer
   (1877–79) *31*
Still Life with Pitcher and Fruit
   (1893–94) *38*
Still Life with Plaster Cupid
   (c. 1894) *40*
Still Life with Pomegranates,
   Carafe, Sugar Bowl, Bottle and
   Watermelon (1900–06) *44*
Still Life, Drapery, Pitcher and Fruit
   Bowl (1893–94) *37*

T

Tall Trees at Jas de Bouffan
   (c. 1883) *56*
Temptation of St Anthony, The
   (c. 1870) 8, *110*
Temptation of St Anthony, The
   (c. 1877) 10, 25, *111*

U

Uncle Dominique as a Monk (1866)
   7–8, *81*
Underwood (near Jas de Bouffan)
   (1890–94) 22, *65*

W

Women Bathing (1888–90) *117*

Y

Young Italian Woman at a Table
   (c. 1895–1900) *100*

General Index

A
Académie Suisse, Paris 7
Achille Empéraire (1867–68) 82
Aix-en-Provence 6–7, 12, 14, 17, 18,
   20, 22, 24, 26, 27
Aubert, Anne Elisabeth Honorine 6,
   7, 17, 23
Auvers-sur-Oise 9

B
Barbizon School 12
Baroque 7
bathers 24–26
Bazille, Frédéric 8
Belle Époque 17
Bellevue 20
Bernard, Émile 18–19, 26–27
Bibémus quarry 21–22
Bourron-Marlotte 21
Braque, Georges 27
Brémond, Mme 23

C
Café Guerbois, Batignolles, Paris 8
Caillebotte, Gustave 11, 21
Cézanne, Louis-Auguste 6, 7, 12, 16,
   17, 19
Cézanne, Marie 12, 15, 16, 23
Cézanne, Paul (son) 9, 12, 15,
   19–20, 21
Cézanne, Paul 6
   Bibémus quarry 21–22
   birth of son 9
   bourgeois background 6
   change of scenery 19–20
   Château Noir 22–23
   Chocquet, Victor 11
   construction of vision 11–12
   critical attention 18–19
   death 26–27
   fantasy and reality 25–26
   'Father of Modern Art' 6, 26–27
   fear of influence 19
   fresh perspective 17
   friends and influences 7
   Gardanne 15
   Hortense 8, 12, 16, 17 18
   Impressionism 9–10, 12–13
   L'Estaque 15
   Les Lauves studio 23–24
   male gaze 10–11
   Paris 7
   Renoir, Auguste 14–15
   romantic visions 7–8
   structure of feeling 13–14
   Vollard, Ambroise 20–21
   Zola, Émile 14, 16–17, 24–25
Cézanne, Rose 20
Chantilly 12, 18
Château Noir 22–23
Chocquet, Victor 11, 12, 18, 21
Cloisonnism 18
Conil, Maxime 20
Courbet, Gustave 7, 8
Cravache, La 18
Cubism 27

D
Degas, Edgar 8, 21
Delacroix, Eugène 7
Duret, Théodore 11

E
École des Beaux-Arts, Paris 7
Empéraire, Achille 8
en plein air 9, 15
Exposition Universelle, Paris 1889 18

F
Fauvism 11, 27
Fiquet, Marie-Hortense 8, 9, 10–11,
   12, 15, 17–18
   marriage to Cézanne 16, 19–21,
   22, 23
Fontainebleu 12, 21
Franco-Prussian War 8

G
Gachet, Paul 9–10
Gardanne 15, 16, 17
Gasquet, Joachim 22
Gauguin, Paul 18, 21, 27
Geffroy, Gustave 19
Group of Seven 27
Groupe des Batignolles 8
Guillaumin, Armand 7
Guillemet, Antoine 7, 13

H
Huysmans, Joris-Karl 18

I
Impressionism 8, 9–10, 11, 14, 16,
   18, 22, 25
   crisis of Impressionism 12–13

J
Jas de Bouffan, Aix-en-Provence 6,
   12, 14, 15, 17, 20, 23, 25

K
Klimt, Gustave 27

L
L'Estaque 8, 12, 14. 17
   paintings of the Bay of Marseille 15
Lake Annecy 22
Le Tholonet 22
Les Lauves 23–24, 26
life painting 10
Louvre, Paris 7, 15, 21

M
Manet, Édouard 8
   Le déjeuner sur l'herbe 7
   Olympia 7
Marseille 8, 12, 14, 15
Matisse, Henri 11, 27
Médan 12, 14
Melun 12
Millet, Jean-François 20
Monet, Claude 8, 13, 15, 16, 19, 21
Mont Sainte-Victoire, Provence 6,
   21–22, 23, 26, 27
Monticelli, Adolphe 14
Musée du Luxembourg 21

N
Nabis 18, 27
Napoleon III 7, 16
nudes 8, 12, 25

P
Paris 7, 8, 9, 12, 18, 21, 23, 24
Picasso, Pablo 27
Pissarro, Camille 7, 8, 9, 13, 14,
   21, 27
Pontoise 9, 14, 21
portraits 10–11
Poussin, Nicolas 13, 15

R
Realism 7
Renoir, Pierre-Auguste 8, 11, 13,
   14–15, 16, 19, 22
Rodin, Auguste 19
Romanticism 7, 13, 25
Rue Boulegon, Aix 23, 26

S
Salon 7, 8, 13, 17
Salon d'Automne 24
Salon des Indépendants 24
Salon des Refusés 7
Schiele, Egon 27
Sisley, Alfred 8
Solari, Philippe 9, 24
sur le motif 10, 13, 24

T
Talloires, Lake Annecy 22
Tanguy, Julien-François 21
Tintoretto 7
Titian 7

V
Valenciennes, Pierre-Henri de 15, 20
Vallier, M. 24, 26
Van Gogh, Vincent 10
Velázquez, Diego 7
Veronese, Paolo 7
Vingts 18
Vollard, Ambroise 20–21
Voltaire, Le 13

Z
Zola, Émile 7, 8, 9, 12, 14
   critique of Impressionism 13
   death 24–25
   L'Oeuvre 16–17
Zurbarán, Francisco de 7

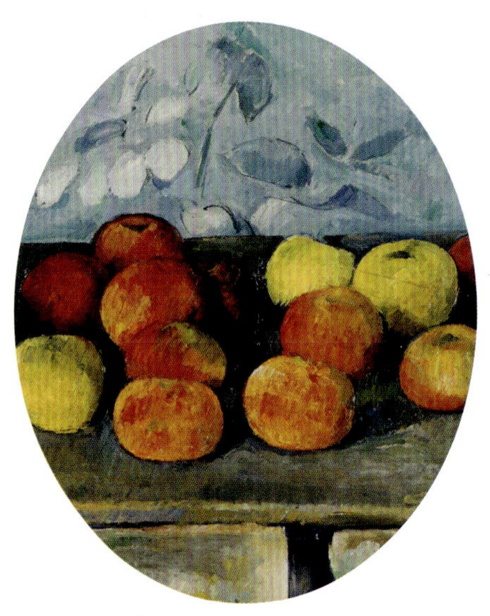

Masterpieces of Art
FLAME TREE PUBLISHING

A new series of carefully curated print and digital books covering the world's greatest art, artists and art movements.

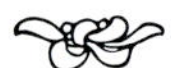